CHEAT CODE EXPLOSION

EXPLOSION

⬥ FOR CONSOLES ⬥

DANGER   COMBUSTIBLE

**FLIP THIS BOOK OVER
FOR HANDHELD SYSTEMS**

Nintendo DS™

PlayStation® Portable

Game Boy® Advance

LOOK FOR CODEY

When you see
Codey's face, you've
found the newest
and coolest codes!

SPECIAL SECTION: GUITAR HERO & ROCK BAND

GAMES LIST

GUITAR HERO

UNLOCK ALL

At the Main menu, press Yellow, Orange, Blue, Blue, Orange, Yellow, Yellow.

GUITAR HERO GUITAR CHEAT

At the Main menu, press Blue, Orange, Yellow, Blue, Blue.

CROWD METER CHEAT

At the Main menu, press Yellow, Blue, Orange, Orange, Blue, Blue, Yellow, Orange.

MONKEY HEAD CROWD CHEAT

At the Main menu, press Blue, Orange, Yellow, Yellow, Yellow, Blue, Orange.

SKULL HEAD CROWD CHEAT

At the Main menu, press Orange, Yellow, Blue, Blue, Orange, Yellow, Blue, Blue.

AIR GUITAR CHEAT

At the Main menu, press Orange, Orange, Blue, Yellow, Orange.

NO VENUE CHEAT

At the Main menu, press Blue, Yellow, Orange, Blue, Yellow, Orange.

GUITAR HERO II

AIR GUITAR

At the Main menu, press Yellow, Yellow, Blue, Orange, Yellow, Blue.

EYEBALL HEAD CROWD

At the Main menu, press Blue, Orange, Yellow, Orange, Yellow, Orange, Blue.

MONKEY HEAD CROWD

At the Main menu, press Orange, Blue, Yellow, Yellow, Orange, Blue, Yellow, Yellow.

FLAMING HEAD

At the Main menu, press Orange, Yellow, Orange, Orange, Yellow, Orange, Yellow, Yellow.

HORSE HEAD

At the Main menu, press Blue, Orange, Orange, Blue, Orange, Orange, Blue, Orange, Orange, Blue.

HYPER SPEED

At the Main menu, press Orange, Blue, Orange, Yellow, Orange, Blue, Orange, Yellow.

PERFORMANCE MODE

At the Main menu, press Yellow, Yellow, Blue, Yellow, Yellow, Orange, Yellow, Yellow.

GUITAR HERO III: LEGENDS OF ROCK

To enter the following cheats, strum the guitar while holding the listed buttons. For example, if the code lists Yellow + Orange, hold the Yellow and Orange buttons as you strum. Air Guitar, Precision Mode and Performance Mode can be toggled on and off from the Cheats menu. You can also change between five different levels of Hyperspeed at this menu.

UNLOCK EVERYTHING

Select Cheats from the Options. Choose Enter Cheat and enter the following (no sounds play while this code is entered):

Green + Red + Blue + Orange
Green + Red + Yellow + Blue
Green + Red + Yellow + Orange
Green + Yellow + Blue + Orange
Green + Red + Yellow + Blue
Red + Yellow + Blue + Orange
Green + Red + Yellow + Blue
Green + Yellow + Blue + Orange
Green + Red + Yellow + Blue
Green + Red + Yellow + Orange
Green + Red + Yellow + Orange
Green + Red + Yellow + Blue
Green + Red + Yellow + Orange

An easier way to illustrate this code is to represent Green as 1, progressing down the guitar neck to Orange as 5. For example, if you have 1345, you would hold Green + Yellow + Blue + Orange while strumming: 1245 + 1234 + 1235 + 1345 + 1234 + 2345 + 1234 + 1345 + 1234 + 1235 + 1235 + 1234 + 1235.

ALL SONGS

Select Cheats from the Options. Choose Enter Cheat and enter:

Yellow + Orange
Red + Blue
Red + Orange
Green + Blue
Red + Yellow
Yellow + Orange
Red + Yellow
Red + Blue
Green + Yellow
Green + Yellow
Yellow + Blue
Yellow + Blue
Yellow + Orange
Yellow + Orange
Yellow + Blue
Yellow
Red
Red + Yellow
Red
Yellow
Orange

NO FAIL

Select Cheats from the Options. Choose Enter Cheat and enter:

Green + Red
Blue
Green + Red
Green + Yellow
Blue
Green + Yellow
Red + Yellow
Orange
Red + Yellow
Green + Yellow
Yellow
Green + Yellow
Green + Red

AIR GUITAR

Select Cheats from the Options. Choose Enter Cheat and enter:

Blue + Yellow
Green + Yellow
Green + Yellow
Red + Blue
Red + Blue
Red + Yellow
Red + Yellow
Blue + Yellow
Green + Yellow
Green + Yellow
Red + Blue
Red + Blue
Red + Yellow
Red + Yellow
Green + Yellow
Green + Yellow
Red + Yellow
Red + Yellow

HYPERSPEED

Select Cheats from the Options. Choose Enter Cheat and enter:

Orange
Blue
Orange
Yellow
Orange
Blue
Orange
Yellow

PERFORMANCE MODE

Select Cheats from the Options. Choose Enter Cheat and enter:

Red + Yellow
Red + Blue
Red + Orange
Red + Blue
Red + Yellow
Green + Blue
Red + Yellow
Red + Blue

EASY EXPERT

Select Cheats from the Options. Choose Enter Cheat and enter:

Green + Red
Green + Yellow
Yellow + Blue
Red + Blue
Blue + Orange
Yellow + Orange
Red + Yellow
Red + Blue

PRECISION MODE

Select Cheats from the Options. Choose Enter Cheat and enter:

Green + Red
Green + Red
Green + Red
Red + Yellow
Red + Yellow
Red + Blue
Red + Blue
Yellow + Blue
Yellow + Orange
Yellow + Orange
Green + Red
Green + Red
Green + Red
Red + Yellow
Red + Yellow
Red + Blue
Red + Blue
Yellow + Blue
Yellow + Orange
Yellow + Orange

BRET MICHAELS SINGER

Select Cheats from the Options. Choose Enter Cheat and enter:

Green + Red
Green + Red
Green + Red
Green + Blue
Green + Blue
Green + Blue
Red + Blue
Red
Red
Red
Red + Blue
Red
Red
Red
Red + Blue
Red
Red
Red

5

GUITAR HERO ENCORE: ROCKS THE 80S

UNLOCK EVERYTHING

At the Main menu, press Blue, Orange, Yellow, Red, Orange, Yellow, Blue, Yellow, Red, Yellow, Blue, Yellow, Red, Yellow, Blue, Yellow.

HYPERSPEED

At the Main menu, press Yellow, Blue, Orange, Orange, Blue, Yellow, Yellow, Orange.

PERFORMANCE MODE

At the Main menu, press Blue, Blue, Orange, Yellow, Yellow, Blue, Orange, Blue.

AIR GUITAR

At the Main menu, press Yellow, Blue, Yellow, Orange, Blue, Blue.

EYEBALL HEAD CROWD

At the Main menu, press Yellow, Blue, Orange, Orange, Orange, Blue, Yellow.

MONKEY HEAD CROWD

At the Main menu, press Blue, Blue, Orange, Yellow, Blue, Blue, Orange, Yellow.

FLAME HEAD

At the Main menu, press Yellow, Orange, Yellow, Orange, Yellow, Orange, Blue, Orange.

HORSE HEAD

At the Main menu, press Blue, Orange, Orange, Blue, Yellow, Blue, Orange, Orange, Blue, Yellow.

GUITAR HERO: AEROSMITH

To enter the following cheats, strum the guitar while holding the listed buttons. For example, if the codes lists Yellow + Orange, hold Yellow and Orange as you strum. Air Guitar, Precision Mode, and Performance Mode can be toggled on and off from the Cheats menu. You can also change between five different levels of Hyperspeed at this menu.

ALL SONGS

Red + Yellow
Green + Red
Green + Red
Red + Yellow
Red + Yellow
Green + Red
Red + Yellow
Red + Yellow
Green + Red
Green + Red
Red + Yellow
Red + Yellow
Green + Red
Red + Yellow
Red + Blue

AIR GUITAR

Red + Yellow
Green + Red
Red + Yellow
Red + Yellow
Red + Blue
Red + Blue
Red + Blue
Red + Blue
Red + Blue
Yellow + Blue
Yellow + Blue
Yellow + Orange

HYPERSPEED

Yellow + Orange
Yellow + Orange
Yellow + Orange
Yellow + Orange
Yellow + Orange
Red + Yellow
Red + Yellow
Red + Yellow
Red + Yellow
Red + Blue
Red + Blue
Red + Blue
Red + Blue
Red + Blue
Yellow + Blue
Yellow + Orange
Yellow + Orange

NO FAIL

Green + Red
Blue
Green + Red
Green + Yellow
Blue
Green + Yellow
Red + Yellow
Orange
Red + Yellow
Green + Yellow
Yellow
Green + Yellow
Green + Red

PERFORMANCE MODE

Green + Red
Green + Red
Red + Orange
Red + Blue
Green + Red
Green + Red
Red + Orange
Red + Blue

PRECISION MODE

Red + Yellow
Red + Blue
Red + Blue
Red + Yellow
Red + Yellow
Yellow + Blue
Yellow + Blue
Yellow + Blue
Red + Blue
Red + Yellow
Red + Blue
Red + Blue
Red + Yellow
Red + Yellow
Yellow + Blue
Yellow + Blue
Yellow + Blue
Red + Blue

GUITAR HERO WORLD TOUR

The following cheats can be toggled on and off at the Cheats menu.

QUICKPLAY SONGS

Select Cheats from the Options menu, choose Enter New Cheat and press Blue, Blue, Red, Green, Green, Blue, Blue, Yellow.

ALWAYS SLIDE

Select Cheats from the Options menu, choose Enter New Cheat and press Green, Green, Red, Red, Yellow, Red, Yellow, Blue.

AT&T BALLPARK

Select Cheats from the Options menu, choose Enter New Cheat and press Yellow, Green, Red, Red, Green, Blue, Red, Yellow.

AUTO KICK

Select Cheats from the Options menu, choose Enter New Cheat and press Yellow, Green, Red, Blue (x4), Red.

EXTRA LINE 6 TONES

Select Cheats from the Options menu, choose Enter New Cheat and press Green, Red, Yellow, Blue, Red, Yellow, Blue, Green.

FLAME COLOR

Select Cheats from the Options menu, choose Enter New Cheat and press Green, Red, Green, Blue, Red, Red, Yellow, Blue.

GEM COLOR

Select Cheats from the Options menu, choose Enter New Cheat and press Blue, Red, Red, Green, Red, Green, Red, Yellow.

STAR COLOR

Select Cheats from the Options menu, choose Enter New Cheat and press Red, Red, Yellow, Red, Blue, Red, Red, Blue.

AIR INSTRUMENTS

Select Cheats from the Options menu, choose Enter New Cheat and press Red, Red, Blue, Yellow, Green (x3), Yellow.

HYPERSPEED

Select Cheats from the Options menu, choose Enter New Cheat and press Green, Blue, Red, Yellow, Yellow, Red, Green, Green. These show up in the menu as HyperGuitar, HyperBass, and HyperDrums.

PERFORMANCE MODE

Select Cheats from the Options menu, choose Enter New Cheat and press Yellow, Yellow, Blue, Red, Blue, Green, Red, Red.

INVISIBLE ROCKER

Select Cheats from the Options menu, choose Enter New Cheat and press Green, Red, Yellow (x3), Blue, Blue, Green.

VOCAL FIREBALL

Select Cheats from the Options menu, choose Enter New Cheat and press Red, Green, Green, Yellow, Blue, Green, Yellow, Green.

AARON STEELE!

Select Cheats from the Options menu, choose Enter New Cheat and press Blue, Red, Yellow (x5), Green.

JONNY VIPER

Select Cheats from the Options menu, choose Enter New Cheat and press Blue, Red, Blue, Blue, Yellow (x3), Green.

NICK

Select Cheats from the Options menu, choose Enter New Cheat and press Green, Red, Blue, Green, Red, Blue, Blue, Green.

RINA

Select Cheats from the Options menu, choose Enter New Cheat and press Blue, Red, Green, Green, Yellow (x3), Green.

GUITAR HERO 5

ALL HOPOS

Select Input Cheats from the Options menu and enter Green, Green, Blue, Green, Green, Green, Yellow, Green.

ALWAYS SLIDE

Select Input Cheats from the Options menu and enter Green, Green, Red, Red, Yellow, Blue, Yellow, Blue.

AUTO KICK

Select Input Cheats from the Options menu and enter Yellow, Green, Red, Blue, Blue, Blue, Blue, Red.

FOCUS MODE

Select Input Cheats from the Options menu and enter Yellow, Green, Red, Green, Yellow, Blue, Green, Green.

HUD FREE MODE

Select Input Cheats from the Options menu and enter Green, Red, Green, Green, Yellow, Green, Green, Green.

PERFORMANCE MODE

Select Input Cheats from the Options menu and enter Yellow, Yellow, Blue, Red, Blue, Green, Red, Red.

AIR INSTRUMENTS

Select Input Cheats from the Options menu and enter Red, Red, Blue, Yellow, Green, Green, Green, Yellow.

INVISIBLE ROCKER

Select Input Cheats from the Options menu and enter Green, Red, Yellow, Yellow, Yellow, Blue, Blue, Green.

ALL CHARACTERS

Select Input Cheats from the Options menu and enter Blue, Blue, Green, Green, Red, Green, Red, Yellow.

CONTEST WINNER 1

Select Input Cheats from the Options menu and enter Green, Green, Red, Red, Yellow, Red, Yellow, Blue.

GUITAR HERO: METALLICA

Once entered, the cheats must be activated in the Cheats menu.

METALLICA COSTUMES

Select Cheats from Settings and enter Green, Red, Yellow, Blue, Blue, Yellow, Red, Green.

HYPERSPEED

Select Cheats from Settings and enter Green, Blue, Red, Yellow, Yellow, Red, Green, Green.

PERFORMANCE MODE

Select Cheats from Settings and enter Yellow, Yellow, Blue, Red, Blue, Green, Red, Red.

INVISIBLE ROCKER

Select Cheats from Settings and enter Green, Red, Yellow (x3), Blue, Blue, Green.

AIR INSTRUMENTS

Select Cheats from Settings and enter Red, Red, Blue, Yellow, Green (x3), Yellow.

ALWAYS DRUM FILL

Select Cheats from Settings and enter Red (x3), Blue, Blue, Green, Green, Yellow.

AUTO KICK

Select Cheats from Settings and enter Yellow, Green, Red, Blue (x4), Red. With this cheat activated, the bass pedal is automatically hit.

ALWAYS SLIDE
Select Cheats from Settings and enter Green, Green, Red, Red, Yellow, Red, Yellow, Blue. All Guitar Notes Become Touch Pad Sliding Notes.

BLACK HIGHWAY
Select Cheats from Settings and enter Yellow, Red, Green, Red, Green, Red, Red, Blue.

FLAME COLOR
Select Cheats from Settings and enter Green, Red, Green, Blue, Red, Red, Yellow, Blue.

GEM COLOR
Select Cheats from Settings and enter Blue, Red, Red, Green, Red, Green, Red, Yellow.

STAR COLOR
Select Cheats from Settings and enter Press Red, Red, Yellow, Red, Blue, Red, Red, Blue.

ADDITIONAL LINE 6 TONES
Select Cheats from Settings and enter Green, Red, Yellow, Blue, Red, Yellow, Blue, Green.

VOCAL FIREBALL
Select Cheats from Settings and enter Red, Green, Green, Yellow, Blue, Green, Yellow, Green.

GUITAR HERO: SMASH HITS

Enter the following in the cheats menu which can be found in the options menu.

ALWAYS DRUM FILL
Green, Green, Red, Red, Blue, Blue, Yellow, Yellow

ALWAYS SLIDE
Blue, Yellow, Red, Green, Blue, Green, Green, Yellow

HYPERSPEED
Red, Green, Blue, Yellow, Green, Yellow, Red, Red

AIR INSTRUMENTS
Yellow, Red, Blue, Green, Yellow, Red, Red, Red

INVISIBLE ROCKER
Blue, Red, Red, Red, Red, Yellow, Blue, Green

GEM COLOR
Red, Red, Red, Blue, Blue, Blue, Yellow, Green

STAR COLOR
Green, Red, Green, Yellow, Green, Blue, Yellow, Red

LINE 6 UNLOCK

Green, Red, Yellow, Blue, Red, Yellow, Blue, Green

VOCAL FIREBALL

Green, Blue, Red, Red, Yellow, Yellow, Blue, Blue

ROCK BAND

ALL SONGS

At the title screen, press Red, Yellow, Blue, Red, Red, Blue, Blue, Red, Yellow, Blue. Saving and all network features are disabled with this code.

TRANSPARENT INSTRUMENTS

Complete the hall of fame concert with that instrument.

GOLD INSTRUMENT

Complete the solo tour with that instrument.

SILVER INSTRUMENT

Complete the bonus tour with that instrument.

ROCK BAND 2

Most of these codes disable saving, achievements, and Xbox LIVE play.

UNLOCK ALL SONGS

Select Modify Game from the Extras menu, choose Enter Unlock Code and press Red, Yellow, Blue, Red, Red, Blue, Blue, Red, Yellow, Blue or Y, B, X, Y, Y, X, X, Y, B, X. Toggle this cheat on or off from the Modify Game menu.

SELECT VENUE SCREEN

Select Modify Game from the Extras menu, choose Enter Unlock Code and press Blue, Orange, Orange, Blue, Yellow, Blue, Orange, Orange, Blue, Yellow or (for Xbox 360) X, Left Bumper, Left Bumper, X, B, X, Left Bumper, Left Bumper, X, B. Toggle this cheat on or off from the Modify Game menu.

NEW VENUES ONLY

Select Modify Game from the Extras menu, choose Enter Unlock Code and press Red, Red, Red, Red, Yellow, Yellow, Yellow, Yellow or (for Xbox 360) Y (x4), B (x4). Toggle this cheat on or off from the Modify Game menu.

PLAY THE GAME WITHOUT A TRACK

Select Modify Game from the Extras menu, choose Enter Unlock Code and press Blue, Blue, Red, Red, Yellow, Yellow, Blue, Blue or (for Xbox 360) X, X, Y, Y, B, B, X, X. Toggle this cheat on or off from the Modify Game menu.

AWESOMENESS DETECTION

Select Modify Game from the Extras menu, choose Enter Unlock Code and press Yellow, Blue, Orange, Yellow, Blue, Orange, Yellow, Blue, Orange or (for Xbox 360) B, X, Left Bumper, B, X, Left Bumper, B, X, Left Bumper. Toggle this cheat on or off from the Modify Game menu.

STAGE MODE

Select Modify Game from the Extras menu, choose Enter Unlock Code and press Blue, Yellow, Red, Blue, Yellow, Red, Blue, Yellow, Red or (for Xbox 360) X, B, Y, X, B, Y, X, B, Y. Toggle this cheat on or off from the Modify Game menu.

THE BEATLES: ROCK BAND

BONUS PHOTOS

At the title screen, press Blue, Yellow, Orange, Orange, Orange, Blue, Blue, Blue, Yellow, Orange.

PLAYSTATION® 3

CONTENTS

BAJA: EDGE OF CONTROL

CAREER COMPLETE 100%

Select Cheat Codes from the Options menu and enter SHOWTIME.

INSTALL ALL PARTS

Select Cheat Codes from the Options menu and enter SUPERMAX.

BEJEWELED 2

TOGGLE CLASSIC STYLE GEMS

During a game, hold L1 + L2 + R1 + R2 and press ❎.

TOGGLE GAME BORDERS

During a game, hold L1 + L2 + R1 + R2 and press ◉.

THE BIGS

START A ROOKIE WITH HIGHER STATS

When you create a rookie, name him HOT DOG. His stats will be higher than when you normally start.

BLAZING ANGELS 2: SECRET MISSIONS OF WWII

ALL MISSIONS AND PLANES UNLOCKED

At the main menu, hold L2 + R2, and press ◉, L1, R1, ▲, ▲, R1, L1, ◉.

GOD MODE

Pause the game, hold L2, and press ◉, ▲, ▲, ◉. Release L2, hold R2 and press ▲, ◉, ◉, ▲. Re-enter the code to disable it.

INCREASED DAMAGE WITH ALL WEAPONS

Pause the game, hold L2, and press L1, L1, R1. Release L2, hold R2, and press R1, R1, L1. Re-enter the code to disable it.

BOLT

Many of the following cheats can be toggled on/off by pausing the game and selecting Cheats.

LEVEL SELECT

Select Cheats from the Extras menu and enter Right, Up, Left, Right, Up, Right.

ALL MINIGAMES

Select Cheats from the Extras menu and enter Right, Up, Right, Right.

UNLIMITED ENHANCED VISION

Select Cheats from the Extras menu and enter Left, Right, Up, Down.

UNLIMITED GROUND POUND

Select Cheats from the Extras menu and enter Right, Up, Right, Up, Left, Down.

UNLIMITED INVULNERABILITY

Select Cheats from the Extras menu and enter Down, Down, Up, Left.

UNLIMITED GAS MINES

Select Cheats from the Extras menu and enter Right, Left, Left, Up, Down, Right.

UNLIMITED LASER EYES

Select Cheats from the Extras menu and enter Left, Left, Up, Right.

UNLIMITED STEALTH CAMO

Select Cheats from the Extras menu and enter Left, Down (x3).

UNLIMITED SUPERBARK

Select Cheats from the Extras menu and enter Right, Left, Left, Up, Down, Up.

BURNOUT PARADISE

BEST BUY CAR

Pause the game and select Sponsor Product Code from the Under the Hood menu. Enter Bestbuy. Need A License to use this car offline.

CIRCUIT CITY CAR

Pause the game and select Sponsor Product Code from the Under the Hood menu. Enter Circuitcity. Need Burnout Paradise License to use this car offline.

GAMESTOP CAR

Pause the game and select Sponsor Product Code from the Under the Hood menu. Enter Gamestop. Need A License to use this car offline.

WALMART CAR

Pause the game and select Sponsor Product Code from the Under the Hood menu.. Enter Walmart. Need Burnout Paradise License to use this car offline.

"STEEL WHEELS" GT

Pause the game and select Sponsor Product Code from the Under the Hood menu. Enter G23X 5K8Q GX2V 04B1 or E60J 8Z7T MS8L 51U6.

LICENSES

LICENSE	NUMBER OF WINS NEEDED
D	2
C	7
B	16
A	26
Burnout Paradise	45
Elite License	All events

CARS MATER-NATIONAL

ALL ARCADE RACES, MINI-GAMES, AND WORLDS

Select Codes/Cheats from the options and enter PLAYALL.

ALL CARS

Select Codes/Cheats from the options and enter MATTEL07.

ALTERNATE LIGHTNING MCQUEEN COLORS

Select Codes/Cheats from the options and enter NCEDUDZ.

ALL COLORS FOR OTHERS

Select Codes/Cheats from the options and enter PAINTIT.

UNLIMITED TURBO

Select Codes/Cheats from the options and enter ZZOOOOM.

EXTREME ACCELERATION

Select Codes/Cheats from the options and enter OTO200X.

EXPERT MODE

Select Codes/Cheats from the options and enter VRYFAST.

ALL BONUS ART

Select Codes/Cheats from the options and enter BUYTALL.

DIRT 2

Win the given events to earn the following cars:

GET THIS CAR	BY WINNING THIS EVENT
Ford RS200 Evolution	Rally Cross World Tour
Toyota Stadium Truck	Landrush World Tour
Mitsubishi Pajero Dakar 1993	Raid World Tour
Dallenbach Special	Trailblazer World Tour
1995 Subaru Impreza WRX STi	Colin McRae Challenge
Colin McRae R4 [X Games]	X Games Europe
Mitsubishi Lancer Evolution X [X Games]	X Games Asia
Subaru Impreza WRX STi [X Games]	X Games America
Ford Escort MKII and MG Metro 6R4	All X Games events

G.I. JOE: THE RISE OF COBRA

CLASSIC DUKE

At the main menu, press Left, Up, ⬤, Up, Right, ▲.

SHANA "SCARLETT" O'HARA

At the main menu, press Right, Up, Down, Down, ▲.

GRID

ALL DRIFT CARS

Select Bonus Codes from the Options. Then choose Enter Code and enter TUN58396.

ALL MUSCLE CARS

Select Bonus Codes from the Options. Then choose Enter Code and enter MUS59279.

BUCHBINDER EMOTIONAL ENGINEERING BMW 320SI

Select Bonus Codes from the Options. Then choose Enter Code and enter F93857372. You can use this in Race Day or in GRID World once you've started your own team.

EBAY MOTORS MUSTANG

Select Bonus Codes from the Options. Then choose Enter Code and enter DAFJ55E01473M0. You can use this in Race Day or in GRID World once you've started your own team.

GAMESTATION BMW 320SI

Select Bonus Codes from the Options. Then choose Enter Code and enter G29782655. You can use this in Race Day or in GRID World once you've started your own team.

MICROMANIA PAGANI ZONDA R

Select Bonus Codes from the Options. Then choose Enter Code and enter M38572343. You can use this in Race Day or in GRID World once you've started your own team.

PLAY.COM ASTON MARTIN DBR9

Select Bonus Codes from the Options. Then choose Enter Code and enter P47203845. You can use this in Race Day or in GRID World once you've started your own team.

IRON MAN

CLASSIC ARMOR

Clear One Man Army vs. Mercs.

EXTREMIS ARMOR

Clear One Man Army vs. Maggia.

MARK II ARMOR

Clear One Man Army vs. Ten Rings.

HULKBUSTER ARMOR

Clear One Man Army vs. AIM-X. Can also be unlocked when clear game save data from Incredible Hulk is stored on the same console.

CLASSIC MARK I ARMOR

Clear One Man Army vs. AIM.

ULTIMATE ARMOR

Clear Mission 13: Showdown.

JUICED 2: HOT IMPORT NIGHTS

ASCARI KZ1

Select Cheats and Codes from the DNA Lab menu and enter KNOX. Defeat the challenge to earn the car.

AUDI TT 1.8L QUATTRO

Select Cheats and Codes from the DNA Lab menu and enter YTHZ. Defeat the challenge to earn the car.

BMW Z4 ROADSTER

Select Cheats and Codes from the DNA Lab menu and enter GVDL. Defeat the challenge to earn the car.

FRITO-LAY INFINITI G35

Select Cheats and Codes from the DNA Lab menu and enter MNCH. Defeat the challenge to earn the car.

HOLDEN MONARO

Select Cheats and Codes from the DNA Lab menu and enter RBSG. Defeat the challenge to earn the car.

HYUNDAI COUPE 2.7L V6

Select Cheats and Codes from the DNA Lab menu and enter BSLU. Defeat the challenge to earn the car.

INFINITI G35

Select Cheats and Codes from the DNA Lab menu and enter MRHC. Defeat the challenge to earn the car.

KOENIGSEGG CCX

Select Cheats and Codes from the DNA Lab menu and enter KDTR. Defeat the challenge to earn the car.

MITSUBISHI PROTOTYPE X

Select Cheats and Codes from the DNA Lab menu and enter DOPX. Defeat the challenge to earn the car.

NISSAN 350Z

Select Cheats and Codes from the DNA Lab menu and enter PRGN. Defeat the challenge to earn the car.

NISSAN SKYLINE R34 GT-R

Select Cheats and Codes from the DNA Lab menu and enter JWRS. Defeat the challenge to earn the car.

SALEEN S7

Select Cheats and Codes from the DNA Lab menu and enter WIKF. Defeat the challenge to earn the car.

SEAT LEON CUPRA R

Select Cheats and Codes from the DNA Lab menu and enter FAMQ. Defeat the challenge to earn the car.

KUNG FU PANDA

UNLIMITED CHI

Select Cheats from the Extra menu and enter Down, Right, Left, Up, Down.

INVULNERABILITY

Select Cheats from the Extra menu and enter Down, Down, Right, Up, Left.

FULL UPGRADES

Select Cheats from the Extra menu and enter Left, Right, Down, Left, Up.

FULL AWESOME METER

Select Cheats from the Extra menu and enter Up, Down, Up, Right, Left. This gives Po 4X damage.

MULTIPLAYER CHARACTERS

Select Cheats from the Extra menu and enter Left, Down, Left, Right, Down.

OUTFITS

Select Cheats from the Extra menu and enter Right, Left, Down, Up, Right.

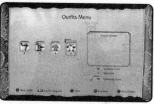

LAIR

CHICKEN VIDEO

At the cheat menu, enter chicken.

COFFEE VIDEO

At the cheat menu, enter 686F7420636F66666565.

UNLOCKS STABLE OPTION FOR ALL LEVELS

At the cheat menu, enter koelsch. Saving is disabled with this code.

THE LEGEND OF SPYRO: DAWN OF THE DRAGON

UNLIMITED LIFE

Pause the game, hold L1 and press Right, Right, Down, Down, Left with the Left Analog Stick.

UNLIMITED MANA

Pause the game, hold R1 and press Up, Right, Up, Left, Down with the Left Analog Stick.

MAXIMUM XP

Pause the game, hold R1 and press Left, Right, Right, Up, Up with the Left Analog Stick.

ALL ELEMENTAL UPGRADES

Pause the game, hold L1 and press Left, Up, Down, Up, Right with the Left Analog Stick.

LEGO BATMAN

BATCAVE CODES

Using the computer in the Batcave, select Enter Code and enter the following codes.

CHARACTERS

CHARACTER	CODE	CHARACTER	CODE
Alfred	ZAQ637	Penguin Henchman	BJH782
Batgirl	JKR331	Penguin Minion	KJP748
Bruce Wayne	BDJ327	Poison Ivy Goon	GTB899
Catwoman (Classic)	M1AAWW	Police Marksman	HKG984
Clown Goon	HJK327	Police Officer	JRY983
Commissioner Gordon	DDP967	Riddler Goon	CRY928
Fishmonger	HGY748	Riddler Henchman	XEU824
Freeze Girl	XVK541	S.W.A.T.	HTF114
Joker Goon	UTF782	Sailor	NAV592
Joker Henchman	YUN924	Scientist	JFL786
Mad Hatter	JCA283	Security Guard	PLB946
Man-Bat	NYU942	The Joker (Tropical)	CCB199
Military Policeman	MKL382	Yeti	NJL412
Nightwing	MVY759	Zoo Sweeper	DWR243
Penguin Goon	NKA238		

VEHICLES

VEHICLE	CODE	VEHICLE	CODE
Bat-Tank	KNTT4B	Mr. Freeze's Kart	BCT229
Bruce Wayne's Private Jet	LEA664	Penguin Goon Submarine	BTN248
Catwoman's Motorcycle	HPL826	Police Bike	LJP234
Garbage Truck	DUS483	Police Boat	PLC999
Goon Helicopter	GCH328	Police Car	KJL832
Harbor Helicopter	CHP735	Police Helicopter	CWR732
Harley Quinn's Hammer Truck	RDT637	Police Van	MAC788
Mad Hatter's Glider	HS000W	Police Watercraft	VJD328
Mad Hatter's Steamboat	M4DM4N	Riddler's Jet	HAHAHA
Mr. Freeze's Iceberg	ICYICE	Robin's Submarine	TTF453
The Joker's Van	JUK657	Two-Face's Armored Truck	EFE933

CHEATS

CHEAT	CODE	CHEAT	CODE
Always Score Multiply	9LRGNB	More Batarang Targets	XWP645
Fast Batarangs	JRBDCB	Piece Detector	KHJ554
Fast Walk	Z0LM6N	Power Brick Detector	MMN786
Flame Batarang	D8NYWH	Regenerate Hearts	HJH7HJ
Freeze Batarang	XPN4NG	Score x2	N4NR3E
Extra Hearts	ML3KHP	Score x4	CX9MAT
Fast Build	EVG26J	Score x6	MLVNF2
Immune to Freeze	JXUDY6	Score x8	WCCDB9
Invincibility	WYD5CP	Score x10	18HW07
Minikit Detector	ZXGH9J		

22

LEGO INDIANA JONES: THE ORIGINAL ADVENTURES

CHARACTERS

Approach the blackboard in the Classsroom and enter the following codes.

CHARACTER	CODE	CHARACTER	CODE
Bandit	12N68W	Fedora	V75YSP
Bandit Swordsman	1MK4RT	First Mate	0GIN24
Barranca	04EM94	Grail Knight	NE6THI
Bazooka Trooper (Crusade)	MK83R7	Hovitos Tribesman	HOV1SS
Bazooka Trooper (Raiders)	S93Y5R	Indiana Jones (Desert Disguise)	4J8S4M
Belloq	CHN3YU	Indiana Jones (Officer)	VJ850S
Belloq (Jungle)	TDR197	Jungle Guide	24PF34
Belloq (Robes)	VEO29L	Kao Kan	WM046L
British Commander	B73EUA	Kazim	NRH23J
British Officer	VJ5TI9	Kazim (Desert)	3M29TJ
British Soldier	DJ5I2W	Lao Che	2NK479
Captain Katanga	VJ3TT3	Maharajah	NFK5N2
Chatter Lal	ENW936	Major Toht	13NS01
Chatter Lal (Thuggee)	CNH4RY	Masked Bandit	N48SF0
Chen	3NK48T	Mola Ram	FJUR31
Colonel Dietrich	2K9RKS	Monkey Man	3RF6YJ
Colonel Vogel	8EAL4H	Pankot Assassin	2NKT72
Dancing Girl	C7EJ21	Pankot Guard	VN28RH
Donovan	3NFTU8	Sherpa Brawler	VJ37WJ
Elsa (Desert)	JSNRT9	Sherpa Gunner	ND762W
Elsa (Officer)	VMJ5US	Slave Child	OE3ENW
Enemy Boxer	8246RB	Thuggee	VM683E
Enemy Butler	VJ48W3	Thuggee Acolyte	T2R3F9
Enemy Guard	VJ7R51	Thuggee Slave Driver	VBS7GW
Enemy Guard (Mountains)	YR47WM	Village Dignitary	KD48TN
Enemy Officer	572E61	Village Elder	4682E1
Enemy Officer (Desert	2MK450	Willie (Dinner Suit)	VK93R7
Enemy Pilot	B84ELP	Willie (Pajamas)	MEN4IP
Enemy Radio Operator	1MF94R	Wu Han	3NSLT8
Enemy Soldier (Desert)	4NSU7Q		

EXTRAS

Approach the blackboard in the Classsroom and enter the following codes. Some cheats need to be enabled by selecting Extras from the pause menu.

CHEAT	CODE	CHEAT	CODE
Artifact Detector	VIKED7	Regenerate Hearts	MDLP69
Beep Beep	VNF59Q	Secret Characters	3X44AA
Character Treasure	VIES2R	Silhouettes	3HE85H
Disarm Enemies	VKRNS9	Super Scream	VN3R7S
Disguises	4ID1N6	Super Slap	OP1TA5
Fast Build	VB3SLO	Treasure Magnet	H86LA2
Fast Dig	378RS6	Treasure x10	VI3PS8
Fast Fix	FJ59WS	Treasure x2	VM4TS9
Fertilizer	B1GW1F	Treasure x4	VLWEN3
Ice Rink	33GM7J	Treasure x6	V84RYS
Parcel Detector	VUT673	Treasure x8	A72E1M
Poo Treasure	WWQ1SA		

LEGO STAR WARS: THE COMPLETE SAGA

The following still need to be purchase after entering the codes.

CHARACTERS

ADMIRAL ACKBAR

At the bar in Mos Eisley Cantina, select Enter Code and enter ACK646.

BATTLE DROID (COMMANDER)

At the bar in Mos Eisley Cantina, select Enter Code and enter KPF958.

BOBA FETT (BOY)

At the bar in Mos Eisley Cantina, select Enter Code and enter GGF539.

BOSS NASS

At the bar in Mos Eisley Cantina, select Enter Code and enter HHY697.

CAPTAIN TARPALS

At the bar in Mos Eisley Cantina, select Enter Code and enter QRN714.

COUNT DOOKU

At the bar in Mos Eisley Cantina, select Enter Code and enter DDD748.

DARTH MAUL

At the bar in Mos Eisley Cantina, select Enter Code and enter EUK421.

EWOK

At the bar in Mos Eisley Cantina, select Enter Code and enter EWK785.

GENERAL GRIEVOUS

At the bar in Mos Eisley Cantina, select Enter Code and enter PMN576.

GREEDO

At the bar in Mos Eisley Cantina, select Enter Code and enter ZZR636.

IG-88

At the bar in Mos Eisley Cantina, select Enter Code and enter GIJ989.

IMPERIAL GUARD

At the bar in Mos Eisley Cantina, select Enter Code and enter GUA850.

JANGO FETT

At the bar in Mos Eisley Cantina, select Enter Code and enter KLJ897.

KI-ADI MUNDI

At the bar in Mos Eisley Cantina, select Enter Code and enter MUN486.

LUMINARA

At the bar in Mos Eisley Cantina, select Enter Code and enter LUM521.

PADMÉ

At the bar in Mos Eisley Cantina, select Enter Code and enter VBJ322.

R2-Q5

At the bar in Mos Eisley Cantina, select Enter Code and enter EVILR2.

STORMTROOPER

At the bar in Mos Eisley Cantina, select Enter Code and enter NBN431.

TAUN WE

At the bar in Mos Eisley Cantina, select Enter Code and enter PRX482.

VULTURE DROID

At the bar in Mos Eisley Cantina, select Enter Code and enter BDC866.

WATTO

At the bar in Mos Eisley Cantina, select Enter Code and enter PLL967.

ZAM WESELL

At the bar in Mos Eisley Cantina, select Enter Code and enter 584HJF.

SKILLS

DISGUISE

At the bar in Mos Eisley Cantina, select Enter Code and enter BRJ437.

FORCE GRAPPLE LEAP

At the bar in Mos Eisley Cantina, select Enter Code and enter CLZ738.

VEHICLES

DROID TRIFIGHTER

At the bar in Mos Eisley Cantina, select Enter Code and enter AAB123.

IMPERIAL SHUTTLE

At the bar in Mos Eisley Cantina, select Enter Code and enter HUT845.

TIE INTERCEPTOR

At the bar in Mos Eisley Cantina, select Enter Code and enter INT729.

TIE FIGHTER

At the bar in Mos Eisley Cantina, select Enter Code and enter DBH897.

ZAM'S AIRSPEEDER

At the bar in Mos Eisley Cantina, select Enter Code and enter UUU875.

MARVEL ULTIMATE ALLIANCE

UNLOCK ALL SKINS

At the Team Menu, press Up, Down, Left, Right, Left, Right, Start.

UNLOCKS ALL HERO POWERS

At the Team Menu, press Left, Right, Up, Down, Up, Down, Start.

ALL HEROES TO LEVEL 99

At the Team Menu, press Up, Left, Up, Left, Down, Right, Down, Right, Start.

UNLOCK ALL HEROES

At the Team Menu, press Up, Up, Down, Down, Left, Left, Left, Start.

UNLOCK DAREDEVIL

At the Team Menu, press Left, Left, Right, Right, Up, Down, Up, Down, Start.

UNLOCK SILVER SURFER

At the Team Menu, press Down, Left, Left, Up, Right, Up, Down, Left, Start.

GOD MODE

During gameplay, press Up, Down, Up, Down, Up, Left, Down, Right, Start.

TOUCH OF DEATH

During gameplay, press Left, Right, Down, Down, Right, Left, Start.

SUPER SPEED

During gameplay, press Up, Left, Up, Right, Down, Right, Start.

FILL MOMENTUM

During gameplay, press Left, Right, Right, Left, Up, Down, Down, Up, Start.

UNLOCK ALL COMICS

At the Review menu, press Left, Right, Right, Left, Up, Up, Right, Start.

UNLOCK ALL CONCEPT ART

At the Review menu, press Down, Down, Down, Right, Right, Left, Down, Start.

UNLOCK ALL CINEMATICS

At the Review menu, press Up, Left, Left, Up, Right, Right, Up, Start.

UNLOCK ALL LOAD SCREENS

At the Review menu, press Up, Down, Right, Left, Up, Up Down, Start.

UNLOCK ALL COURSES

At the Comic Missions menu, press Up, Right, Left, Down, Up, Right, Left, Down, Start.

MARVEL: ULTIMATE ALLIANCE 2

These codes will disable the ability to save.

GOD MODE

During a game, press Up, Down, Up, Down, Up, Left, Down, Right, Start.

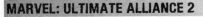

UNLIMITED FUSION

During a game, press Right, Right, Up, Down, Up, Up, Left, Start.

UNLOCK ALL POWERS

During a game, press Left, Right, Up, Down, Up, Down, Start.

UNLOCK ALL HEROES

During a game, press Up, Up, Down, Down, Left, Left, Left, Start.

UNLOCK ALL SKINS

During a game, press Up, Down, Left, Right, Left, Right, Start.

UNLOCK JEAN GREY

During a game, press Left, Left, Right, Right, Up, Down, Up, Down, Start.

UNLOCK HULK

During a game, press Down, Left, Left, Up, Right, Up, Down, Left, Start.

UNLOCK THOR

During a game, press Up, Right, Right, Down, Right, Down, Left, Right, Start.

UNLOCK ALL AUDIO LOGS

At the main menu, press Left, Right, Right, Left, Up, Up, Right, Start.

UNLOCK ALL DOSSIERS

At the main menu, press Down, Down, Down, Right, Right, Left, Down, Start.

UNLOCK ALL MOVIES

At the main menu, press Up, Left, Left, Up, Right, Right, Up, Start.

MLB 07: THE SHOW

CLASSIC STADIUMS

At the Main Menu, press Down, Up, Right, Down, Up, Left, Down, Up.

GOLDEN/SLIVER ERA PLAYERS

At the Main Menu, press Left, Up, Right, Down, Down, Left, Up, Down.

MLB 08: THE SHOW

ALL CLASSIC STADIUMS

At the main menu, press Down, Right, Circle, Square, Left, Triangle, Up, L1. The controller will vibrate if entered correctly.

MX VS. ATV UNTAMED

ALL RIDING GEAR

Select Cheat Codes from the Options and enter crazylikea.

ALL HANDLEBARS

Select Cheat Codes from the Options and enter nohands.

NASCAR 08

ALL CHASE MODE CARS

Select cheat codes from the options menu and enter checkered flag.

EA SPORTS CAR

Select cheat codes from the options menu and enter ea sports car.

FANTASY DRIVERS

Select cheat codes from the options menu and enter race the pack.

WALMART CAR AND TRACK

Select cheat codes from the options menu and enter walmart everyday.

NASCAR 09

WAL-MART CAR & CHICAGO PIER RACETRACK

Select EA Extras from My Nascar, then choose Cheat Codes and enter WALMART EVERYDAY.

NBA 09: THE INSIDE

EASTERN ALL-STARS 09 JERSEY

Select Extras from the Progression menu. Then choose nba.com from the Jerseys menu. Press ● and enter SHPNV2K699.

WESTERN ALL-STARS 09 JERSEY

Select Extras from the Progression menu. Then choose nba.com from the Jerseys menu. Press ● and enter K8AV6YMLNF.

L.A. LAKERS LATIN NIGHT JERSEY

Select Extras from the Progression menu. Then choose nba.com from the Jerseys menu. Press ● and enter NMTWCTC84S.

MIAMI HEAT LATIN NIGHT JERSEY

Select Extras from the Progression menu. Then choose nba.com from the Jerseys menu. Press ● and enter WCTGSA8SPD.

PHOENIX SUNS LATIN NIGHT JERSEY

Select Extras from the Progression menu. Then choose nba.com from the Jerseys menu. Press ● and enter LKUTSENFJH.

SAN ANTONIO SPURS LATIN NIGHT JERSEY

Select Extras from the Progression menu. Then choose nba.com from the Jerseys menu. Press ● and enter JFHSY73MYD.

NBA 2K8

ABA BALL

Select Codes from the Features menu and enter Payrespect.

2KSPORTS TEAM

Select Codes from the Features menu and enter 2ksports.

NBA DEVELOPMENT TEAM

Select Codes from the Features menu and enter nba2k.

SUPERSTARS TEAM

Select Codes from the Features menu and enter Ilmohffaae.

VISUAL CONCEPTS TEAM

Select Codes from the Features menu and enter Vcteam.

2008 ALL-STAR NBA JERSEYS

Select Codes from the Features menu and enter haeitgyebs.

BOBCATS RACING JERSEY

Select Codes from the Features menu and enter agtaccsinr.

PACERS SECOND ROAD JERSEY

Select Codes from the Features menu and enter cpares.

ST. PATRICK'S DAY JERSEYS

Select Codes from the Features menu and enter uclerehanp.

VALENTINE'S DAY JERSEYS

Select Codes from the Features menu and enter amcnreo.

NBA 2K9

2K SPORTS TEAM

Select Codes from the Features menu and enter 2ksports.

NBA 2K TEAM

Select Codes from the Features menu and enter nba2k.

SUPERSTARS

Select Codes from the Features menu and enter llmohffaae.

VC TEAM

Select Codes from the Features menu and enter vcteam.

ABA BALL

Select Codes from the Features menu and enter payrespect.

NBA 2K10

ABA BALL

Select Codes from Options and enter payrespect.

2K CHINA TEAM

Select Codes from Options and enter 2kchina.

NBA 2K TEAM

Select Codes from Options and enter nba2k.

2K SPORTS TEAM

Select Codes from Options and enter 2ksports.

VISUAL CONCEPTS TEAM

Select Codes from Options and enter vcteam.

NBA LIVE 07

AIR JORDAN V
Select NBA Codes from My NBA Live 07 and enter PNBBX1EVT5.

AIR JORDAN V
Select NBA Codes from My NBA Live 07 and enter VIR13PC451.

AIR JORDAN V
Select NBA Codes from My NBA Live 07 and enter IB7G8NN91Z.

JORDAN MELO M3
Select NBA Codes from My NBA Live 07 and enter JUL38TC485.

C-BILLUPS ALL-STAR EDITION
Select NBA Codes from My NBA Live 07 and enter BV6877HB9N.

ADIDAS C-BILLUPS VEGAS EDITION
Select NBA Codes from My NBA Live 07 and enter 85NVLDMWS5.

ADIDAS GARNETT BOUNCE ALL-STAR EDITION
Select NBA Codes from My NBA Live 07 and enter HYIOUHCAAN.

ADIDAS GARNETT BOUNCE VEGAS EDITION
Select NBA Codes from My NBA Live 07 and enter KDZ2MQL17W.

ADIDAS GIL-ZERO ALL-STAR EDITION
Select NBA Codes from My NBA Live 07 and enter 23DN1PPOG4.

ADIDAS GIL-ZERO VEGAS EDITION
Select NBA Codes from My NBA Live 07 and enter QQQ3JCUYQ7.

ADIDAS GIL-ZERO MID
Select NBA Codes from My NBA Live 07 and enter 1GSJC8JWRL.

ADIDAS GIL-ZERO MID
Select NBA Codes from My NBA Live 07 and enter 369V6RVU3G.

ADIDAS STEALTH ALL-STAR EDITION
Select NBA Codes from My NBA Live 07 and enter FE454DFJCC.

ADIDAS T-MAC 6 ALL-STAR EDITION
Select NBA Codes from My NBA Live 07 and enter MCJK843NNC.

ADIDAS T-MAC 6 VEGAS EDITION
Select NBA Codes from My NBA Live 07 and enter 84GF7EJG8V.

CHARLOTTE BOBCATS SECOND ROAD JERSEY
Select NBA Codes from My NBA Live 07 and enter WEDX671H7S.

UTAH JAZZ SECOND ROAD JERSEY
Select NBA Codes from My NBA Live 07 and enter VCBI89FK83.

NEW JERSEY NETS SECOND ROAD JERSEY
Select NBA Codes from My NBA Live 07 and enter D4SAA98U5H.

WASHINGTON WIZARDS SECOND ROAD JERSEY
Select NBA Codes from My NBA Live 07 and enter QV93NLKXQC.

EASTERN ALL-STARS 2007 ROAD JERSEY
Select NBA Codes from My NBA Live 07 and enter WOCNW4KL7L.

EASTERN ALL-STARS 2007 HOME JERSEY

Select NBA Codes from My NBA Live 07 and enter 5654ND43N6.

WESTERN ALL-STARS 2007 ROAD JERSEY

Select NBA Codes from My NBA Live 07 and enter XX93BVL20U.

WESTERN ALL-STARS 2007 HOME JERSEY

Select NBA Codes from My NBA Live 07 and enter 993NSKL199.

NBA LIVE 08

ADIDAS GIL-ZERO - ALL-STAR EDITION

Select NBA Codes from My NBA and enter 23DN1PPOG4.

ADIDAS TIM DUNCAN STEALTH - ALL-STAR EDITION

Select NBA Codes from My NBA and enter FE454DFJCC.

NBA LIVE 09

SUPER DUNKS MODE

Use the Sprite vending machine in the practice area and enter spriteslam.

NBA STREET HOMECOURT

ALL TEAMS

At the Main menu, hold **R1** + **L1** and press Left, Right, Left, Right.

ALL COURTS

At the Main menu, hold **R1** + **L1** and press Up, Right, Down, Left.

BLACK/RED BALL

At the Main menu, hold **R1** + **L1** and press Up, Down, Left, Right.

NEED FOR SPEED PROSTREET

$2,000

Select Career and then choose Code Entry. Enter 1MA9X99.

$4,000

Select Career and then choose Code Entry. Enter W2IOLL01.

$8,000

Select Career and then choose Code Entry. Enter L1IS97A1.

$10,000

Select Career and then choose Code Entry. Enter 1MI9K7E1.

$10,000

Select Career and then choose Code Entry. Enter CASHMONEY.

$10,000

Select Career and then choose Code Entry. Enter REGGAME.

AUDI TT

Select Career and then choose Code Entry. Enter ITSABOUTYOU.

CHEVELLE SS

Select Career and then choose Code Entry. Enter HORSEPOWER.

COKE ZERO GOLF GTI

Select Career and then choose Code Entry. Enter COKEZERO.

DODGE VIPER

Select Career and then choose Code Entry. Enter WORLDSLONGESTLASTING.

MITSUBISHI LANCER EVOLUTION

Select Career and then choose Code Entry. Enter MITSUBISHIGOFAR.

UNLOCK ALL BONUSES

Select Career and then choose Code Entry. Enter UNLOCKALLTHINGS.

5 REPAIR MARKERS

Select Career and then choose Code Entry. Enter SAFETYNET.

ENERGIZER VINYL

Select Career and then choose Code Entry. Enter ENERGIZERLITHIUM.

CASTROL SYNTEC VINYL

Select Career and then choose Code Entry. Enter CASTROLSYNTEC. This also gives you $10,000.

NEED FOR SPEED UNDERCOVER

$10,000

Select Secret Codes from the Options menu and enter %%S3/".

DIE-CAST BMW M3 E92

Select Secret Codes from the Options menu and enter)B7@B=.

DIE-CAST LEXUS IS F

Select Secret Codes from the Options menu and enter 0;5M2;.

NEEDFORSPEED.COM LOTUS ELISE

Select Secret Codes from the Options menu and enter -KJ3=E.

DIE-CAST NISSAN 240SX (S13)

Select Secret Codes from the Options menu and enter ?P:COL.

DIE-CAST PORSCHE 911 TURBO

Select Secret Codes from the Options menu and enter >8P:I;.

SHELBY TERLINGUA

Select Secret Codes from the Options menu and enter NeedForSpeedShelbyTerlingua.

DIE-CAST VOLKWAGEN R32

Select Secret Codes from the Options menu and enter!2ODBJ:.

NHL 08

ALL RBK EDGE JERSEYS

At the RBK Edge Code option, enter h3oyxpwksf8ibcgt.

NHL 2K9

3RD JERSEYS

From the Features menu, enter R6y34bsH52 as a code.

PRINCE OF PERSIA

SANDS OF TIME PRINCE/FARAH SKINS

Select Skin Manager from the Extras menu. Press ⬤ and enter 52585854. This gives you the Sands of Time skin for the Prince and Farah from Sands of Time for the Princess. Access them from the Skin Manager

PRINCE ALTAIR IBN LA-AHAD SKIN

Create an Ubisoft account. Then select "Altair Skin for Prince" to unlock.

RATATOUILLE

Select Gusteau's Shop from the Extras menu. Choose Secrets, select the appropriate code number, and then enter the code. Once the code is entered, select the cheat you want to activate it.

CODE NUMBER	CODE	EFFECT
1	Pieceocake	Very Easy difficulty mode
2	Myhero	no impact and no damage from enemies
3	Shielded	No damage from enemies
4	Spyagent	Move undetected by any enemy
5	Ilikeonions	Fart every time Remy jumps
6	Hardfeelings	Head butt when attacking instead of tailswipe
7	Slumberparty	Multiplayer mode
8	Gusteauart	All Concept Art
9	Gusteauship	All four championship modes
10	Mattelme	All single player and multiplayer minigames
11	Gusteauvid	All Videos
12	Gusteaures	All Bonus Artworks
13	Gusteaudream	All Dream Worlds in Gusteau's Shop
14	Gusteauslide	All Slides in Gusteau's Shop
15	Gusteaulevel	All single player minigames
16	Gusteaucombo	All items in Gusteau's Shop
17	Gusteaupot	5,000 Gusteau points
18	Gusteaujack	10,000 Gusteau points
19	Gusteauomni	50,000 Gusteau points

RATCHET & CLANK FUTURE: TOOLS OF DESTRUCTION

CHALLENGE MODE

After defeating the game, you can replay the game in Challenge Mode with all of Ratchet's current upgraded weapons and armor.

SKILL POINTS

Complete the following objectives to earn skill points. Each one is worth 10 to 40 points and you can use these points to unlock Cheats in the Cheats Menu. The following table lists the skill points with a location and description.

SKILL POINT	LOCATION	DESCRIPTION
Smashing Good Time	Cobalia	Destroy all crates and consumer bots in the trade port and gel factory.
I Should Have Gone Down in a Barrel	Cobalia	Jump into each of the two gel waterfall areas in Cobalia gel factory.
Giant Hunter	Cobalia	Kill several Basilisk Leviathans in the Cobalia wilderness.
Wrench Ninja 3	Stratus City	Use only the Omniwrench to get through the level to the Robo-Wings segment.
We Don't Need No Stinkin' Bridges!	Stratus City	Cross the tri-pad sequence using gel-cube bounces.
Surface-to-Air Plasma Beasts	Stratus City	Take out several flying targets using a specific weapon.
Been Around	Stratus City	Take off from every Robo-wing launch pad in Stratus City.
Collector's Addition	Voron	Be very thorough in your collection of goodies.
Minesweeper	Voron	Clear out a bunch of mines.
What's That, R2?	Voron	Barrel roll multiple times.
I Think I'm Gonna Be Sick	IFF	Ride the Ferris wheel for 5 loops without getting off or taking damage.
Fast and the Fire-ious	IFF	Use the Charge Boots to cross the bridge to the arena without being burned.
One Heckuva Peephole	IFF	Return after receiving the Geo-laser and complete the Geo-laser setup.
Alphabet City	Apogee	Teleport to each of the six asteroids in alphabetical order.
Knock You Down to Size	Apogee	Wrench Slam 5 centipedes.
Dancin' with the Stars	Apogee	Make 5 enemies dance at once on an asteroid.
Taste o' Yer Own Medicine	Pirate Base	Destroy all of the Shooter Pirates with the Combuster.
Preemptive Strike	Pirate Base	Destroy all of the "sleeping bats" while they are still sleeping.
It's Mutant-E Cap'n!	Pirate Base	Change 5 pirates into penguins in one blast.
You Sunk My Battleship!	Rakar	Shoot down a large percentage of the big destroyers.
Pretty Lights	Rakar	Complete the level without destroying any of the snatchers that fire beams at Ratchet.
I've Got Places To Be	Rakar	Destroy the boss in under 2:30.
The Consumer Is Not (Always) Right	Rykan V	Destroy a bunch of consumer bots in the level.
Live Strong	Rykan V	Complete the Gryo Cycle in 1:45.
Untouchable	Rykan V	Don't take damage in the Gyro-Cycle.
It Sounded Like a Freight Train	Sargasso	Get 10 Swarmers in one tornado.
Head Examiner	Sargasso	Land on all of the dinosaur heads in Sargasso.
Extinction	Sargasso	Kill all of the Sargasso Predators.
Lombaxes Don't Like Cold	Iris	Break all the breakable icicles.
Mow Down Ho-Down	Iris	Use turrets to destroy 10 dancing pirates.
Dancin' on the Ceiling	Zordoom	Successfully use a Groovitron while on a Magboot surface.

SKILL POINT	LOCATION	DESCRIPTION
Seared Ahi	Zordoom	Use the Pyroblaster on 3 Drophid creatures after freeing them from their robotic suits.
Shocking Ascent	Zordoom	Destroy all enemies on the elevator using just the Shock Ravager.
Expert Marksman	Borag	Kill 75% of all of the enemies.
Can't Touch This	Borag	Don't take damage before fighting the boss.
Pyoo, Pyoo!	Borag	Complete the level without secondary fire.
Dead Aim	Kerchu	Destroy several destructible towers while on the pirate barge.
Fire With Fire	Kerchu	Kill a few Kerchu Flamethrowers with the Pyro Blaster.
Rocket Jump	Kerchu	Successfully jump over a row of three rockets while on the grindrail during the boss fight in Kerchu City.
Your Friendly Neighborhood...	Slag Fleet	Destroy 5 enemies while on the grav ramp before Slag's ship.
Turret Times Two	Slag Fleet	Destroy at least 2 pirates with each turret in the level.
Six Gun Salute	Slag Fleet	Get six pirates in a row to salute Ratchet while in the Pirate Disguise.
Gotta Catch 'Em All	Cragmite Ruins	Hit all Cragmite soldiers with the Mag-Net Launcher.
Ratchet and Goliath	Cragmite Ruins	Destroy multiple walkers using just the Nano-Swarmers.
Ratchet &...Not Clank?!	Cragmite Ruins	Use Mr. Zurkon in Cragmite's Ratchet-only segment.
Stay Still So I Can Shoot You!	Meridian	Use strafe-flip 10 times while fighting the Cragmite soldiers.
Now Boarding...	Meridian	Complete the Gyro-Cycle in 55 seconds.
Low Flying Howls	Meridian	Fly under an electrified barrier in the Robo-wings segment.
Extreme Alien Makeover	Fastoon2	Turn 10 Cragmites into penguins.
Empty Bag o' Tricks	Fastoon2	Complete the level without using any devices.
Nowhere to Hide	Fastoon2	Destroy every piece of breakable cover.
No, Up Your Arsenal	Global	Upgrade every weapon to the max.
Roflcopter	Global	Turn enemies into penguins, then use the Visicopter to destroy the penguins.
Stir Fry	Global	Kill 2 different enemy types using the Shock Ravager while they are trapped in a tornado.
Golden Children	Overall	Find all of the Gold Bolts.
Sacagawea	Global	Complete all of the maps 100%, leaving no area undiscovered.
Cheapskate	Global	Purchase a single Combustor round.
Everybody Dance Now	Global	Make every type of enemy in the game dance.
F5 on the Fujita Scale	Global	Pick up more than 10 enemies with one tornado.
Chorus Line	Global	Get 10+ enemies to dance together.
Happy Feet	Global	Get several penguins to dance on-screen.
Disco Inferno	Global	Use the Groovitron followed by the Pyro Blaster.
Bolts in the Bank	Global	Sell a bunch of Leviathan Souls to the Smuggler.
It's Like the North Pole Here	Global	Have at least 12-15 enemies and/or citizens turned into penguins at one time.
Say Hello to My Little Friend	Global	Kill 15 enemies with one RYNO shot.
For the Hoard!	Global	Get every item.
Promoted to Inspector	Global	Get every gadget.
Global Thermonuclear War	Global	Get every weapon.
It's Even Better the Second Time!	Global	Complete Challenge Mode.
The Hardest of Core	Global	Get all skill points and everything else in the game.

ROCK REVOLUTION

ALL CHARACTERS

At the main menu, press ●, ■, ●, ■, ●, ■, ●, ▲, ■.

ALL VENUES

At the main menu, press ■, ●, ▲, ●, ■, ●, ▲, ■, ▲.

SEGA SUPERSTARS TENNIS

UNLOCK CHARACTERS

Complete the following missions to unlock the corresponding character.

CHARACTER	MISSION TO COMPLETE
Alex Kidd	Mission 1 of Alex Kidd's World
Amy Rose	Mission 2 of Sonic the Hedgehog's World
Gilius	Mission 1 of Golden Axe's World
Gum	Mission 12 of Jet Grind Radio's World
Meemee	Mission 8 of Super Monkey Ball's World
Pudding	Mission 1 of Space Channel 5's World
Reala	Mission 2 of NiGHTs' World
Shadow The Hedgehog	Mission 14 of Sonic the Hedgehog's World

THE SIMPSONS GAME

After unlocking the following, the outfits can be changed at the downstairs closet in the Simpson's house. The Trophies can be viewed at different locations in the house: Bart's room, Lisa's room, Marge's room, and the garage.

BART'S OUTFITS AND TROPHIES (POSTER COLLECTION)

At the main menu, press Right, Left, ●, ●, ▲, R3.

HOMER'S OUTFITS AND TROPHIES (BEER BOTTLE COLLECTION)

At the main menu, press Left, Right, ▲, ▲, ●, L3.

LISA'S OUTFITS AND TROPHIES (DOLLS)

At the main menu, press ●, ▲, ●, ●, ●, Triangle, L3.

MARGE'S OUTFITS AND TROPHIES (HAIR PRODUCTS)

At the main menu, press ▲, ●, ▲, ▲, ●, R3.

SKATE

BEST BUY CLOTHES

At the Main menu, press Up, Down, Left, Right, ●, R1, ▲, L1.

SKATE 2

BIG BLACK

Select Enter Cheat from the Extras menu and enter letsdowork.

3D MODE

Select Enter Cheat from the Extras menu and enter strangeloops. Use glasses to view in 3D.

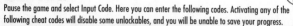

CHEAT CODES

Pause the game and select Input Code. Here you can enter the following codes. Activating any of the following cheat codes will disable some unlockables, and you will be unable to save your progress.

CHEAT	CODE
All Force Powers at Max Power	KATARN
All Force Push Ranks	EXARKUN
All Saber Throw Ranks	ADEGAN
All Repulse Ranks	DATHOMIR
All Saber Crystals	HURRIKANE
All Talents	JOCASTA
Deadly Saber	LIGHTSABER

COMBOS

Pause the game and select Input Code. Here you can enter the following codes. Activating any of the following cheat codes will disable some unlockables, and you will be unable to save your progress.

COMBO	CODE
All Combos	MOLDYCROW
Aerial Ambush	VENTRESS
Aerial Assault	EETHKOTH
Aerial Blast	YADDLE
Impale	BRUTALSTAB
Lightning Bomb	MASSASSI
Lightning Grenade	RAGNOS
Saber Slam	PLOKOON
Saber Sling	KITFISTO
Sith Saber Flurry	LUMIYA
Sith Slash	DARAGON
Sith Throw	SAZEN
New Combo	FREEDON
New Combo	MARAJADE

ALL DATABANK ENTRIES

Pause the game and select Input Code. Enter OSSUS.

MIRRORED LEVEL

Pause the game and select Input Code. Enter MINDTRICK. Re-enter the code to return level to normal.

SITH MASTER DIFFICULTY

Pause the game and select Input Code. Enter SITHSPAWN.

COSTUMES

Pause the game and select Input Code. Here you can enter the following codes.

COSTUME	CODE
All Costumes	SOHNDANN
Bail Organa	VICEROY
Ceremonial Jedi Robes	DANTOOINE
Drunken Kota	HARDBOILED
Emperor	MASTERMIND
Incinerator Trooper	PHOENIX
Jedi Adventure Robe	HOLOCRON
Kashyyyk Trooper	TK421GREEN
Kota	MANDALORE
Master Kento	WOOKIEE
Proxy	PROTOTYPE
Scout Trooper	FERRAL
Shadow Trooper	BLACKHOLE
Sith Stalker Armor	KORRIBAN
Snowtrooper	SNOWMAN
Stormtrooper	TK421WHITE
Stormtrooper Commander	TK421BLUE

STAR WARS THE CLONE WARS: REPUBLIC HEROES

SPIDER DROID-JAK UPGRADE

Pause the game, select Cheats from the Shop, and press Up, Left, Down, Left, Right, Left, Left Left.

STUNTMAN IGNITION

3 PROPS IN STUNT CREATOR MODE

Select Cheats from Extras and enter COOLPROP.

ALL ITEMS UNLOCKED FOR CONSTRUCTION MODE

Select Cheats from Extras and enter NOBLEMAN.

MVX SPARTAN

Select Cheats from Extras and enter fastride.

ALL CHEATS

Select Cheats from Extras and enter Wearefrozen.

This unlocks the following cheats: Slo-mo Cool, Thrill Cam, Vision Switcher, Nitro Addiction, Freaky Fast, and Ice Wheels.

ALL CHEATS

Select Cheats from Extras and enter Kungfoopete.

ICE WHEELS CHEAT
Select Cheats from Extras and enter IceAge.

NITRO ADDICTION CHEAT
Select Cheats from Extras and enter TheDuke.

VISION SWITCHER CHEAT
Select Cheats from Extras and enter GFXMODES.

SUPER PUZZLE FIGHTER II TURBO HD REMIX

PLAY AS AKUMA
At the character select, highlight Hsien-Ko and press Down.

PLAY AS DAN
At the character select, highlight Donovan and press Down.

PLAY AS DEVILOT
At the character select, highlight Morrigan and press Down.

PLAY AS ANITA
At the character select, hold L1 + R1 and choose Donovan.

PLAY AS HSIEN-KO'S TALISMAN
At the character select, hold L1 + R1 and choose Hsien-Ko.

PLAY AS MORRIGAN AS A BAT
At the character select, hold L1 + R1 and choose Morrigan.

SURF'S UP

ALL CHAMPIONSHIP LOCATIONS
Select Cheat Codes from the Extras menu and enter FREEVISIT.

ALL LEAF SLIDE STAGES
Select Cheat Codes from the Extras menu and enter GOINGDOWN.

ALL MULTIPLAYER LEVELS
Select Cheat Codes from the Extras menu and enter MULTIPASS.

ALL BOARDS
Select Cheat Codes from the Extras menu and enter MYPRECIOUS.

ASTRAL BOARD
Select Cheat Codes from the Extras menu and enter ASTRAL.

MONSOON BOARD
Select Cheat Codes from the Extras menu and enter MONSOON.

TINE SHOCKWAVE BOARD
Select Cheat Codes from the Extras menu and enter TINYSHOCKWAVE.

ALL CHARACTER CUSTOMIZATIONS
Select Cheat Codes from the Extras menu and enter TOPFASHION.

PLAY AS ARNOLD
Select Cheat Codes from the Extras menu and enter TINYBUTSTRONG.

PLAY AS ELLIOT
Select Cheat Codes from the Extras menu and enter SURPRISEGUEST.

PLAY AS GEEK
Select Cheat Codes from the Extras menu and enter SLOWANDSTEADY.

PLAY AS TANK EVANS
Select Cheat Codes from the Extras menu and enter IMTHEBEST.

PLAY AS TATSUHI KOBAYASHI

Select Cheat Codes from the Extras menu and enter KOBAYASHI.

PLAY AS ZEKE TOPANGA

Select Cheat Codes from the Extras menu and enter THELEGEND.

ALL VIDEOS AND SPEN GALLERY

Select Cheat Codes from the Extras menu and enter WATCHAMOVIE.

ART GALLERY

Select Cheat Codes from the Extras menu and enter NICEPLACE.

TIGER WOODS PGA TOUR 08

ALL COURSES

Select Password from EA Sports Extras and enter greensfees.

ALL GOLFERS

Select Password from EA Sports Extras and enter allstars.

WAYNE ROONEY

Select Password from EA Sports Extras and enter playfifa08.

INFINITE MONEY

Select Password from EA Sports Extras and enter cream.

TOM CLANCY'S HAWX

A-12 AVENGER II

At the hangar, hold L2 and press ●, L1, ●, R1, ▲, ■.

F-18 HARV

At the hangar, hold L2 and press L1, ▲, L1, ▲, L1, ■.

FB-22 STRIKE RAPTOR

At the hangar, hold L2 and press R1, ●, R1, ●, R1, ▲.

TONY HAWK'S PROVING GROUND

Select Cheat Codes from the Options and enter the following cheats. Some codes need to be enabled by selecting Cheats from the Options during a game.

UNLOCK	CHEAT	UNLOCK	CHEAT
Unlocks Boneman	CRAZYBONEMAN	Unlock FDR	THEPREZPARK
Unlocks Bosco	MOREMILK	Unlock Lansdowne	THELOCALPARK
Unlocks Cam	NOTACAMERA	Unlock Air & Space Museum	THEINDOORPARK
Unlocks Cooper	THECOOP	Unlocks all Fun Items	OVERTHETOP
Unlocks Eddie X	SKETCHY	Unlocks all CAS items	GIVEMESTUFF
Unlocks El Patinador	PILEDRIVER	Unlocks all Decks	LETSGOSKATE
Unlocks Eric	FLYAWAY	Unlock all Game Movies	WATCHTHIS
Unlocks Mad Dog	RABBIES	Unlock all Lounge Bling Items	SWEETSTUFF
Unlocks MCA	INTERGALACTIC		
Unlocks Mel	NOTADUDE	Unlock all Lounge Themes	LAIDBACKLOUNGE
Unlocks Rube	LOOKSSMELLY	Unlock all Rigger Pieces	IMGONNABUILD
Unlocks Spence	DAPPER	Unlock all Video Editor Effects	TRIPPY
Unlocks Shayne	MOVERS		
Unlocks TV Producer	SHAKER	Unlock all Video Editor Overlays	PUTEMONTOP

UNLOCK	CHEAT
All specials unlocked and in player's special list	LOTSOFTRICKS
Full Stats	BEEFEDUP

UNLOCK	CHEAT
Give player +50 skill points	NEEDSHELP

The following cheats lock you out of the Leaderboards:

UNLOCK	CHEAT
Unlocks Perfect Manual	STILLAINTFALLIN
Unlocks Perfect Rail	AINTFALLIN
Unlock Super Check	BOOYAH
Unlocks Unlimited Focus	MYOPIC
Unlimited Slash Grind	SUPERSLASHIN

UNLOCK	CHEAT
Unlocks 100% branch completion in NTT	FOREVERNAILED
No Bails	ANDAINTFALLI

You can not use the Video Editor with the following cheats:

UNLOCK	CHEAT
Unlocks Invisible Man	THEMISSING
Mini Skater	TINYTATER
No Board	MAGICMAN

TRANSFORMERS: THE GAME

INFINITE HEALTH

At the Main menu, press Left, Left, Up, Left, Right, Down, Right.

INFINITE AMMO

At the Main menu, press Up, Down, Left, Right, Up, Up, Down.

NO MILITARY OR POLICE

At the Main menu, press Right, Left, Right, Left, Right, Left, Right.

ALL MISSIONS

At the Main menu, press Down, Up, Left, Right, Right, Right, Up, Down.

BONUS CYBERTRON MISSIONS

At the Main menu, press Right, Up, Up, Down, Right, Left, Left.

GENERATION 1 SKIN: JAZZ

At the Main menu, press Left, Up, Down, Down, Left, Up, Right.

GENERATION 1 SKIN: MEGATRON

At the Main menu, press Down, Left, Left, Down, Right, Right, Up.

GENERATION 1 SKIN: OPTIMUS PRIME

At the Main menu, press Down, Right, Left, Up, Down, Down, Left.

GENERATION 1 SKIN: ROBOVISION OPTIMUS PRIME

At the Main menu, press Down, Down, Up, Up, Right, Right, Right.

GENERATION 1 SKIN: STARSCREAM

At the Main menu, press Right, Down, Left, Left, Down, Up, Up.

TRANSFORMERS REVENGE OF THE FALLEN

LOW GRAVITY MODE

Select Cheat Code and enter ✖, ●, ▲, L3, ▲, L3.

NO WEAPON OVERHEAT

Select Cheat Code and enter L3, ●, ✖, L3, ▲, L1.

41

ALWAYS IN OVERDRIVE MODE

Select Cheat Code and enter L1, ●, L1, ✕, ●, R3.

UNLIMITED TURBO

Select Cheat Code and enter ●, L3, ●, R3, ✕, ▲

NO SPECIAL COOLDOWN TIME

Select Cheat Code and enter R3, ●, R3, R3, ●, ✕.

INVINCIBILITY

Select Cheat Code and enter R3, ✕, ●, L3, ●, ●.

4X ENERGON FROM DEFEATED ENEMIES

Select Cheat Code and enter ▲, ●, ●, R3, ✕, ▲.

INCREASED WEAPON DAMAGE(ROBOT FORM)

Select the Cheat Code option and enter ▲, ▲, R3, ✕, L1, ▲.

INCREASED WEAPON DAMAGE(VEHICLE FORM)

Select Cheat Code and enter ▲, ●, R1, ✕, R3, L3.

MELEE INSTANT KILLS

Select the Cheat Code option and enter R3, ✕, L1, ●, R3, L1.

LOWER ENEMY ACCURACY

Select Cheat Code and enter ✕, L3, R3, L3, R3, R1.

INCREASED ENEMY HEALTH

Select Cheat Code and enter ●, ✕, L1, ●, R3, ▲.

INCREASED ENEMY DAMAGE

Select Cheat Code and enter L1, ▲, ✕, ▲, R3, R3.

INCREASED ENEMY ACCURACY

Select Cheat Code and enter ▲, ▲, ●, ✕, A, L1.

SPECIAL KILLS ONLY MODE

Select Cheat Code and enter ●, ●, R1, ●, ✕, L3.

UNLOCK ALL SHANGHAI MISSIONS & ZONES

Select Cheat Code and enter ▲, L3, R3, L1, ▲, ✕.

UNLOCK ALL WEST COAST MISSIONS & ZONES

Select Cheat Code and enter L1, R1, R3, ▲, R3, ●.

UNLOCK ALL DEEP SIX MISSIONS & ZONES

Select Cheat Code and enter ✕, R1, ▲, ●, ✕, L1.

UNLOCK ALL EAST COAST MISSIONS & ZONES

Select Cheat Code and enter R3, L3, R1, ✕, ●, ✕.

UNLOCK ALL CAIRO MISSIONS & ZONES

Select Cheat Code and enter R3, ▲, ✕, ▲, L3, L1.

UNLOCK & ACTIVATE ALL UPGRADES

Select Cheat Code and enter L1, ▲, L1, ●, ✕, ✕.

UNCHARTED 2: AMONG THIEVES

In Uncharted 2: Among Thieves, upon opening the store you'll have the option to hit the Square button to check for Uncharted: Drake's Fortune save data. You'll obtain cash for having save data! This cash can be used in the single and multiplayer stores. Could be useful if you want a head start online!

$20,000

Have a saved game of Uncharted: Drake's Fortune.

$80,000

Have a saved game of Uncharted: Drake's Fortune with the story completed at least once.

VIRTUA FIGHTER 5

WATCH MODE

Select Exhibition Mode, then at the character select, hold **L1** + **R1** and press ✖.

WALL-E

The following cheats will disable saving. The five possible characters starting with Wall-E and going down are:
Wall-E, Auto, EVE, M-O, GEL-A Steward.

ALL BONUS FEATURES UNLOCKED

Select Cheats from the Bonus Features menu and enter Wall-E, Auto, EVE, GEL-A Steward.

ALL GAME CONTENT UNLOCKED

Select Cheats from the Bonus Features menu and enter M-O, Auto, GEL-A Steward, EVE.

ALL SINGLE-PLAYER LEVELS UNLOCKED

Select Cheats from the Bonus Features menu and enter Auto, GEL-A Steward, M-O, Wall-E.

ALL MULTIPLAYER MAPS UNLOCKED

Select Cheats from the Bonus Features menu and enter EVE, M-O, Wall-E, Auto.

ALL HOLIDAY COSTUMES UNLOCKED

Select Cheats from the Bonus Features menu and enter Auto, Auto, GEL-A Steward, GEL-A Steward.

ALL MULTIPLAYER COSTUMES UNLOCKED

Select Cheats from the Bonus Features menu and enter GEL-A Steward, Wall-E, M-O, Auto.

UNLIMITED HEALTH UNLOCKED

Select Cheats from the Bonus Features menu and enter Wall-E, M-O, Auto, M-O.

WALL-E: MAKE ANY CUBE AT ANY TIME

Select Cheats from the Bonus Features menu and enter Auto, M-O, Auto, M-O.

WALL-EVE: MAKE ANY CUBE AT ANY TIME

Select Cheats from the Bonus Features menu and enter M-O, GEL-A Steward, EVE, EVE.

WALL-E WITH A LASER GUN AT ANY TIME

Select Cheats from the Bonus Features menu and enter Wall-E, EVE, EVE, Wall-E.

WALL-EVE WITH A LASER GUN AT ANY TIME

Select Cheats from the Bonus Features menu and enter GEL-A Steward, EVE, M-O, Wall-E.

WALL-E: PERMANENT SUPER LASER UPGRADE

Select Cheats from the Bonus Features menu and enter Wall-E, Auto, EVE, M-O.

EVE: PERMANENT SUPER LASER UPGRADE

Select Cheats from the Bonus Features menu and enter EVE, Wall-E, Wall-E, Auto.

CREDITS

Select Cheats from the Bonus Features menu and enter Auto, Wall-E, GEL-A Steward, M-O.

WORLD SERIES OF POKER 2008: BATTLE FOR THE BRACELETS

PHILLIP J. HELLMUTH

Enter BEATTHEBRAT as the player name.

WWE SMACKDOWN! VS. RAW 2008

HBK AND HHH'S DX OUTFIT

Select Cheat Codes from the Options and enter DXCostume69K2.

KELLY KELLY'S ALTERNATE OUTFIT

Select Cheat Codes from the Options and enter KellyKG12R.

BRET HART

Complete the March 31, 1996 Hall of Fame challenge by defeating Bret Hart with Shawn Michaels in a One-On-One 30-Minute Iron Man Match on Legend difficulty. Purchase from WWE Shop for $210,000.

MICK FOLEY

Complete the June 28, 1998 Hall of Fame challenge by defeating Mick Foley with The Undertaker in a H*** In a Cell Match on Legend difficulty. Purchase from WWE Shop for $210,000.

MR. MCMAHON

Win or successfully defend a championship (WWE or World Heavyweight) at WrestleMania in WWE 24/7 GM Mode. Purchase from WWE Shop for $110,000.

THE ROCK

Complete the April 1, 2001 Hall of Fame challenge by defeating The Rock with Steve Austin in a Single Match on Legend Difficulty. Purchase from WWE Shop for $210,000.

STEVE AUSTIN

Complete the March 23, 1997 Hall of Fame challenge by defeating Steve Austin with Bret Hart in a Submission Match on Legend Difficulty. Purchase from WWE Shop for $210,000.

TERRY FUNK

Complete the April 13, 1997 Hall of Fame challenge by defeating Tommy Dreamer, Sabu and Sandman with any Superstar in an ECW Extreme Rules 4-Way Match on Legend difficulty. Purchase from WWE Shop for $210,000.

MR. MCMAHON BALD

Must unlock Mr. McMahon as a playable character first. Purchase from WWE Shop for $60,000.

WWE SMACKDOWN VS. RAW 2010

THE ROCK

Select Cheat Codes from the Options menu and enter The Great One.

VINCE'S OFFICE AND DIRT SHEET FOR BACKSTAGE BRAWL

Select Cheat Codes from the Options menu and enter BonusBrawl.

SHAWN MICHAELS' NEW COSTUME

Select Cheat Codes from the Options menu and enter Bow Down.

RANDY ORTON'S NEW COSTUME

Select Cheat Codes from the Options menu and enter ViperRKO.

TRIPLE H'S NEW COSTUME

Select Cheat Codes from the Options menu and enter Suck IT!.

NINTENDO Wii™

CONTENTS

NINTENDO Wii™ VIRTUAL CONSOLE GAMES

CONTENTS

ASTRO BOY: THE VIDEO GAME

INVULNERABLE
Pause the game and press Up, Down, Down, Up, 1, 2.

MAX STATS
Pause the game and press Left, Left, 2, Down, Down, 1.

INFINITE SUPERS
Pause the game and press Left, 1, Right, 1, Up, Down.

INFINITE DASHES

Pause the game and press 2, 2, 1, 2, Left, Up.

DISABLE SUPERS

Pause the game and press 1, 1, 2, 2, 1, Left.

COSTUME SWAP (ARENA AND CLASSIC COSTUMES)

Pause the game and press 2, Up, 1, Up, Down, 2.

UNLOCK LEVELS

Pause the game and press Up, 1, Right, 1, Down, 1. This allows you to travel to any level from the Story menu.

AVATAR: THE LAST AIRBENDER

UNLIMITED HEALTH

Select Code Entry from Extras and enter 94677.

UNLIMITED CHI

Select Code Entry from Extras and enter 24463.

UNLIMITED COPPER

Select Code Entry from Extras and enter 23637.

NEVERENDING STEALTH

Select Code Entry from Extras and enter 53467.

1 HIT DISHONOR

Select Code Entry from Extras and enter 54641.

DOUBLE DAMAGE

Select Code Entry from Extras and enter 34743.

ALL TREASURE MAPS

Select Code Entry from Extras and enter 37437.

THE CHARACTER CONCEPT ART GALLERY

Select Code Entry from Extras and enter 97831.

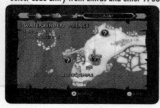 

AVATAR: THE LAST AIRBENDER-THE BURNING EARTH

DOUBLE DAMAGE
Go to the code entry section and enter 90210.

INFINITE LIFE
Go to the code entry section and enter 65049.

INFINITE SPECIAL ATTACKS
Go to the code entry section and enter 66206.

MAX LEVEL
Go to the code entry section and enter 89121.

ONE-HIT DISHONOR
Go to the code entry section and enter 28260.

ALL BONUS GAMES
Go to the code entry section and enter 99801.

ALL GALLERY ITEMS
Go to the code entry section and enter 85061.

AVATAR - THE LAST AIRBENDER: INTO THE INFERNO

After you have defeated the first level, The Awakening, go to Ember Island. Walk to the left past the volleyball net to a red and yellow door. Select Game Secrets and then Code Entry. Now you can enter the following cheats.

MAX COINS
Enter 66639224.

ALL ITEMS AVAILABLE FROM SHOP
Enter 34737253.

ALL CHAPTERS
Enter 52993833.

UNLOCK CONCEPT ART IN GALLERY
Enter 27858343.

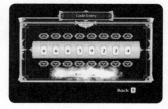

BEN 10: PROTECTOR OF EARTH

INVINCIBILITY
Select a game from the Continue option. Go to the Map Selection screen, press Plus and choose Extras. Select Enter Secret Code and enter XLR8, Heatblast, Wildvine, Fourarms.

ALL COMBOS
Select a game from the Continue option. Go to the Map Selection screen, press Plus and choose Extras. Select Enter Secret Code and enter Cannonblot, Heatblast, Fourarms, Heatblast.

ALL LOCATIONS

Select a game from the Continue option. Go to the Map Selection screen, press Plus and choose Extras. Select Enter Secret Code and enter Heatblast, XLR8, XLR8, Cannonblot.

DNA FORCE SKINS

Select a game from the Continue option. Go to the Map Selection screen, press Plus and choose Extras. Select Enter Secret Code and enter Wildvine, Fourarms, Heatblast, Cannonbolt.

DARK HEROES SKINS

Select a game from the Continue option. Go to the Map Selection screen, press Plus and choose Extras. Select Enter Secret Code and enter Cannonbolt, Cannonbolt, Fourarms, Heatblast.

ALL ALIEN FORMS

Select a game from the Continue option. Go to the Map Selection screen, press Plus and choose Extras. Select Enter Secret Code and enter Wildvine, Fourarms, Heatblast, Wildvine.

MASTER CONTROL

Select a game from the Continue option. Go to the Map Selection screen, press Plus and choose Extras. Select Enter Secret Code and enter Cannonbolt, Heatblast, Wildvine, Fourarms.

BLAZING ANGELS: SQUADRONS OF WWII

ALL AIRCRAFT AND CAMPAIGNS

After you have chosen a pilot, hold Minus + Plus and press Left, Right, 1, 2, 2, 1.

GOD MODE

Pause the game, hold Minus and press 1, 2, 1, 2.

WEAPON DAMAGE INCREASED

Pause the game, hold Minus and press 2, 1, 1, 2.

BOOM BLOX

ALL TOYS IN CREATE MODE

At the title screen, press Up, Right, Down, Left to bring up a cheats menu. Enter Tool Pool.

SLOW-MO IN SINGLE PLAYER

At the title screen, press Up, Right, Down, Left to bring up a cheats menu. Enter Blox Time.

CHEERLEADERS BECOME PROFILE CHARACTER

At the title screen, press Up, Right, Down, Left to bring up a cheats menu. Enter My Team.

FLOWER EXPLOSIONS

At the title screen, press Up, Right, Down, Left to bring up a cheats menu. Enter Flower Power.

JINGLE BLOCKS

At the title screen, press Up, Right, Down, Left to bring up a cheats menu. Enter Maestro.

BUILD-A-BEAR WORKSHOP: A FRIEND FUR ALL SEASONS

ALL ISLANDS, MINIGAMES, OUTFITS, AND ACCESSORIES

At the main menu, press Up, Down, Left, Right, A, B.

CARS MATER-NATIONAL

ALL ARCADE RACES, MINI-GAMES, AND WORLDS
Select Codes/Cheats from the options and enter PLAYALL.

ALL CARS
Select Codes/Cheats from the options and enter MATTEL07.

ALTERNATE LIGHTNING MCQUEEN COLORS
Select Codes/Cheats from the options and enter NCEDUDZ.

ALL COLORS FOR OTHERS
Select Codes/Cheats from the options and enter PAINTIT.

UNLIMITED TURBO
Select Codes/Cheats from the options and enter ZZOOOOM.

EXTREME ACCELERATION
Select Codes/Cheats from the options and enter OTO200X.

EXPERT MODE
Select Codes/Cheats from the options and enter VRYFAST.

ALL BONUS ART
Select Codes/Cheats from the options and enter BUYTALL.

CARS RACE-O-RAMA

ALL ARCADE MODE EVENTS
Select Cheats from the Options menu and enter SLVRKEY.

ALL STORY MODE EVENTS
Select Cheats from the Options menu and enter GOLDKEY.

ALL OF LIGHTNING MCQUEEN'S FRIENDS
Select Cheats from the Options menu and enter EVRYBDY.

ALL LIGHTNING MCQUEEN CUSTOM KIT PARTS
Select Cheats from the Options menu and enter GR8MODS.

ALL PAINT JOBS FOR ALL NON-LIGHTNING MCQUEEN CHARACTERS
Select Cheats from the Options menu and enter CARSHOW.

CODE LYOKO: QUEST FOR INFINITY

UNLOCK EVERYTHING
Pause the game and press 2, 1, C, Z, 2, 1.

UNLIMITED HEALTH AND POWER
Pause the game and press 2, 2, Z, Z, 1, 1.

INCREASE SPEED
Pause the game and press Z, 1, 2, 1 (x3).

INCREASE DAMAGE
Pause the game and press 1, Z, Z, C (x3).

CONFIGURATION A
Pause the game and press 2, Z, 1, Z, C, Z.

CONFIGURATION B
Pause the game and press C, C, 1, C, Z, C.

ALL ABILITIES
Pause the game and press Z, C, Z, C (x3).

ALL BONUSES
Pause the game and press 1, 2, C, 2 (x3).

ALL GOODIES
Pause the game and press C, 2, 2, Z, C, Z.

CONTRA REBIRTH

DEBUG MENU
At the title screen, press Plus + 1 + 2.

CORALINE

UNLIMITED LEVEL SKIP
Select Cheats from the Options menu and enter Beldam.

UNLIMITED HEALTH
Select Cheats from the Options menu and enter beets.

UNLIMITED FIREFLYS
Select Cheats from the Options menu and enter garden.

FREE HALL PASSES
Select Cheats from the Options menu and enter well.

BUTTON EYE CORALINE
Select Cheats from the Options menu and enter cheese.

DE BLOB

INVULNERABILITY
During a game, hold C and press 1, 1, 1, 1.
Re-enter the code to disable.

LIFE UP
During a game, hold C and press 1, 1, 2, 2

TIME BONUS
During a game, hold C and press 1, 2, 1, 2.
This adds 10 minutes to your time.

ALL MOODS
At the main menu, hold C and press B, B, 1, 2, 1, 2, B, B.

ALL MULTIPLAYER LEVELS

At the main menu, hold C and press 2, 2, B, B, 1, 1, B, B.

DEFEND YOUR CASTLE

GIANT ENEMIES

Select Credits and click SMB3W4 when it appears.

TINY UNITS

Select Credits and click Chuck Norris when it appears.

EASY LEVEL COMPLETE

Pause the game and wait for the sun to set. Unpause to complete the level.

DISNEY PRINCESS: ENCHANTED JOURNEY

BELLE'S KINGDOM

Select Secrets and enter GASTON.

GOLDEN SET

Select Secrets and enter BLUEBIRD.

FLOWER WAND

Select Secrets and enter SLEEPY.

HEART WAND

Select Secrets and enter BASHFUL.

SHELL WAND

Select Secrets and enter RAJAH.

SHIELD WAND

Select Secrets and enter CHIP.

STAR WAND

Select Secrets and enter SNEEZY.

DONKEY KONG COUNTRY 2: DIDDY'S KONG QUEST

SOUND TEST

Highlight Two Player and press Down (x5).

CHEAT MODE

Press Down (x5) again after getting Sound Test to access the cheat mode. Now you can enter the following:

50 LIVES

Press Y, A, Select, A, Down, Left, A, Down.

HARD MODE

Press B, A, Right, Right, A, Left, A, X. This gets rid of the barrels.

DRAGON BALL Z: BUDOKAI TENKAICHI 2

Hold Z + Minus to clear codes.

DOUBLE FIST POWER

At the Stage Select in vs mode, hold Z + Plus to start code input. Swing the Nunchuk Right, Wiimote Left, Wiimote Left + Nunchuk Right, Wiimote and Nunchuk Down.

TAIL POWER

At the Stage Select in vs mode, hold Z + Plus to start code input. Swing the Wiimote Down, Up, Left, Right.

DRAGON BALL Z: BUDOKAI TENKAICHI 3

SURVIVAL MODE

Clear 30 missions in Mission 100 mode.

DRAGON BLADE: WRATH OF FIRE

ALL LEVELS

At the title screen, hold Plus + Minus and select New Game or Load game. Hold the buttons until the stage select appears.

EASY DIFFICULTY

At the title screen, hold Z + 2 when selecting "New Game."

HARD DIFFICLUTY

At the title screen, hold C + 2 when selecting "New Game."
To clear the following codes, hold Z at the stage select.

DRAGON HEAD

At the stage select, hold Z and press Plus. Immediately Swing Wii Remote Right, swing Wii Remote Down, swing Nunchuk Left, swing Nunchuk Right.

DRAGON WINGS

At the stage select, hold Z and press Plus. Immediately Swing Nunchuk Up + Wii Remote Up, swing Nunchuk Down + Wii Remote Down, swing Nunchuk Right + Wii Remote Left, swing Nunchuk Left + Wii Remote Right.

TAIL POWER

At the stage select, hold Z and press Plus. Immediately Swing your Wii Remote Down, Up, Left, and Right.

DOUBLE FIST POWER

At the stage select, hold Z and press Plus. Immediately swing your Nunchuk Right; swing your Wii Remote left; swing your Nunchuk right while swinging your Wii Remote left; swing both the Wii Remote and the Nunchuk down.

FAMILY FEUD 2010 EDITION

NEW WARDROBE

Select the lock tab from the Wardrobe screen and enter FAMILY.

GHOST SQUAD

COSTUMES

Reach the following levels in single-player to unlock the corresponding costume.

LEVEL	COSTUME	LEVEL	COSTUME
07	Desert Camouflage	30	Urban Camouflage
10	Policeman	34	Virtua Cop
15	Tough Guy	38	Future Warrior
18	Sky Camouflage	50	Ninja
20	World War II	60	Panda Suit
23	Cowboy	99	Gold Uniform

NINJA MODE

Play through Arcade Mode.

PARADISE MODE

Play through Ninja Mode.

G.I. JOE: THE RISE OF COBRA

CLASSIC DUKE

At the title screen press Left, Up, -, Up, Right, +.

CLASSIC SCARLETT

At the title screen press Right, Up, Down, Down, +.

GODZILLA UNLEASHED

UNLOCK ALL

At the main menu, press A + Up to bring up the cheat entry screen. Enter 204935.

90000 STORE POINTS

At the main menu, press A + Up to bring up the cheat entry screen. Enter 031406.

SET DAY

At the main menu, press A + Up to bring up the cheat entry screen. Enter 0829XX, where XX represents the day. Use 00 for day one.

SHOW MONSTER MOVES

At the main menu, press A + Up to bring up the cheat entry screen. Enter 411411.

VERSION NUMBER

At the main menu, press A + Up to bring up the cheat entry screen. Enter 787321.

MOTHERSHIP LEVEL

Playing as the Aliens, destroy the mothership in the Invasion level.

GRADIUS REBIRTH

4 OPTIONS

Pause the game and press Up, Up, Down, Down, Left, Right, Left, Right, Fire, Powerup. This code can be used once for each stage you have attempted.

GRAVITRONIX

VERSUS OPTIONS AND LEVEL SELECT

At the Options menu, press 1, 2, 2, 2, 1.

THE GRIM ADVENTURES OF BILLY & MANDY

CONCEPT ART

At the Main menu, hold 1 and press Up, Up, Down, Down, Left, Right, Left, Right.

ICE AGE 2: THE MELTDOWN

INFINITE PEBBLES

Pause the game and press Down, Down, Left, Up, Up, Right, Up, Down.

INFINITE ENERGY

Pause the game and press Down, Left, Right, Down, Down, Right, Left, Down.

INFINITE HEALTH

Pause the game and press Up, Right, Down, Up, Left, Down, Right, Left.

INDIANA JONES AND THE STAFF OF KINGS

FATE OF ATLANTIS GAME

At the main menu, hold Z and press A, Up, Up, B, Down, Down, Left, Right, Left, B.

IRON MAN

ARMOR SELECTION

Iron Man's different armor suits are unlocked by completing certain missions. Refer to the following tables for when each is unlocked. After selecting a mission to play, you get the opportunity to pick the armor you wish to use.

COMPLETE MISSION	SUIT UNLOCKED
1: Escape	Mark I
2: First Flight	Mark II
3: Fight Back	Mark III
6: Flying Fortress	Comic Tin Can
9: Home Front	Classic
13: Showdown	Silver Centurion

CONCEPT ART

Concept Art is unlocked after finding certain numbers of Weapon Crates.

CONCEPT ART UNLOCKED	NUMBER OF WEAPON CRATES FOUND
Environments Set 1	6
Environments Set 2	12
Iron Man	18
Environments Set 3	24
Enemies	30
Environments Set 4	36
Villains	42
Vehicles	48
Covers	50

KUNG FU PANDA

INFINITE CHI

Select Cheats from the Extra menu and press Down, Right, Left, Up, Down.

INVINCIBILITY

Select Cheats from the Extra menu and press Down, Down, Right, Up, Left.

4X DAMAGE MULTIPLYER

Select Cheats from the Extra menu and press Up, Down, Up, Right, Left.

ALL MULTIPLAYER CHARACTERS

Select Cheats from the Extra menu and press Left, Down, Left, Right, Down.

DRAGON WARRIOR OUTFIT IN MULTIPLAYER

Select Cheats from the Extra menu and press Left, Down, Right, Left, Up.

THE LEGEND OF SPYRO: DAWN OF THE DRAGON

INFINITE HEALTH

Pause the game, hold Z and move the Nunchuk Right, Right, Down, Down, Left.

INFINITE MANA

Pause the game, hold Z and move the Nunchuk Up, Right, Up, Left, Down.

MAX XP

Pause the game, hold Z and move the Nunchuk Up, Left, Left, Down, Up.

ALL ELEMENTAL UPGRADES

Pause the game, hold Z and move the Nunchuk Left, Up, Down, Up, Right.

LEGO BATMAN

BATCAVE CODES

Using the computer in the Batcave, select Enter Code and enter the following codes.

CHARACTERS

CHARACTER	CODE	CHARACTER	CODE
Alfred	ZAQ637	Penguin Henchman	BJH782
Batgirl	JKR331	Penguin Minion	KJP748
Bruce Wayne	BDJ327	Poison Ivy Goon	GTB899
Catwoman (Classic)	M1AAWW	Police Marksman	HKG984
Clown Goon	HJK327	Police Officer	JRY983
Commissioner Gordon	DDP967	Riddler Goon	CRY928
Fishmonger	HGY748	Riddler Henchman	XEU824
Freeze Girl	XVK541	S.W.A.T.	HTF114
Joker Goon	UTF782	Sailor	NAV592
Joker Henchman	YUN924	Scientist	JFL786
Mad Hatter	JCA283	Security Guard	PLB946
Man-Bat	NYU942	The Joker (Tropical)	CCB199
Military Policeman	MKL382	Yeti	NJL412
Nightwing	MVY759	Zoo Sweeper	DWR243
Penguin Goon	NKA238		

VEHICLES

VEHICLE	CODE	VEHICLE	CODE
Bat-Tank	KNTT4B	Mr. Freeze's Kart	BCT229
Bruce Wayne's Private Jet	LEA664	Penguin Goon Submarine	BTN248
Catwoman's Motorcycle	HPL826	Police Bike	LJP234
Garbage Truck	DUS483	Police Boat	PLC999
Goon Helicopter	GCH328	Police Car	KJL832
Harbor Helicopter	CHP735	Police Helicopter	CWR732
Harley Quinn's Hammer Truck	RDT637	Police Van	MAC788
Mad Hatter's Glider	HS000W	Police Watercraft	VJD328
Mad Hatter's Steamboat	M4DM4N	Riddler's Jet	HAHAHA
Mr. Freeze's Iceberg	ICYICE	Robin's Submarine	TTF453
The Joker's Van	JUK657	Two-Face's Armored Truck	EFE933

CHEATS

CHEAT	CODE	CHEAT	CODE
Always Score Multiply	9LRGNB	More Batarang Targets	XWP645
Fast Batarangs	JRBDCB	Piece Detector	KHJ554
Fast Walk	ZOLM6N	Power Brick Detector	MMN786
Flame Batarang	D8NYWH	Regenerate Hearts	HJH7HJ
Freeze Batarang	XPN4NG	Score x2	N4NR3E
Extra Hearts	ML3KHP	Score x4	CX9MAT
Fast Build	EVG26J	Score x6	MLVNF2
Immune to Freeze	JXUDY6	Score x8	WCCDB9
Invincibility	WYD5CP	Score x10	18HW07
Minikit Detector	ZXGH9J		

LEGO INDIANA JONES: THE ORIGINAL ADVENTURES

CHARACTERS

Approach the blackboard in the Classsroom and enter the following codes.

CHARACTER	CODE	CHARACTER	CODE
Bandit	12N68W	Enemy Boxer	8246RB
Bandit Swordsman	1MK4RT	Enemy Butler	VJ48W3
Barranca	04EM94	Enemy Guard	VJ7R51
Bazooka Trooper (Crusade)	MK83R7	Enemy Guard (Mountains)	YR47WM
Bazooka Trooper (Raiders)	S93Y5R	Enemy Officer	572E61
Belloq	CHN3YU	Enemy Officer (Desert)	2MK450
Belloq (Jungle)	TDR197	Enemy Pilot	B84ELP
Belloq (Robes)	VEO29L	Enemy Radio Operator	1MF94R
British Commander	B73EUA	Enemy Soldier (Desert)	4NSU7Q
British Officer	VJ5TI9	Fedora	V75YSP
British Soldier	DJ512W	First Mate	0GIN24
Captain Katanga	VJ3TT3	Grail Knight	NE6THI
Chatter Lal	ENW936	Hovitos Tribesman	HOV1SS
Chatter Lal (Thuggee)	CNH4RY	Indiana Jones (Desert Disguise)	4J8S4M
Chen	3NK48T	Indiana Jones (Officer)	VJ850S
Colonel Dietrich	2K9RKS	Jungle Guide	24PF34
Colonel Vogel	8EAL4H	Kao Kan	WM046L
Dancing Girl	C7EJ21	Kazim	NRH23J
Donovan	3NFTU8	Kazim (Desert)	3M29TJ
Elsa (Desert)	JSNRT9	Lao Che	2NK479
Elsa (Officer)	VMJ5US	Maharajah	NFK5N2

CHARACTER	CODE
Major Toht	13NS01
Masked Bandit	N48SF0
Mola Ram	FJUR31
Monkey Man	3RF6YJ
Pankot Assassin	2NKT72
Pankot Guard	VN28RH
Sherpa Brawler	VJ37WJ
Sherpa Gunner	ND762W
Slave Child	0E3ENW

CHARACTER	CODE
Thuggee	VM683E
Thuggee Acolyte	T2R3F9
Thuggee Slave Driver	VBS7GW
Village Dignitary	KD48TN
Village Elder	4682E1
Willie (Dinner Suit)	VK93R7
Willie (Pajamas)	MEN4IP
Wu Han	3NSLT8

EXTRAS

Approach the blackboard in the Classsroom and enter the following codes. Some cheats need to be enabled by selecting Extras from the pause menu.

CHEAT	CODE
Artifact Detector	VIKED7
Beep Beep	VNF59Q
Character Treasure	VIES2R
Disarm Enemies	VKRNS9
Disguises	4ID1N6
Fast Build	V83SL0
Fast Dig	378RS6
Fast Fix	FJ59WS
Fertilizer	B1GW1F
Ice Rink	33GM7J
Parcel Detector	VUT673
Poo Treasure	WWQ1SA

CHEAT	CODE
Regenerate Hearts	MDLP69
Secret Characters	3X44AA
Silhouettes	3HE85H
Super Scream	VN3R7S
Super Slap	0P1TA5
Treasure Magnet	H86LA2
Treasure x10	VI3PS8
Treasure x2	VM4TS9
Treasure x4	VLWEN3
Treasure x6	V84RYS
Treasure x8	A72E1M

LEGO STAR WARS: THE COMPLETE SAGA

The following still need to be purchase after entering the codes.

CHARACTERS

ADMIRAL ACKBAR

At the bar in Mos Eisley Cantina, select Enter Code and enter ACK646.

BATTLE DROID (COMMANDER)

At the bar in Mos Eisley Cantina, select Enter Code and enter KPF958.

BOBA FETT (BOY)

At the bar in Mos Eisley Cantina, select Enter Code and enter GGF539.

BOSS NASS

At the bar in Mos Eisley Cantina, select Enter Code and enter HHY697.

CAPTAIN TARPALS

At the bar in Mos Eisley Cantina, select Enter Code and enter QRN714.

COUNT DOOKU

At the bar in Mos Eisley Cantina, select Enter Code and enter DDD748.

DARTH MAUL

At the bar in Mos Eisley Cantina, select Enter Code and enter EUK421.

EWOK

At the bar in Mos Eisley Cantina, select Enter Code and enter EWK785.

GENERAL GRIEVOUS

At the bar in Mos Eisley Cantina, select Enter Code and enter PMN576.

GREEDO

At the bar in Mos Eisley Cantina, select Enter Code and enter ZZR636.

IG-88

At the bar in Mos Eisley Cantina, select Enter Code and enter GIJ989.

IMPERIAL GUARD

At the bar in Mos Eisley Cantina, select Enter Code and enter GUA850.

JANGO FETT

At the bar in Mos Eisley Cantina, select Enter Code and enter KLJ897.

KI-ADI MUNDI

At the bar in Mos Eisley Cantina, select Enter Code and enter MUN486.

LUMINARA

At the bar in Mos Eisley Cantina, select Enter Code and enter LUM521.

PADMÉ

At the bar in Mos Eisley Cantina, select Enter Code and enter VBJ322.

R2-Q5

At the bar in Mos Eisley Cantina, select Enter Code and enter EVILR2.

STORMTROOPER

At the bar in Mos Eisley Cantina, select Enter Code and enter NBN431.

TAUN WE

At the bar in Mos Eisley Cantina, select Enter Code and enter PRX482.

VULTURE DROID

At the bar in Mos Eisley Cantina, select Enter Code and enter BDC866.

WATTO

At the bar in Mos Eisley Cantina, select Enter Code and enter PLL967.

ZAM WESELL

At the bar in Mos Eisley Cantina, select Enter Code and enter 584HJF.

SKILLS

DISGUISE

At the bar in Mos Eisley Cantina, select Enter Code and enter BRJ437.

FORCE GRAPPLE LEAP

At the bar in Mos Eisley Cantina, select Enter Code and enter CLZ738.

VEHICLES

DROID TRIFIGHTER

At the bar in Mos Eisley Cantina, select Enter Code and enter AAB123.

IMPERIAL SHUTTLE

At the bar in Mos Eisley Cantina, select Enter Code and enter HUT845.

TIE INTERCEPTOR

At the bar in Mos Eisley Cantina, select Enter Code and enter INT729.

TIE FIGHTER

At the bar in Mos Eisley Cantina, select Enter Code and enter DBH897.

ZAM'S AIRSPEEDER

At the bar in Mos Eisley Cantina, select Enter Code and enter UUU875.

MADDEN NFL 10

UNLOCK EVERYTHING

Select Enter Game Code from Extras and enter THEWORKS.

FRANCHISE MODE

Select Enter Game Code from Extras and enter TEAMPLAYER.

SITUATION MODE

Select Enter Game Code from Extras and enter YOUCALLIT.

SUPERSTAR MODE

Select Enter Game Code from Extras and enter EGOBOOST.

PRO BOWL STADIUM

Select Enter Game Code from Extras and enter ALLSTARS.

SUPER BOWL STADIUM

Select Enter Game Code from Extras and enter THEBIGSHOW.

MADSTONE

HIGH GRAVITY

At the main menu press Down, Down, Down, Down, Right, Left, Right, Left.

LOW GRAVITY

At the main menu press Up, Up, Left, Left, Up, Up, Right, Right.

PLAYER SKULLS IN ARCADE MODE

At the difficulty select press Up, Right, Down, Left, Up, Right, Down, Left.

SAVANT MODE IN ARCADE MODE

At the difficulty select, press Down (x10).

MARBLE SAGA: KORORINPA

MASTER HIGGINS BALL

Select ??? from the Options. Press A on the right lamp, the left lamp twice, and the right lamp again. Now select the right icon and enter TV, Car, Sunflower, Bike, Helicopter, Strawberry.

MIRROR MODE

Select ??? from the Options. Press A on the right lamp, the left lamp twice, and the right lamp again. Now select the right icon and enter Beetle, Clover, Boy, Plane, Car, Bike.

MARIO & SONIC AT THE OLYMPIC GAMES

UNLOCK 4X100M RELAY EVENT
Medal in Mercury, Venus, Jupiter, and Saturn.

UNLOCK SINGLE SCULLS EVENT
Medal in Mercury, Venus, Jupiter, and Saturn.

UNLOCK DREAM RACE EVENT
Medal in Mercury, Venus, Jupiter, and Saturn.

UNLOCK ARCHERY EVENT
Medal in Moonlight Circuit.

UNLOCK HIGH JUMP EVENT
Medal in Stardust Circuit.

UNLOCK 400M EVENT
Medal in Planet Circuit.

UNLOCK DREAM FENCING EVENT
Medal in Comet Circuit.

UNLOCK DREAM TABLE TENNIS EVENT
Medal in Satellite Circuit.

UNLOCK 400M HURDLES EVENT
Medal in Sunlight Circuit.

UNLOCK POLE VAULT EVENT
Medal in Meteorite Circuit.

UNLOCK VAULT EVENT
Medal in Meteorite Circuit.

UNLOCK DREAM PLATFORM EVENT
Medal in Cosmos Circuit.

CROWNS
Get all gold medals in all events with a character to unlock their crown.

MARIO KART WII

CHARACTERS

CHARACTER	HOW TO UNLOCK
Baby Daisy	Earn 1 Star in 50cc for Mushroom, Flower, Star, and Special Cups
Baby Luigi	Unlock 8 Expert Staff Ghost Data in Time Trials
Birdo	Race 16 different courses in Time Trials or win 250 versus races
Bowser Jr.	Earn 1 Star in 100cc for Shell, Banana, Leaf, and Lightning Cups
Daisy	Win 150cc Special Cup
Diddy Kong	Win 50cc Lightning Cup
Dry Bones	Win 100cc Leaf Cup
Dry Bowser	Earn 1 Star in 150cc for Mushroom, Flower, Star, and Special Cups
Funky Kong	Unlock 4 Expert Staff Ghost Data in Time Trials
King Boo	Win 50cc Star Cup
Mii Outfit A	Win 100cc Special Cup
Mii Outfit B	Unlock all 32 Expert Staff Ghost Data in Time Trials
Mii Outfit C	Get 15,000 points in Versus Mode
Rosalina	Have a Super Mario Galaxy save file and she is unlocked after 50 races or earn 1 Star in all Mirror Cups
Toadette	Race 32 different courses in Time Trials

KARTS

KART	HOW TO UNLOCK
Blue Falcon	Win Mirror Lightning Cup
Cheep Charger	Earn 1 Star in 50cc for Mushroom, Flower, Star, and Special Cups
Rally Romper	Unlock an Expert Staff Ghost Data in Time Trials
B Dasher Mk. 2	Unlock 24 Expert Staff Ghost Data in Time Trials
Royal Racer	Win 150cc Leaf Cup
Turbo Blooper	Win 50cc Leaf Cup
Aero Glider	Earn 1 Star in 150cc for Mushroom, Flower, Star, and Special Cups
Dragonetti	Win 150cc Lightning Cup
Piranha Prowler	Win 50cc Special Cup

BIKES

KART	HOW TO UNLOCK
Bubble Bike	Win Mirror Leaf Cup
Magikruiser	Race 8 different courses in Time Trials
Quacker	Win 150cc Star Cup
Dolphin Dasher	Win Mirror Star Cup
Nitrocycle	Earn 1 Star in 100cc for all cups
Rapide	Win 100cc Lightning Cup
Phantom	Win Mirror Special Cup
Torpedo	Unlock 12 Expert Staff Ghost Data in Time Trials
Twinkle Star	Win 100cc Star Cup

MARVEL SUPER HERO SQUAD

IRON MAN BONUS COSTUMES

Select Enter Code from the Options and enter 111111.

HULK BONUS COSTUMES

Select Enter Code from the Options and enter 222222.

WOLVERINE BONUS COSTUMES

Select Enter Code from the Options and enter 333333.

THOR BONUS COSTUMES

Select Enter Code from the Options and enter 444444.

SILVER SURFER BONUS COSTUMES

Select Enter Code from the Options and enter 555555.

FALCON BONUS COSTUMES

Select Enter Code from the Options and enter 666666.

CHEAT SUPER KNOCKBACK

Select Enter Code from the Options and enter 777777.

CHEAT NO BLOCK MODE
Select Enter Code from the Options and enter 888888.

DR. DOOM BONUS COSTUMES
Select Enter Code from the Options and enter 999999.

MARVEL ULTIMATE ALLIANCE

UNLOCK ALL SKINS
At the Team menu, press Up, Down, Left, Right, Left, Right, Plus.

UNLOCKS ALL HERO POWERS
At the Team menu, press Left, Right, Up, Down, Up, Down, Plus.

ALL HEROES TO LEVEL 99
At the Team menu, press Up, Left, Up, Left, Down, Right, Down, Right, Plus.

UNLOCK ALL HEROES
At the Team menu, press Up, Up, Down, Down, Left, Left, Left, Plus.

UNLOCK DAREDEVIL
At the Team menu, press Left, Left, Right, Right, Up, Down, Up, Down, Plus.

UNLOCK SILVER SURFER
At the Team menu, press Down, Left, Left, Up, Right, Up, Down, Left, Plus.

GOD MODE
During gameplay, press Up, Down, Up, Down, Up, Left, Down, Right, Plus.

TOUCH OF DEATH
During gameplay, press Left, Right, Down, Down, Right, Left, Plus.

SUPER SPEED
During gameplay, press Up, Left, Up, Right, Down, Right, Plus.

FILL MOMENTUM
During gameplay, press Left, Right, Right, Left, Up, Down, Down, Up, Plus.

UNLOCK ALL COMICS
At the Review menu, press Left, Right, Right, Left, Up, Up, Right, Plus.

UNLOCK ALL CONCEPT ART
At the Review menu, press Down, Down, Down, Right, Right, Left, Down, Plus.

UNLOCK ALL CINEMATICS
At the Review menu, press Up, Left, Left, Up, Right, Right, Up, Plus.

UNLOCK ALL LOAD SCREENS
At the Review menu, press Up, Down, Right, Left, Up, Up Down, Plus.

UNLOCK ALL COURSES
At the Comic Missions menu, press Up, Right, Left, Down, Up, Right, Left, Down, Plus.

MARVEL: ULTIMATE ALLIANCE 2

GOD MODE
At any point during a game, press Up, Up, Down, Down, Left, Right, Down.

GIVE MONEY
At the Team Select or Hero Details screen press Up, Down, Down, Up, Up, Up, Down.

UNLOCK ALL POWERS
At the Team Select or Hero Details screen press Up, Up, Down, Down, Left, Right, Right, Left.

ADVANCE ALL CHARACTERS TO L99
At the Hero Details screen press Down, Up, Left, Up, Right, Up, Left, Down.

UNLOCK ALL BONUS MISSIONS
While using the Bonus Mission Simulator, press Up, Right, Down, Left, Left, Right, Up, Up.

ADD 1 CHARACTER LEVEL

During a game, press Down, Up, Right, Up, Right, Up, Right, Down.

ADD 10 CHARACTER LEVELS

During a game, press Down, Up, Left, Up, Left, Up, Left, Down.

MLB POWER PROS

EXTRA FORMS

At the main menu, press Right, Left, Up, Down, Down, Right, Right, Up, Up, Left, Down, Left.

VIEW MLB PLAYERS AT CUSTOM PLAYER MENU

Select View or Delete Custom Players/Password Display from My Data and press Up, Up, Down, Down, Left, Right, Left, Right, 1, 2.

MONSTER JAM

TRUCKS

As you collect monster points, they are tallied toward your Championship Score. Trucks are unlocked when you reach certain point totals.

TRUCK	POINTS
Destroyer	10,000
Blacksmith	50,000
El Toro Loco	70,000
Suzuki	110,000
Maximum Destruction	235,000

MYSIMS

PASSWORD SCREEN

Press the Minus button to bring up the pause screen. Then enter the following with the Wii Remote: 2, 1, Down, Up, Down, Up, Left, Left, Right, Right. Now you can enter the following passwords:

OUTFITS

Camouflage pants	N10ng5g
Diamond vest	Tglg0ca
Genie outfit	Gvsb3k1
Kimono dress	I3hkdvs
White jacket	R705aan

FURNITURE

Bunk bed	F3nevr0
Hourglass couch	Ghtymba
Modern couch	T7srhca
Racecar bed	Ahvmrva
Rickshaw bed	Itha7da

MYSIMS KINGDOM

DETECTIVE OUTFIT

Pause the game and press Left, Right, Left, Right, Left, Right.

SWORDSMAN OUTFIT

Pause the game and press Down, Up, Down, Up, Down, Up, Down, Up.

TATTOO VEST OUTFIT

Pause the game and press C, Z, C, Z, B, A, B, A.

MYSIMS AGENTS

ASTRONAUT SUIT

At the Create-a-Sim screen, press Up, Down, Up, Down, Left, Right, Left, Right.

BLACK NINJA OUTFIT

At the Create-a-Sim screen, press Right, Up, Right, Up, Down, Left, Down, Left.

STEALTH SUIT

At the Create-a-Sim screen, press Left, Right, Left, Right, Up, Down, Up, Down.

NASCAR KART RACING

JOEY LOGANO

Select Enter Cheat from the Profile Info menu and enter 426378.

NBA LIVE 08

AGENT ZERO SHOES

At the extras menu, enter ADGILLIT6BE as a code.

CUBA SHOES

At the extras menu, enter ADGILLIT4BC as a code.

CUSTOMIZE SHOES

At the extras menu, enter ADGILLIT5BD as a code.

DUNCAN ALL STAR SHOES

At the extras menu, enter FE454DFJCC as a code.

GIL WOOD SHOES

At the extras menu, enter ADGILLIT1B9 as a code.

GIL ZERO ALL STAR SHOES

At the extras menu, enter 23DN1PPOG4 as a code.

TS LIGHTSWITCH AWAY SHOES

At the extras menu, enter ADGILLIT0B8 as a code.

TS LIGHTSWITCH HOME SHOES

At the extras menu, enter ADGILLIT2BA as a code.

NEED FOR SPEED PROSTREET

$2,000
Select Career and then choose Code Entry. Enter 1MA9X99.

$4,000
Select Career and then choose Code Entry. Enter W2IOLL01.

$8,000
Select Career and then choose Code Entry. Enter L1IS97A1.

$10,000
Select Career and then choose Code Entry. Enter 1MI9K7E1.

$10,000
Select Career and then choose Code Entry. Enter CASHMONEY.

$10,000
Select Career and then choose Code Entry. Enter REGGAME.

AUDI TT
Select Career and then choose Code Entry. Enter ITSABOUTYOU.

CHEVELLE SS
Select Career and then choose Code Entry. Enter HORSEPOWER.

COKE ZERO GOLF GTI
Select Career and then choose Code Entry. Enter COKEZERO.

DODGE VIPER
Select Career and then choose Code Entry. Enter WORLDSLONGESTLASTING.

MITSUBISHI LANCER EVOLUTION
Select Career and then choose Code Entry. Enter MITSUBISHIGOFAR.

UNLOCK ALL BONUSES
Select Career and then choose Code Entry. Enter UNLOCKALLTHINGS.

5 REPAIR MARKERS
Select Career and then choose Code Entry. Enter SAFETYNET.

ENERGIZER VINYL
Select Career and then choose Code Entry. Enter ENERGIZERLITHIUM.

CASTROL SYNTEC VINYL
Select Career and then choose Code Entry. Enter CASTROLSYNTEC. This also gives you $10,000.

NERF N-STRIKE

BLACK HEART VENGEANCE
Select Codes from the main menu and enter BHDETA8.

CRUSHER SAD-G
Select Codes from the main menu and enter CRUSH14.

FIREFLY ELITE
Select Codes from the main menu and enter HELIOX6.

GOLIATHAN NITRO
Select Codes from the main menu and enter FIERO2.

HABANERO
Select Codes from the main menu and enter 24KGCON4.

HYDRA
Select Codes from the main menu and enter HRANGEL3.

LONGSHOT STREET
Select Codes from the main menu and enter LONGST5.

MAVERICK CRYSTAL
Select Codes from the main menu and enter CRISTOL10.

MAVERICK MIDNIGHT
Select Codes from the main menu and enter MAVMID7.

MERCURIO
Select Codes from the main menu and enter RSMERC9.

SEMPER FIRE ULTRA

Select Codes from the main menu and enter CROM01.

SPARTAN NCS-12

Select Codes from the main menu and enter THISIS12.

STAMPEDE

Select Codes from the main menu and enter DOGIE15.

VULCAN MAGMA

Select Codes from the main menu and enter MAGMA3.

NHL 2K9

3RD JERSEYS

At the codes menu enter R6y34bsH52.

NICKTOONS: ATTACK OF THE TOYBOTS

DAMAGE BOOST

Select Cheats from the Extras menu. Choose Enter Cheat Code and enter 456645.

INVULNERABILITY

Select Cheats from the Extras menu. Choose Enter Cheat Code and enter 313456.

UNLOCK EXO-HUGGLES 9000

Select Cheats from the Extras menu. Choose Enter Cheat Code and enter 691427.

UNLOCK MR. HUGGLES

Select Cheats from the Extras menu. Choose Enter Cheat Code and enter 654168.

UNLIMITED LOBBER GOO

Select Cheats from the Extras menu. Choose Enter Cheat Code and enter 118147.

UNLIMITED SCATTER GOO

Select Cheats from the Extras menu. Choose Enter Cheat Code and enter 971238.

UNLIMITED SPLITTER GOO

Select Cheats from the Extras menu. Choose Enter Cheat Code and enter 854511.

THE PRICE IS RIGHT 2010 EDITION

AVATAR UPGRADES

Select the lock tab from the Wardrobe screen and enter PRIZES.

PUNCH-OUT!!

REGAIN HEALTH BETWEEN ROUNDS

Press minus between rounds to regain health at the start of the next round.

DONKEY KONG IN EXHIBITION

Fight Donkey Kong in Last Stand mode.

CHAMPIONS MODE

Win 10 bouts in Mac's Last Stand.

RATATOUILLE

Select Gusteau's Shop from the Extras menu. Choose Secrets, select the appropriate code number, and then enter the code. Once the code is entered, select the cheat you want to activate it.

CODE NO.	CODE	EFFECT
1	Pieceocake	Very Easy difficulty mode
2	Myhero	No impact and no damage from enemies
3	Shielded	No damage from enemies
4	Spyagent	Move undetected by any enemy
5	Ilikeonions	Fart every time Remy jumps
6	Hardfeelings	Head butt when attacking instead of tailswipe
7	Slumberparty	Multiplayer mode
8	Gusteauart	All concept art
9	Gusteauship	All four championship modes
10	Mattelme	All single-player and multiplayer minigames
11	Gusteauvid	All videos
12	Gusteaures	All bonus artworks
13	Gusteaudream	All dream worlds in Gusteau's shop
14	Gusteauslide	All slides in Gusteau's shop
15	Gusteaulevel	All single-player minigames
16	Gusteaucombo	All items in Gusteau's shop
17	Gusteaupot	5,000 Gusteau points
18	Gusteaujack	10,000 Gusteau points
19	Gusteauomni	50,000 Gusteau points

RAYMAN RAVING RABBIDS 2

FUNKYTOWN

Play each game at least once.

RABBID COSTUMES

Costumes are unlocked as you score 12,000 points in certain games and when you shoot the correct rabbid in the shooting games.

COSTUME	MINIGAME	HOW TO UNLOCK
Cossack	Chess	Earn 12,000 points
Crash Test Dummy	Shopping Cart Downhill	Earn 12,000 points
Cupid	Burgerinnii	Earn 12,000 points
Doctor	Anesthetics	Earn 12,000 points
Fireman	Paris, Pour Troujours	Shoot fireman rabbid
French Maid	Little Chemist	Earn 12,000 points
Fruit-Hat Dancer	Year of the Rabbids	Shoot rabbid wearing fruit hat
Gingerbread	Hot Cake	Earn 12,000 points
HAZE Armor	Big City Fights	Shoot rabbid with armor
Indiana Jones	Rolling Stone	Earn 12,000 points
Jet Trooper	Greatest Hits	Earn 12,000 points
Ken	RRR Xtreme Beach Volleyball	Earn 12,000 points
Martian	Bumper Cars	Earn 12,000 points
Party Girl	Paris, Mon Amour	Once inside boat, shoot girl rabbid
Raider's	American Football	Earn 12,000 points
Sam Fisher	Rabbid School	Earn 12,000 points
Samurai	The Office	Earn 12,000 points
Space	Year of the Rabbids	Earn 12,000 points
Spider-	Spider Rabbid	Play the "Spider Rabbid" Game
TMNT, Leonardo	Usual Rabbids	Earn 12,000 points

COSTUME	MINIGAME	HOW TO UNLOCK
Transformer	Plumber Rabbids	Earn 12,000 points
Vegas Showgirl	Burp	Earn 12,000 points
Voodoo	Voodoo Rabbids	Earn 12,000 points
Wrestler	Greatest Hits	Shoot rabbid in green outfit

RUBIK'S PUZZLE WORLD

ALL LEVELS AND CUBIES

At the main menu, press A, B, B, A, A.

SCOOBY-DOO! FIRST FRIGHTS

DAPHNE'S SECRET COSTUME

Select Codes from the Extras menu and enter 2839.

FRED'S SECRET COSTUME

Select Codes from the Extras menu and enter 4826.

SCOOBY DOO'S SECRET COSTUME

Select Codes from the Extras menu and enter 1585.

SHAGGY'S SECRET COSTUME

Select Codes from the Extras menu and enter 3726.

VELMA'S SECRET COSTUME

Select Codes from the Extras menu and enter 6588.

SHREK THE THIRD

10,000 GOLD COINS

At the gift shop, press Up, Up, Down, Up, Right, Left.

THE SIMS 2: CASTAWAY

CHEAT GNOME

During a game, press B, Z, Up, Down, B. You can now use this Gnome to get the following:

MAX ALL MOTIVES

During a game, press Minus, Plus, Z, Z, A.

MAX CURRENT INVENTORY

During a game, press Left, Right, Left, Right, A.

MAX RELATIONSHIPS

During a game, press Z, Plus, A, B, 2.

ALL RESOURCES

During a game, press A, A, Down, Down, A.

ALL CRAFTING PLANS

During a game, press Plus, Plus, Minus, Minus, Z.

ADD 1 TO SKILL

During a game, press 2, Up, Right, Z, Right.

SIMANIMALS

FERRET

Begin a game in an unlocked forest area, press 2 to pause, and select Enter Codes. Enter Ferret.

PANDA

Begin a game in an unlocked forest area, press 2 to pause, and select Enter Codes. Enter PANDA.

RED PANDA

Begin a game in an unlocked forest area, press 2 to pause, and select Enter Codes. Enter Red Panda.

SIMCITY CREATOR

EGYPTIAN BUILDING SET

Name your city Mummy's desert.

GREEK BUILDING SET

Name your city Ancient culture.

JUNGLE BUILDING SET

Name your city Become wild.

SCI-FI BUILDING SET

Name your city Future picture.

THE SIMPSONS GAME

UNLIMITED POWER FOR ALL CHARACTERS

At the Extras menu, press Plus, Left, Right, Plus, Minus, Z.

ALL MOVIES

At the Extras menu, press Minus, Left, Minus, Right, Plus, C.

ALL CLICHÉS

At the Extras menu, press Left, Minus, Right, Plus, Right, Z.

SPACE HARRIER

CONTINUE AFTER GAME OVER

At the Game Over screen, press Up, Up, Down, Down, Left, Right, Left, Right, Down, Up, Down, Up.

SPECTROBES: ORIGINS

METALIC LEO AND RYZA

At the title screen, before creating a game save, press Up, Down, Left, Right, A.

SPEED RACER

INVULNERABILITY

Select Enter Code from the Options menu and enter A, B, A, Up, Left, Down, Right.

UNLIMITED BOOST

Select Enter Code from the Options menu and enter B, A, Down, Up, B, A, Down.

LAST 3 CARS

Select Enter Code from the Options menu and enter 1, 2, 1, 2, B, A, Plus.

GRANITE CAR

Select Enter Code from the Options menu and enter B, Up, Minus, Plus, 1, Up, Plus.

MONSTER TRUCK

Select Enter Code from the Options menu and enter B, Up, Minus, 2, B, Up, Minus.

AGGRESSIVE OPPONENTS

Select Enter Code from the Options menu and enter Up, Left, Down, Right, Up, Left, Down.

PACIFIST OPPONENTS

Select Enter Code from the Options menu and enter Up, Right, Down, Left, Up, Right, Down.

TINY OPPONENTS

Select Enter Code from the Options menu and enter B, A, Left, Down, Minus, Up, Minus.

HELIUM

Select Enter Code from the Options menu and enter Minus, Up, Minus, 2, Minus, Up, Minus.

MOON GRAVITY

Select Enter Code from the Options menu and enter Up, Plus, Up, Right, Minus, Up, Minus.

OVERKILL

Select Enter Code from the Options menu and enter A, Minus, Plus, Down, Up, Plus, 1.

PSYCHEDELIC

Select Enter Code from the Options menu and enter Left, A, Right, Down, B, Up, Minus.

SPIDER-MAN: FRIEND OR FOE

NEW GREEN GOBLIN AS A SIDEKICK

While standing in the Helicarrier between levels, press Left, Down, Right, Right, Down, Left.

SANDMAN AS A SIDEKICK

While standing in the Helicarrier between levels, press Right, Right, Right, Up, Down, Left.

VENOM AS A SIDEKICK

While standing in the Helicarrier between levels, press Left, Left, Right, Up, Down, Down.

5000 TECH TOKENS

While standing in the Helicarrier between levels, press Up, Up, Down, Down, Left, Right.

SPONGEBOB SQUAREPANTS FEATURING NICKTOONS: GLOBS OF DOOM

When entering the following codes, the order of the characters going down is: SpongeBob SquarePants, Nicolai Technus, Danny Phantom, Dib, Zim, Tlaloc, Tak, Beautiful Gorgeous, Jimmy Neutron, Plankton. These names are shortened to the first name in the following.

ATTRACT COINS

Using the Upgrade Machine on the bottom level of the lair, select "Input cheat codes here". Enter Tlaloc, Plankton, Danny, Plankton, Tak. Coins are attracted to you making them much easier to collect.

DON'T LOSE COINS

Using the Upgrade Machine on the bottom level of the lair, select "Input cheat codes here". Enter Plankton, Jimmy, Beautiful, Jimmy, Plankton. You don't lose coins when you get knocked out.

GOO HAS NO EFFECT

Using the Upgrade Machine on the bottom level of the lair, select "Input cheat codes here". Enter Danny, Danny, Danny, Nicolai, Nicolai. Goo does not slow you down.

MORE GADGET COMBO TIME

Using the Upgrade Machine on the bottom level of the lair, select "Input cheat codes here". Enter SpongeBob, Beautiful, Danny, Plankton, Nicolai. You have more time to perform gadget combos.

PATRICK TUX IN STARFISHMAN TO THE RESCUE

Select Cheat Codes from the Extras menu and enter PATRICK. Select Activate Bonus Items to enable this bonus item.

SPONGEBOB PLANKTON IN SUPER-SIZED PATTY

Select Cheat Codes from the Extras menu and enter PANTS. Select Activate Bonus Items to enable this bonus item.

PATRICK LASER COLOR IN ROCKET RODEO

Select Cheat Codes from the Extras menu and enter ROCKET. Select Activate Bonus Items to enable this bonus item.

PATRICK ROCKET SKIN COLOR IN ROCKET RODEO

Select Cheat Codes from the Extras menu and enter SPACE. Select Activate Bonus Items to enable this bonus item.

PLANKTON ASTRONAUT SUIT IN REVENGE OF THE GIANT PLANKTON MONSTER

Select Cheat Codes from the Extras menu and enter ROBOT. Select Activate Bonus Items to enable this bonus item.

PLANKTON EYE LASER COLOR IN REVENGE OF THE GIANT PLANKTON MONSTER

Select Cheat Codes from the Extras menu and enter LASER. Select Activate Bonus Items to enable this bonus item.

PIRATE PATRICK IN ROOFTOP RUMBLE

Select Cheat Codes from the Extras menu and enter PIRATE. Select Activate Bonus Items to enable this bonus item.

HOVERCRAFT VEHICLE SKIN IN HYPNOTIC HIGHWAY—PLANKTON

Select Cheat Codes from the Extras menu and enter HOVER. Select Activate Bonus Items to enable this bonus item.

STAR WARS: THE FORCE UNLEASHED

CHEATS

Once you have accessed the Rogue Shadow, select Enter Code from the Extras menu. Now you can enter the following codes:

CHEAT	CODE
Invincibility	CORTOSIS
Unlimited Force	VERGENCE
1,000,000 Force Points	SPEEDER
All Force Powers	TYRANUS
Max Force Power Level	KATARN
Max Combo Level	COUNTDOOKU
Stronger Lightsaber	LIGHTSABER

COSTUMES

Once you have accessed the Rogue Shadow, select Enter Code from the Extras menu. Now you can enter the following codes:

COSTUME	CODE	COSTUME	CODE
All Costumes	GRANDMOFF	Juno Eclipse	ECLIPSE
501st Legion	LEGION	Kento's Robe	WOOKIEE
Aayla Secura	AAYLA	Kleef	KLEEF
Admiral Ackbar	ITSATWAP	Lando Calrissian	SCOUNDREL
Anakin Skywalker	CHOSENONE	Luke Skywalker	T16WOMPRAT
Asajj Ventress	ACOLYTE	Luke Skywalker (Yavin)	YELLOWJCKT
Ceremonial Jedi Robes	DANTOOINE	Mace Windu	JEDIMASTER
Chop'aa Notimo	NOTIMO	Mara Jade	MARAJADE
Classic stormtrooper	TK421	Maris Brook	MARISBROOD
Count Dooku	SERENNO	Navy commando	STORMTROOP
Darth Desolous	PAUAN	Obi Wan Kenobi	BENKENOBI
Darth Maul	ZABRAK	Proxy	HOLOGRAM
Darth Phobos	HIDDENFEAR	Qui Gon Jinn	MAVERICK
Darth Vader	SITHLORD	Shaak Ti	TOGRUTA
Drexl Roosh	DREXLROOSH	Shadow trooper	INTHEDARK
Emperor Palpatine	PALPATINE	Sith Robes	HOLOCRON
General Rahm Kota	MANDALORE	Sith Stalker Armor	KORRIBAN
Han Solo	NERFHERDER	Twi'lek	SECURA
Heavy trooper	SHOCKTROOP		

STRONG BAD'S COOL GAME FOR ATTRACTIVE PEOPLE EPISODE 1: HOMESTAR RUINER

COBRA MODE IN SNAKE BOXER 5

At the Snake Boxer 5 title screen, press Up, Up, Down, Up, Plus.

SUPER C

RETAIN LIVES AND SCORE ON NEW GAME
After defeating the game, press A, Start.

RETAIN SCORE ON NEW GAME
After defeating the game, press A, B, Start.

10 LIVES
At the title screen press Right, Left, Down, Up, A, B, Start.

SOUND TEST
At the title screen hold A + B and press Start.

SUPER MARIO GALAXY

PLAY AS LUIGI
Collect all 120 stars and fight Bowser. After the credits you will get a message that Luigi is playable.

GRAND FINALE GALAXY
Collect all 120 stars with Luigi and beat Bowser.

STAR 121
Collect 100 purple coins.

SWORDS AND SOLDIERS

ALL LEVELS AND MODES
Pause the game and press Down, Up, B, Left, B, Up, Right, B.

10,000 MANA
Pause the game and press B, Left, Up, B, B, Left, Up, B.

10,000 MONEY
Pause the game and press Right, Up, B, B, B, Left, Up, Down.

LOSE LEVEL
Pause the game and press Down, Up, Left, Left, B, Up, Left, Left.

WIN LEVEL
Pause the game and press B, Right, Up, Left, B, Up, Left, Left.

TEENAGE MUTANT NINJA TURTLES: SMASH-UP

NINJA RABBID AND UNDERGROUND STAGE
At the Bonus Content menu, press Up, Up, Down, Down, Down, Right, Up, Left, Right, Left.

SHREDDER AND CYBER SHREDDER OUTFIT
At the Bonus Content menu, press Up, Down, Right, Up, Down, Right, Left, Up, Right, Down.

THRILLVILLE: OFF THE RAILS

$50,000
During a game, press C, Z, B, C, Z, B, A.

500 THRILL POINTS
During a game, press Z, C, B, Z, C, B, C.

ALL MISSIONS
During a game, press C, Z, B, C, Z, B, Z.

ALL PARKS
During a game, press C, Z, B, C, Z, B, C.

ALL RIDES
During a game, press C, Z, B, C, Z, B, B.

ALL MINIGAMES
During a game, press C, Z, B, C, Z, B, Right.

TIGER WOODS PGA TOUR 08

ALL CLUBS
Select Passwords from the Options and enter PROSHOP.

ALL GOLFERS
Select Passwords from the Options and enter GAMEFACE.

BRIDGESTONE ITEMS
Select Passwords from the Options and enter NOTJUSTTIRES.

BUICK ITEMS
Select Passwords from the Options and enter THREESTRIPES.

CLEVELAND GOLF ITEMS
Select Passwords from the Options and enter CLEVELAND.

COBRA ITEMS
Select Passwords from the Options and enter SNAKEKING.

EA ITEMS
Select Passwords from the Options and enter INTHEGAME.

GRAFALLOY ITEMS
Select Passwords from the Options and enter JUSTSHAFTS.

MIZUNO ITEMS
Select Passwords from the Options and enter RIHACHINRIZO.

NIKE ITEMS
Select Passwords from the Options and enter JUSTDOIT.

PRECEPT ITEMS
Select Passwords from the Options and enter GUYSAREGOOD.

TIGER WOODS PGA TOUR 09 ALL-PLAY

SPECTATORS BIG HEAD MODE
Select EA SPORTS Extras from My Tiger '09, choose Password and enter cephalus.

TIGER WOODS PGA TOUR 10

TW ITEMS IN PRO SHOP
Select Password from the Options and enter eltigre.

TONY HAWK'S PROVING GROUND

Select Cheat Codes from the Options and enter the following cheats. Some codes need to be enabled by selecting Cheats from the Options during a game.

UNLOCK	CHEAT	UNLOCK	CHEAT
Unlocks Bosco	MOREMILK	Unlocks Shayne	MOVERS
Unlocks Cam	NOTACAMERA	Unlocks TV Producer	SHAKER
Unlocks Cooper	THECOOP	Unlock FDR	THEPREZPARK
Unlocks Eddie X	SKETCHY	Unlock Lansdowne	THELOCALPARK
Unlocks El Patinador	PILEDRIVER	Unlock Air & Space Museum	THEINDOORPARK
Unlocks Eric	FLYAWAY	Unlock all Fun Items	OVERTHETOP
Unlocks Judy Nails	LOVEROCKNROLL	Unlock all Game Movies	WATCHTHIS
Unlocks Mad Dog	RABBIES	Unlock all Rigger Pieces	IMGONNABUILD
Unlocks MCA	INTERGALACTIC	All specials unlocked and in player's special list	LOTSOFTRICKS
Unlocks Mel	NOTADUDE	Full Stats	BEEFEDUP
Unlocks Rube	LOOKSSMELLY	Give player +50 skill points	NEEDSHELP
Unlocks Spence	DAPPER		

The following cheats lock you out of the Leaderboards:

Unlocks Perfect Manual	STILLAINTFALLIN
Unlocks Perfect Rail	AINTFALLIN
Unlocks Unlimited Focus	MYOPIC

You cannot use the Video Editor with the following cheats:

Invisible Man	THEMISSING
Mini Skater	TINYTATER

TRANSFORMERS: THE GAME

INFINITE HEALTH

At the Main menu, press Left, Left, Up, Left, Right, Down, Right.

INFINITE AMMO

At the Main menu, press Up, Down, Left, Right, Up, Up, Down.

NO MILITARY OR POLICE

At the Main menu, press Right, Left, Right, Left, Right, Left, Right.

ALL MISSIONS

At the Main menu, press Down, Up, Left, Right, Right, Right, Up, Down.

BONUS CYBERTRON MISSIONS

At the Main menu, press Right, Up, Up, Down, Right, Left, Left.

GENERATION 1 SKIN: JAZZ

At the Main menu, press Left, Up, Down, Down, Left, Up, Right.

GENERATION 1 SKIN: MEGATRON

At the Main menu, press Down, Left, Left, Down, Right, Right, Up.

GENERATION 1 SKIN: OPTIMUS PRIME

At the Main menu, press Down, Right, Left, Up, Down, Down, Left.

GENERATION 1 SKIN: ROBOVISION OPTIMUS PRIME

At the Main menu, press Down, Down, Up, Up, Right, Right, Right.

GENERATION 1 SKIN: STARSCREAM

At the Main menu, press Right, Down, Left, Left, Down, Up, Up.

ULTIMATE SHOOTING COLLECTION

ROTATE DISPLAY ON SIDE IN TATE MODE

At the main menu, press Left, Right, Left, Right, Up, Up, 1, 2.

WALL-E

The following cheats will disable saving. The five possible characters starting with Wall-E and going down are: Wall-E, Auto, EVE, M-O, GEL-A Steward.

ALL BONUS FEATURES UNLOCKED

Select Cheats from the Bonus Features menu and enter Wall-E, Auto, EVE, GEL-A Steward.

ALL GAME CONTENT UNLOCKED

Select Cheats from the Bonus Features menu and enter M-O, Auto, GEL-A Steward, EVE.

ALL SINGLE-PLAYER LEVELS UNLOCKED

Select Cheats from the Bonus Features menu and enter Auto, GEL-A Steward, M-O, Wall-E.

ALL MULTIPLAYER MAPS UNLOCKED

Select Cheats from the Bonus Features menu and enter EVE, M-O, Wall-E, Auto.

ALL HOLIDAY COSTUMES UNLOCKED

Select Cheats from the Bonus Features menu and enter Auto, Auto, GEL-A Steward, GEL-A Steward.

ALL MULTIPLAYER COSTUMES UNLOCKED

Select Cheats from the Bonus Features menu and enter GEL-A Steward, Wall-E, M-O, Auto.

UNLIMITED HEALTH UNLOCKED

Select Cheats from the Bonus Features menu and enter Wall-E, M-O, Auto, M-O.

WALL-E: MAKE ANY CUBE AT ANY TIME

Select Cheats from the Bonus Features menu and enter Auto, M-O, Auto, M-O.

WALL-EVE: MAKE ANY CUBE AT ANY TIME

Select Cheats from the Bonus Features menu and enter M-O, GEL-A Steward, EVE, EVE.

WALL-E WITH A LASER GUN AT ANY TIME

Select Cheats from the Bonus Features menu and enter Wall-E, EVE, EVE, Wall-E.

WALL-EVE WITH A LASER GUN AT ANY TIME

Select Cheats from the Bonus Features menu and enter GEL-A Steward, EVE, M-O, Wall-E.

WALL-E: PERMANENT SUPER LASER UPGRADE

Select Cheats from the Bonus Features menu and enter Wall-E, Auto, EVE, M-O.

EVE: PERMANENT SUPER LASER UPGRADE

Select Cheats from the Bonus Features menu and enter EVE, Wall-E, Wall-E, Auto.

CREDITS

Select Cheats from the Bonus Features menu and enter Auto, Wall-E, GEL-A Steward, M-O.

WII SPORTS

BOWLING BALL COLOR

After selecting your Mii, hold the following direction on the D-pad and press A at the warning screen:

DIRECTION	COLOR
Up	Blue
Right	Gold
Down	Green
Left	Red

NO HUD IN GOLF

Hold 2 as you select a course to disable the power meter, map, and wind speed meter.

BLUE TENNIS COURT

After selecting your Mii, hold 2 and press A at the warning screen.

WII SPORTS RESORT

MODIFY EVENTS

At the Select a Mii screen, hold 2 while pressing A while on "OK." This will make the following modifications to each event.

EVENT	MODIFICATION
Air Sports Island Flyover	No balloons or I points
Air Sports Skydiving	Play intro event
Archery	More difficult; no aiming reticule
Basketball Pickup Game	Nighttime
Frisbee Golf	No wind display or distance
Golf	No wind display or distance
Swordplay Duel	Evening
Table Tennis Match	11-point match

WWE SMACKDOWN VS. RAW 2010

THE ROCK

Select Cheat Codes from the Options and enter The Great One.

VINCE'S OFFICE AND DIRT SHEET FOR BACKSTAGE BRAWL

Select Cheat Codes from the Options menu and enter BonusBrawl.

Nintendo Wii™: Virtual Console

For the Virtual Console games, a Classic Controller may be needed to enter some codes.

ALTERED BEAST

LEVEL SELECT

At the Title screen, press B + Start.

BEAST SELECT

At the Title screen, hold A + B + C + Down/Left and press Start.

SOUND TEST

At the Title screen, hold A + C + Up/Right and press Start.

CHEW MAN FU

GAME COMPLETE PASSWORDS

Select Password and enter 573300 or 441300.

COMIX ZONE

STAGE SELECT

At the Jukebox menu, press C on the following numbers:

14, 15, 18, 5, 13, 1, 3, 18, 15, 6

A voice says "Oh Yeah" when entered correctly. Then, press C on 1 through 6 to warp to that stage.

INVINCIBLE

At the Jukebox menu, press C on the following numbers:

3, 12, 17, 2, 2, 10, 2, 7, 7, 11

A voice says "Oh Yeah" when entered correctly.

CREDITS

At the Options menu press A + B + C.

DR. ROBOTNIK'S MEAN BEAN MACHINE

EASY PASSWORDS

STAGE	PASSWORD
02: Frankly	Red Bean, Red Bean, Red Bean, Has Bean
03: Humpty	Clear Bean, Purple Bean, Clear Bean, Green Bean
04: Coconuts	Red Bean, Clear Bean, Has Bean, Yellow Bean
05: Davy Sprocket	Clear Bean, Blue Bean, Blue Bean, Purple Bean
06: Skweel	Clear Bean, Red Bean, Clear Bean, Purple Bean

STAGE	PASSWORD
07: Dynamight	Purple Bean, Yellow Bean, Red Bean, Blue Bean
08: Grounder	Yellow Bean, Purple Bean, Has Bean, Blue Bean
09: Spike	Yellow Bean, Purple Bean, Has Bean, Blue Bean
10: Sir Ffuzy-Logik	Red Bean, Yellow Bean, Clear Bean, Has Bean
11: Dragon Breath	Green Bean, Purple Bean, Blue Bean, Clear Bean
12: Scratch	Red Bean, Has Bean, Has Bean, Yellow Bean
13: Dr. Robotnik	Yellow Bean, Has Bean, Blue Bean, Blue Bean

NORMAL PASSWORDS

STAGE	PASSWORD
02: Frankly	Has Bean, Clear Bean, Yellow Bean, Yellow Bean
03: Humpty	Blue Bean, Clear Bean, Red Bean, Yellow Bean
04: Coconuts	Yellow Bean, Blue Bean, Clear Bean, Purple Bean
05: Davy Sprocket	Has Bean, Green Bean, Blue Bean, Yellow Bean
06: Skweel	Green Bean, Purple Bean, Purple Bean, Yellow Bean
07: Dynamight	Purple Bean, Blue Bean, Green Bean, Has Bean
08: Grounder	Green Bean, Has Bean, Clear Bean, Yellow Bean
09: Spike	Blue Bean, Purple Bean, Has Bean, Has Bean
10: Sir Ffuzy-Logik	Has Bean, Red Bean, Yellow Bean, Clear Bean
11: Dragon Breath	Clear Bean, Red Bean, Red Bean, Blue Bean
12: Scratch	Green Bean, Green Bean, Clear Bean, Yellow Bean
13: Dr. Robotnik	Purple Bean, Yellow Bean, Has Bean, Clear Bean

HARD PASSWORDS

STAGE	PASSWORD
02: Frankly	Clear Bean, Green Bean, Yellow Bean, Yellow Bean
03: Humpty	Yellow Bean, Purple Bean, Clear Bean, Purple Bean
04: Coconuts	Blue Bean, Green Bean, Clear Bean, Blue Bean
05: Davy Sprocket	Red Bean, Purple Bean, Green Bean, Green Bean
06: Skweel	Yellow Bean, Yellow Bean, Clear Bean, Green Bean
07: Dynamight	Purple Bean, Clear Bean, Blue Bean, Blue Bean
08: Grounder	Clear Bean, Yellow Bean, Has Bean, Yellow Bean
09: Spike	Purple Bean, Blue Bean, Blue Bean, Green Bean
10: Sir Ffuzy-Logik	Clear Bean, Green Bean, Red Bean, Yellow Bean
11: Dragon Breath	Blue Bean, Yellow Bean, Yellow Bean, Has Bean
12: Scratch	Green Bean, Clear Bean, Clear Bean, Blue Bean
13: Dr. Robotnik	Has Bean, Clear Bean, Purple Bean, Has Bean

HARDEST PASSWORDS

STAGE	PASSWORD
02: Frankly	Blue Bean, Blue Bean, Green Bean, Yellow Bean
03: Humpty	Green Bean, Yellow Bean, Green Bean, Clear Bean
04: Coconuts	Purple Bean, Purple Bean, RedBean, Has Bean
05: Davy Sprocket	Green Bean, Red Bean, Purple Bean, Blue Bean
06: Skweel	Purple Bean, Clear Bean, Green Bean, Yellow Bean
07: Dynamight	Blue Bean, Purple Bean, Green Bean, Has Bean
08: Grounder	Clear Bean, Purple Bean, Yellow Bean, Has Bean
09: Spike	Purple Bean, Green Bean, Has Bean, Clear Bean
10: Sir Ffuzy-Logik	Green Bean, Blue Bean, Yellow Bean, Has Bean
11: Dragon Breath	Green Bean, Purple Bean, Has Bean, Red Bean
12: Scratch	Red Bean, Green Bean, Has Bean, Blue Bean
13: Dr. Robotnik	Red Bean, Red Bean, Clear Bean, Yellow Bean

ECCO THE DOLPHIN

DEBUG MENU

Pause the game with Ecco facing the screen and press Right, B, C, B, C, Down, C, Up.

INFINITE AIR

Enter LIFEFISH as a password.

PASSWORDS

LEVEL	PASSWORD	LEVEL	PASSWORD
The Undercaves	WEFIDNMP	Deep City	DDXPQQLJ
The Vents	BQDPXJDS	City of Forever	MSDBRQLA
The Lagoon	JNSBRIKY	Jurassic Beach	IYCBUNLB
Ridge Water	NTSBZTKB	Pteranodon Pond	DMXEUNLI
Open Ocean	YWGTTJNI	Origin Beach	EGRIUNLB
Ice Zone	HZIFZBMF	Trilobite Circle	IELMUNLB
Hard Water	LRFJRQLI	Dark Water	RKEQUNLN
Cold Water	UYNFRQLC	City of Forever 2	HPQIGPLA
Island Zone	LYTIOQLZ	The Tube	JUMFKMLB
Deep Water	MNOPOQLR	The Machine	GXUBKMLF
The Marble	RJNTQQLZ	The Last Fight	TSONLMLU
The Library	RTGXQQLE		

F-ZERO X

ALL TRACKS, VEHICLES, AND DIFFICULTIES

At the Mode Select screen, press Up on the D-pad, L, R, Up on the Right control stick, X, Y, ZR, Plus.

GOLDEN AXE

LEVEL SELECT

At the Character Select screen, in Arcade mode, hold Down/Left and press B + Start.

START WITH 9 CONTINUES

At the Character Select screen, in Arcade mode, hold Down/Left and then hold A + C. Release the buttons and select a character.

GRADIUS

MAX OUT WEAPONS

Pause the game and press Up, Up, Down, Down, Left, Right, Left, Right, B, A.

GRADIUS III

FULL POWER-UP

Pause the game and press Up, Up, Down, Down, L, R, L, R, B, A.

SUICIDE

Pause the game and press Up, Up, Down, Down, Left, Right, Left, Right, B, A.

MILITARY MADNESS

PASSWORDS

LEVEL	PASSWORD	LEVEL	PASSWORD
01	REVOLT	04	RAMSEY
02	ICARUS	05	NEWTON
03	CYRANO	06	SENECA

LEVEL	PASSWORD	LEVEL	PASSWORD
07	SABINE	20	INAKKA
08	ARATUS	21	TETROS
09	GALIOS	22	ARBINE
10	DARWIN	23	RECTOS
11	PASCAL	24	YEANTA
12	HALLEY	25	MONOGA
13	BORMAN	26	ATTAYA
14	APOLLO	27	DESHTA
15	KAISER	28	NEKOSE
16	NECTOR	29	ERATIN
17	MILTON	30	SOLCIS
18	IRAGAN	31	SAGINE
19	LIPTUS	32	WINNER

SOUND TEST

Enter ONGAKU as a password.

RISTAR

Select Passwords from the Options menu and enter the following:

LEVEL SELECT

ILOVEU

BOSS RUSH MODE

MUSEUM

TIME ATTACK MODE

DOFEEL

TOUGHER DIFFICULTY

SUPER

ONCHI MUSIC

MAGURO. Activate this from the Sound Test.

CLEARS PASSWORD

XXXXXX

GAME COPYRIGHT INFO

AGES

SONIC THE HEDGEHOG

LEVEL SELECT

At the Title screen, press Up, Down, Left, Right. A sound of a ring being collected plays if the code is entered correctly. Hold A and press Start to access the Level Select.

CONTROL MODE

At the Title screen, press Up, C, Down, C, Left, C, Right, C. Then, hold A and press Start.

DEBUG MODE

After entering the Control Mode, hold A and press Start. Press A to change Sonic into another sprite. Press B to change back to Sonic. Press C to place that sprite. Pause the game and press A to restart. Hold B for slow motion and press C to advance a frame.

CHANGE DEMO

During the demo, hold C and Sonic will start making mistakes.

WARIO'S WOODS

HARD BATTLES

Highlight VS. Computer Mode, hold Left and press Start.

81

XBOX 360™

TABLE OF CONTENTS

AMPED 3

ALL SLEDS

Select Cheat Codes from the Options screen and press Right Trigger, ❌, Left Trigger, Down, Right, Left Bumper, Left Trigger, Right Trigger, ❓, ❌.

ALL GEAR

Select Cheat Codes from the Options and press ❓, Down, Up, Left, Right, Left Bumper, Right, Right Trigger, Right Trigger, Right Bumper.

ALL TRICKS

Select Cheat Codes from the Options screen and press Left Bumper, Right Trigger, ⓨ, Up, Down, ⓧ, Left Trigger, Left, Right Bumper, Right Trigger.

ALL LEVELS

Select Cheat Codes from the Options screen and press ⓧ, ⓨ, Up, Left, Left Bumper, Left Bumper, Right Trigger, ⓧ, ⓨ, Left Trigger.

ALL CONFIGS

Select Cheat Codes from the Options screen and press Down, ⓧ, Right, Left Bumper, Right, Right Bumper, ⓧ, Right Trigger, Left Trigger, ⓨ.

SUPER SPINS

Select Cheat Codes from the Options screen and press ⓧ(x4), ⓨ(x3), ⓧ.

AWESOME METER ALWAYS FULL

Select Cheat Codes from the Options screen and press Up, Right Trigger, ⓧ, ⓨ Left Bumper, ⓧ, Down, Left Bumper, Right Trigger, Right Bumper.

ALL AWESOMENESS

Select Cheat Codes from the Options screen and press Right Bumper, Right Bumper, Down, Left, Up, Right Trigger, ⓧ, Right Bumper, ⓧ, ⓧ.

ALL BUILD LICENSES

Select Cheat Codes from the Options screen and press Left, Right Trigger, Left Bumper, Right Trigger, ⓧ, ⓧ, ⓨ, Down, Up, ⓧ.

ALL BUILD OBJECTS

Select Cheat Codes from the Options screen and press Left Trigger, Right Trigger, Up, Up, Right Bumper, Left, Right, ⓧ, ⓨ, Left Bumper.

ALL CHALLENGES

Select Cheat Codes from the Options screen and press Right, Left Bumper, Left Trigger, ⓧ, Left, Right Bumper, Right Trigger, ⓨ, Left Trigger, ⓧ.

LOUD SPEAKERS

Select Cheat Codes from the Options screen and press ⓨ. Right Trigger, Right Trigger, Left Bumper, Down, Down, Left, Left, Right, Left Bumper.

LOW GRAVITY BOARDERS

Select Cheat Codes from the Options screen and press Right Trigger, Down, Down, Up, ⓧ, Left Bumper, ⓨ, Right Trigger, ⓨ, Down.

NO AI

Select Cheat Codes from the Options screen and press ❌, ❌, Left Bumper, Down, Right, Right, Up, ✓, ✓, Left Trigger.

ALL MUSIC

Select Cheat Codes from the Options screen and press Up, Left, Right Trigger, Right Bumper, Right Trigger, Up, Down, Left, ✓, Left Trigger.

AVATAR: THE LAST AIRBENDER - THE BURNING EARTH

UNLIMITED HEALTH

Select Code Entry from the Extras menu and enter 65049.

DOUBLE DAMAGE

Select Code Entry from the Extras menu and enter 90210.

MAXIMUM LEVEL

Select Code Entry from the Extras menu and enter 89121.

UNLIMITED SPECIALS

Select Code Entry from the Extras menu and enter 66206.

ONE-HIT DISHONOR

Select Code Entry from the Extras menu and enter 28260.

ALL BONUS GAMES

Select Code Entry from the Extras menu and enter 99801.

UNLOCKS GALLERY

Select Code Entry from the Extras menu and enter 85061.

BAJA: EDGE OF CONTROL

ALL VEHICLES AND TRACKS

Select Cheat Codes from the Options menu and enter SHOWTIME.

ALL PARTS

Select Cheat Codes from the Options menu and enter SUPERMAX.

BANJO-KAZOOIE

In Treasure Trove Cove, enter the Sandcastle and spell CHEAT by using your Beak Buster on the desired letter. A sound will confirm the entry of the letter. The following cheats will now be available for you. Two things to keep in mind. The first is that no sound will confirm the correct letter. Secondly, ignore the spaces in the phrases...just spell the entire phrase out.

AREA OPENING CHEATS

ACCESS CLANKER'S CAVERN

THERES NOWHERE DANKER THAN IN WITH CLANKER

ACCESS MAD MONSTER MANSION

THE JIGGYS NOW MADE WHOLE INTO THE MANSION YOU CAN STROLL

ACCESS GOBI'S VALLEY

GOBIS JIGGY IS NOW DONE TREK ON IN AND GET SOME SUN

ACCESS RUSTY BUCKET BAY
WHY NOT TAKE A TRIP INSIDE GRUNTYS RUSTY SHIP

ACCESS CLICK CLOCK WOOD
THIS ONES GOOD AS YOU CAN ENTER THE WOOD

ACCESS FREEZEEZY PEAK
THE JIGGYS DONE SO OFF YOU GO INTO FREEZEEZY PEAK AND ITS SNOW

ACCESS BUBBLEGLOOP SWAMP
NOW INTO THE SWAMP YOU CAN STOMP

HIDDEN EGG CHEATS
The Hidden Egg cheats will only work if you have been to the level previously.

REVEAL THE BLUE EGG IN GOBI'S VALLEY BEHIND THE LOCKED GATE IN THE ROCK WALL
A DESERT DOOR OPENS WIDE ANCIENT SECRETS WAIT INSIDE

REVEAL THE PURPLE EGG IN TREASURE TROVE COVE IN SHARKFOOD ISLAND
OUT OF THE SEA IT RISES TO REVEAL MORE SECRET PRIZES

REVEAL THE ICE KEY IN FREEZEEZY PEAK IN THE ICE CAVE
NOW YOU CAN SEE A NICE ICE KEY WHICH YOU CAN HAVE FOR FREE

REVEAL THE LIGHT BLUE EGG IN GRUNTILDA'S LAIR–YOU'LL FIND IT IN THE CASK MARKED WITH AN X
DONT YOU GO AND TELL HER ABOUT THE SECRET IN HER CELLAR

REVEAL THE GREEN EGG IN MAD MONSTER MANSION IN THE SAME ROOM AS LOGGO THE TOILET
AMIDST THE HAUNTED GLOOM A SECRET IN THE BATHROOM

REVEAL THE YELLOW EGG IN CLICK CLOCK WOOD IN NABNUTS' TREE HOUSE
NOW BANJO WILL BE ABLE TO SEE IT ON NABNUTS TABLE

REVEAL THE RED EGG IN RUSTY BUCKET BAY IN THE CAPTAIN'S CABIN
THIS SECRET YOULL BE GRABBIN IN THE CAPTAINS CABIN

NOTE DOOR CHEATS
These will pop those note doors open without having to find the required notes.

DOOR 2
THESE GO RIGHT ON THROUGH NOTE DOOR TWO

DOOR 3
NOTE DOOR THREE GET IN FOR FREE

DOOR 4
TAKE A TOUR THROUGH NOTE DOOR FOUR

DOOR 5
USE THIS CHEAT NOTE DOOR FIVE IS BEAT

DOOR 6
THIS TRICKS USED TO OPEN NOTE DOOR SIX

DOOR 7
THE SEVENTH NOTE DOOR IS NOW NO MORE

SWITCH AND OBSTACLE CHEATS FOR GRUNTILDA'S LAIR

These will allow you to alter certain obstacles throughout Gruntilda's Lair. Sometimes, the cheat will even remove them completely.

RAISE THE PIPES NEAR CLANKER'S CAVERN
BOTH PIPES ARE THERE TO CLANKE❀ LAIR

RAISE THE LARGE PIPE NEAR CLANKER'S CAVERN:
YOULL CEASE TO GRIPE WHEN UP GOES A PIPE

UNLOCK THE PATH NEAR CLANKER'S CAVERN THAT LEADS TO THE CLICK CLOCK WOOD PICTURE
ONCE IT SHONE BUT THE LONG TUNNEL GRILLE IS GONE

REVEAL THE PODIUM FOR THE CLICK CLOCK WOOD JIGGY
DONT DESPAIR THE TREE JIGGY PODIUM IS NOW THERE

UNLOCK THE PATH INSIDE THE GIANT WITCH STATUE, NEAR BUBBLEGLOOP SWAMP (OPEN THE GRILL)
SHES AN UGLY BAT SO LETS REMOVE HER GRILLE AND HAT

UNLOCK THE PATH TO THE FREEZEEZY PEAK PICTURE BEHIND THE ICE CUBE
ITS YOUR LUCKY DAY AS THE ICE BALL MELTS AWAY

UNLOCK PASSAGES BLOCKED BY COBWEBS
WEBS STOP YOUR PLAY SO TAKE THEM AWAY

REVEAL A JIGGY IN GRUNTILDA'S STATUE BY SMASHING THE EYE NEAR MAD MONSTER MANSION
GRUNTY WILL CRY NOW YOUVE SMASHED HER EYE

RAISE THE WATER LEVEL NEAR RUSTY BUCKET BAY
UP YOU GO WITHOUT A HITCH UP TO THE WATER LEVEL SWITCH

UNLOCK THE PATH TO THE CRYPT NEAR MAD MONSTER MANSION (REMOVE THE GATE)
YOU WONT HAVE TO WAIT NOW THERES NO CRYPT GATE

REMOVE THE COFFIN LID IN THE CRYPT
THIS SHOULD GET RID OF THE CRYPT COFFIN LID

CRUMBLE ALL BREAKABLE WALLS
THEY CAUSE TROUBLE BUT NOW THEYRE RUBBLE

ACTIVATE SPECIAL PADS
Skip the lesson from Bottles by entering these codes.

ACTIVATE THE FLY PAD
YOU WONT BE SAD NOW YOU CAN USE THE FLY PAD

ACTIVATE THE SHOCK JUMP PAD
YOULL BE GLAD TO SEE THE SHOCK JUMP PAD

EXTRA HEALTH CHEAT
Skip the note-hunt and get that extra health by entering this cheat.

AN ENERGY BAR TO GET YOU FAR

Remember, to enter a code you must first enter the word CHEAT in the Sandcastle.

BANJO-TOOIE

REGAIN ENERGY

Go to the Code Chamber in the Mayahem Temple and access the scroll on the wall. If you have been awarded this cheat by Cheato, enter HONEYBACK. If not, enter CHEATOKCABYENOH.

FALLS DON'T HURT

Go to the Code Chamber in the Mayahem Temple and access the scroll on the wall. If you have been awarded this cheat by Cheato, enter FALLPROOF. If not, enter CHEATOFOORPLLAF.

HOMING EGGS

Go to the Code Chamber in the Mayahem Temple and access the scroll on the wall. If you have been awarded this cheat, enter HOMING. If not, enter CHEATOGNIMOH.

DOUBLES MAXIMUM EGGS

Go to the Code Chamber in the Mayahem Temple and access the scroll on the wall. If you have been awarded this cheat by Cheato, enter EGGS. If not, enter CHEATOSGGE.

DOUBLES MAXIMUM FEATHERS

Go to the Code Chamber in the Mayahem Temple and access the scroll on the wall. If you have been awarded this cheat by Cheato, enter FEATHE🅱. If not, enter CHEATOSREHTAEF.

JOLLY ROGER LAGOON'S JUKEBOX

Go to the Code Chamber in the Mayahem Temple and access the scroll on the wall. If you have been awarded this cheat, enter JUKEBOX. If not, enter CHEATOXOBEKUJ.

SIGNS IN JIGGYWIGGY'S TEMPLE GIVE HINTS TO GET EACH JIGGY

Go to the Code Chamber in the Mayahem Temple and access the scroll on the wall. If you have been awarded this cheat, enter GETJIGGY. If not, enter CHEATOYGGIJTEG.

ALL LEVELS

Go to the Code Chamber in the Mayahem Temple and enter JIGGYWIGGYSPECIAL.

SPEED BANJO

Go to the Code Chamber in the Mayahem Temple and enter SUPE🅱ANJO.

SPEED ENEMIES

Go to the Code Chamber in the Mayahem Temple and enter SUPE🅱ADDY.

INFINITE EGGS AND FEATHERS

Go to the Code Chamber in the Mayahem Temple and enter NESTKING.

INFINITE HONEY

Go to the Code Chamber in the Mayahem Temple and enter HONEYKING.

BATTLESTATIONS: MIDWAY

ALL CAMPAIGN AND CHALLENGE MISSIONS

At the mission select, hold Right Bumper + Left Bumper + Right Trigger + Left Trigger and press ✖.

BEAT'N GROOVY

ALTERNATE CONTROLS

At the title screen, press Up, Up, Down, Down, Left, Right, Left, Right, Ⓑ, Ⓐ.

BLAZING ANGELS: SQUADRONS OF WWII

ALL MISSIONS, MEDALS, & PLANES

At the Main menu hold Left Trigger + Right Trigger and press ❌, Left Bumper, Right Bumper, ❓, ❓ Right Bumper, Left Bumper, ❌.

GOD MODE

Pause the game, hold Left Trigger and press ❌, ❓, ❓, ❌ Release Left Trigger, hold Right Trigger and press ❓, ❌, ❌, ❓. Re-enter the code to disable it.

INCREASED DAMAGE

Pause the game, hold Left Trigger and press Left Bumper, Left Bumper, Right Bumper.

Release Left Trigger, hold Right Trigger and press Right Bumper, Right Bumper, Left Bumper. Re-enter the code to disable it.

BLAZING ANGELS 2: SECRET MISSIONS OF WWII

Achievements are disabled when using these codes.

ALL MISSIONS AND PLANES UNLOCKED

At the Main menu, hold Left Trigger + Right Trigger, and press ❌, Left Bumper, Right Bumper, ❓, ❓, Right Bumper, Left Bumper, ❌.

GOD MODE

Pause the game, hold Left Trigger, and press ❌, ❓, ❓, ❌. Release Left Trigger, hold Right Trigger and press ❓, ❌, ❌, ❓. Re-enter the code to disable it.

INCREASED DAMAGE WITH ALL WEAPONS

Pause the game, hold Left Trigger, and press Left Bumper, Left Bumper, Right Bumper. Release Left Trigger, hold Right Trigger, and press Right Bumper, Right Bumper, Left Bumper. Re-enter the code to disable it.

BURNOUT PARADISE

BEST BUY CAR

Pause the game and select Sponsor Product Code from the Under the Hood menu. Enter Bestbuy. Need A License to use this car offline.

CIRCUIT CITY CAR

Pause the game and select Sponsor Product Code from the Under the Hood menu. Enter Circuitcity. Need Burnout Paradise License to use this car offline.

GAMESTOP CAR

Pause the game and select Sponsor Product Code from the Under the Hood menu. Enter Gamestop. Need A License to use this car offline.

WALMART CAR

Pause the game and select Sponsor Product Code from the Under the Hood menu. Enter Walmart. Need Burnout Paradise License to use this car offline.

"STEEL WHEELS" GT

Pause the game and select Sponsor Product Code from the Under the Hood menu. Enter G23X 5K8Q GX2V 04B1 or E60J 8Z7T MS8L 51U6.

LICENSES

LICENSE	NUMBER OF WINS NEEDED
D	2
C	7
B	16
A	26
Burnout Paradise	45
Elite License	All events

CARS

UNLOCK EVERYTHING

Select Cheat Codes from the Options and enter IF900HP.

ALL CHARACTERS

Select Cheat Codes from the Options and enter YAYCA⊗.

ALL CHARACTER SKINS

Select Cheat Codes from the Options and enter R4MONE.

ALL MINI-GAMES AND COURSES

Select Cheat Codes from the Options and enter MATTL66.

FAST START

Select Cheat Codes from the Options and enter IMSPEED.

INFINITE BOOST

Select Cheat Codes from the Options and enter VROOOOM.

ART

Select Cheat Codes from the Options and enter CONC3PT.

VIDEOS

Select Cheat Codes from the Options and enter WATCHIT.

CARS MATER-NATIONAL

ALL ARCADE RACES, MINI-GAMES, AND WORLDS

Select Codes/Cheats from the options and enter PLAYALL.

ALL CARS

Select Codes/Cheats from the options and enter MATTEL07.

ALTERNATE LIGHTNING MCQUEEN COLORS

Select Codes/Cheats from the options and enter NCEDUDZ.

ALL COLORS FOR OTHERS

Select Codes/Cheats from the options and enter PAINTIT.

UNLIMITED TURBO

Select Codes/Cheats from the options and enter ZZOOOOM.

EXTREME ACCELERATION

Select Codes/Cheats from the options and enter OTO200X.

EXPERT MODE

Select Codes/Cheats from the options and enter VRYFAST.

ALL BONUS ART

Select Codes/Cheats from the options and enter BUYTALL.

CASTLEVANIA: SYMPHONY OF THE NIGHT

Before using the following codes, complete the game with 170%.

PLAY AS RICHTER BELMONT

Enter RICHTER as your name.

ALUCARD WITH AXELORD ARMOR

Enter AXEARMOR as your name.

ALUCARD WITH 99 LUCK AND OTHER STATS ARE LOW

Enter X-X!V"Q as your name.

CRASH BANDICOOT: MIND OVER MUTANT

A cheat can be deactivated by re-entering the code.

FREEZE ENEMIES WITH TOUCH

Pause the game, hold Right Trigger and press Down, Down, Down, Up.

ENEMIES DROP X4 DAMAGE

Pause the game, hold Right Trigger and press Up, Up, Up, Left.

ENEMIES DROP PURPLE FRUIT

Pause the game, hold Right Trigger and press Up, Down, Down, Up.

ENEMIES DROP SUPER KICK

Pause the game, hold Right Trigger and press Up, Right, Down, Left.

ENIMIES DROP WUMPA FRUIT

Pause the game, hold Right Trigger and press Right, Right, Right, Up.

SHADOW CRASH

Pause the game, hold Right Trigger and press Left, Right, Left, Right.

DEFORMED CRASH

Pause the game, hold Right Trigger and press Left, Left, Left, Down.

CRASH OF THE TITANS

BIG HEAD CRASH

Pause the game, hold the Right Trigger, and press ❌, ❌, ⓨ, Ⓐ.

SHADOW CRASH

Pause the game, hold the Right Trigger, and press ⓨ, ❌, ⓨ, Ⓐ.

DEFENSE GRID: THE AWAKENING

The following cheats will disable Achievements.

100,000 RESOURCES

Click and hold the Right Thumbstick and press Right, Right, Right, Right

CORES CANNOT BE TAKEN

Click and hold the Right Thumbstick and press Up, Left, Down, Right

FREE CAMERA MODE

Click and hold the Right Thumbstick and press Down, Up, Down, Down

INSTANT VICTORY

Click and hold the Right Thumbstick and press Up, Up, Up, Up

KILL ALL ALIENS

Click and hold the Right Thumbstick and press Left, Right, Left, Right

KILL ALL ALIENS CARRYING CORES

Click and hold the Right Thumbstick and press Up, Down, Down, Up

LEVEL SELECT

Click and hold the Right Thumbstick and press Up, Up, Down, Down, Left, Right, Left, Right

SELF-DESTRUCT (INSTANT DEFEAT)

Click and hold the Right Thumbstick and press Down, Down, Down, Down

TOGGLE TARGET RETICULE

Click and hold the Right Thumbstick and press Down, Up, Down, Up

UNLOCK ALL TOWER TYPES

Click and hold the Right Thumbstick and press Up, Down, Left, Right

DIRT 2

Win the given events to earn the following cars:

GET THIS CAR	BY WINNING THIS EVENT
Ford RS200 Evolution	Rally Cross World Tour
Toyota Stadium Truck	Landrush World Tour
Mitsubishi Pajero Dakar 1993	Raid World Tour
Dallenbach Special	Trailblazer World Tour
1995 Subaru Impreza WRX STi	Colin McRae Challenge
Colin McRae R4 [X Games]	X Games Europe
Mitsubishi Lancer Evolution X [X Games]	X Games Asia
Subaru Impreza WRX STi [X Games]	X Games America
Ford Escort MKII and MG Metro 6R4	All X Games events

DON KING PRESENTS: PRIZEFIGHTER

UNLOCK RICARDO MAYORGA

Select Enter Unlock Code from the Extras menu and enter potsemag.

EXCLUSIVE BEST BUY FIGHT FOOTAGE

Select Enter Unlock Code from the Extras menu and enter 1bestbuybest. Select Watch Videos from the Extras menu to find video.

ERAGON

UNLIMITED FURY MODE

Pause the game, hold Left Bumper + Left Trigger + Right Bumper + Right Trigger and press
❌, ❌, Ⓑ, Ⓑ.

EVERY EXTEND EXTRA EXTREME

FINE ADJUSTMENT MENU

At the Start screen, press Left Bumper, Right Bumper, Left Bumper, Right Bumper, Left Bumper, Right Bumper, Left Bumper, Right Bumper.

FATAL FURY SPECIAL

CHEAT MENU

During a game, hold Start and push Ⓐ + Ⓧ + Ⓨ.

FIGHT NIGHT ROUND 3

ALL VENUES

Create a champ with a first name of NEWVIEW.

FLATOUT: ULTIMATE CARNAGE

MOB CAR IN SINGLE EVENTS

Select Enter Code from Extras and enter BIGTRUCK.

 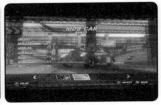

PIMPSTER IN SINGLE EVENTS

Select Enter Code from Extras and enter RUTTO.

ROCKET IN SINGLE EVENTS

Select Enter Code from Extras and enter KALJAKOPPA.

FROGGER

BIG FROGGER

At the one/two player screen, press Up, Up, Down, Down, Left, Right, Left, Right, **B**, **A**.

FUEL

CAMO ARMY HELMET

Select Bonus Codes from the Options and enter 48992519.

ROAD ADDICT JACKET

Select Bonus Codes from the Options and enter 20061977.

SPEED ANGEL SHORTS

Select Bonus Codes from the Options and enter 91031985.

BUTTERFLY LIVERY FOR THE SLUDGERAY VEHICLE

Select Bonus Codes from the Options and enter 18021974.

LIGHTNING BOLT LIVERY FOR THE MUDHOG VEHICLE

Select Bonus Codes from the Options and enter 17121973.

WARRIOR VEHICLE

Select Bonus Codes from the Options and enter 18041851.

FULL AUTO

ALL TRACKS, VEHICLES, & WEAPONS

Create a new profile with the name magicman.

GAROU: MARK OF THE WOLVES

PLAY AS GRANT

Highlight Dong Hwan, hold Start, and press Up, Up, Down, Down, Up, Down. Press any button while still holding Start.

PLAY AS KAIN

Highlight Jae Hoon, hold Start, and press Down, Down, Up, Up, Down, Up. Press any button while still holding Start.

RANDOM CHARACTER SELECT

At the character select, hold Start and press a button.

G.I. JOE: THE RISE OF COBRA

CLASSIC DUKE

At the main menu, press Left, Up, ❸, Up, Right, ❤.

CLASSIC SCARLETT

At the main menu, press Right, Up, Down, Down, ❤.

GRID

ALL DRIFT CARS

Select Bonus Codes from the Options. Then choose Enter Code and enter TUN58396.

ALL MUSCLE CARS

Select Bonus Codes from the Options. Then choose Enter Code and enter MUS59279.

BUCHBINDER EMOTIONAL ENGINEERING BMW 320SI

Select Bonus Codes from the Options. Then choose Enter Code and enter F93857372. You can use this in Race Day or in GRID World once you've started your own team.

EBAY

Select Bonus Codes from the Options. Then choose Enter Code and enter DAFJ55E01473M0. You can use this in Race Day or in GRID World once you've started your own team.

GAMESTATION BMW 320SI

Select Bonus Codes from the Options. Then choose Enter Code and enter G29782655. You can use this in Race Day or in GRID World once you've started your own team.

MICROMANIA PAGANI ZONDA R

Select Bonus Codes from the Options. Then choose Enter Code and enter M38572343. You can use this in Race Day or in GRID World once you've started your own team.

PLAY.COM ASTON MARTIN DBR9

Select Bonus Codes from the Options. Then choose Enter Code and enter P47203845. You can use this in Race Day or in GRID World once you've started your own team.

IDOLMASTER: LIVE FOR YOU!

MAMI

At the character select, press R3 while on Ami.

SHORT-HAIRED MIKI

At the character select, press R3 while on Miki.

96

IRON MAN

CLASSIC ARMOR
Clear One Man Army vs. Mercs.

EXTREMIS ARMOR
Clear One Man Army vs. Maggia.

MARK II ARMOR
Clear One Man Army vs. Ten Rings.

HULKBUSTER ARMOR
Clear One Man Army vs. AIM-X. Can also be unlocked when clear game save data from Incredible Hulk is stored on the same console.

SILVER CENTURION ARMOR
Clear Mission 13: Showdown.

CLASSIC MARK I ARMOR
Clear One Man Army vs. AIM.

JUICED 2: HOT IMPORT NIGHTS

FRITO-LAY INFINITY G35 CAR
Select Cheats and Codes from the DNA Lab menu and enter MNCH.

HIDDEN CHALLENGE AND AN AUDI TT 1.8 QUATTRO
Select Cheats and Codes from the DNA Lab menu and enter YTHZ. Defeat the challenge to earn the Audi TT 1.8 Quattro.

HIDDEN CHALLENGE AND A BMW Z4
Select Cheats and Codes from the DNA Lab menu and enter GVDL. Defeat the challenge to earn the BMW Z4.

HIDDEN CHALLENGE AND A HOLDEN MONARO
Select Cheats and Codes from the DNA Lab menu and enter ⬜ SG. Defeat the challenge to earn the Holden Monaro.

HIDDEN CHALLENGE AND A HYUNDAI COUPE 2.7 V6
Select Cheats and Codes from the DNA Lab menu and enter BSLU. Defeat the challenge to earn the Hyundai Coupe 2.7 V6.

HIDDEN CHALLENGE AND AN INFINITY G35
Select Cheats and Codes from the DNA Lab menu and enter MRHC. Defeat the challenge to earn the Infinity G35.

HIDDEN CHALLENGE AND A KOENIGSEGG CCX
Select Cheats and Codes from the DNA Lab menu and enter KDTR. Defeat the challenge to earn the Koenigsegg CCX.

HIDDEN CHALLENGE AND A MITSUBISHI PROTOTYPE X
Select Cheats and Codes from the DNA Lab menu and enter DOPX. Defeat the challenge to earn the Mitsubishi Prototype X.

HIDDEN CHALLENGE AND A NISSAN 350Z
Select Cheats and Codes from the DNA Lab menu and enter PRGN. Defeat the challenge to earn the Nissan 350Z.

HIDDEN CHALLENGE AND A NISSAN SKYLINE R34 GT-R

Select Cheats and Codes from the DNA Lab menu and enter JW✪. Defeat the challenge to earn the Nissan Skyline R34 GT-R.

HIDDEN CHALLENGE AND A SALEEN S7

Select Cheats and Codes from the DNA Lab menu and enter WIKF. Defeat the challenge to earn the Saleen S7.

HIDDEN CHALLENGE AND A SEAT LEON CUPRA R

Select Cheats and Codes from the DNA Lab menu and enter FAMQ. Defeat the challenge to earn the Seat Leon Cupra R.

KUNG FU PANDA

INFINITE CHI

Select Cheats from the Extra menu and press Down, Right, Left, Up, Down.

INVINCIBILITY

Select Cheats from the Extra menu and press Down, Down, Right, Up, Left.

FULL UPGRADES

Select Cheats from the Extra menu and press Left, Right, Down, Left, Up.

4X DAMAGE MULTIPLIER

Select Cheats from the Extra menu and press Up, Down, Up, Right, Left.

ALL MULTIPLAYER CHARACTERS

Select Cheats from the Extra menu and press Left, Down, Left, Right, Down.

DRAGON WARRIOR OUTFIT IN MULTIPLAYER

Select Cheats from the Extra menu and press Left, Down, Right, Left, Up.

ALL OUTFITS

Select Cheats from the Extra menu and press Right, Left, Down, Up, Right.

THE LEGEND OF SPYRO: DAWN OF THE DRAGON

UNLIMITED LIFE

Pause the game, hold Left Bumper and press Right, Right, Down, Down, Left with the Left Control Stick.

UNLIMITED MANA

Pause the game, hold Right Bumper and press Up, Right, Up, Left, Down with the Left Control Stick.

MAXIMUM XP

Pause the game, hold Right Bumper and press Up, Left, Left, Down, Up with the Left Control Stick.

ALL ELEMENTAL UPGRADES

Pause the game, hold Left Bumper and press Left, Up, Down, Up, Right with the Left Control Stick.

BATCAVE CODES

Using the computer in the Batcave, select Enter Code and enter the following codes.

CHARACTERS

CHARACTER	CODE	CHARACTER	CODE
Alfred	ZAQ637	Penguin Henchman	BJH782
Batgirl	JKR331	Penguin Minion	KJP748
Bruce Wayne	BDJ327	Poison Ivy Goon	GTB899
Catwoman (Classic)	M1AAWW	Police Marksman	HKG984
Clown Goon	HJK327	Police Officer	JRY983
Commissioner Gordon	DDP967	Riddler Goon	CRY928
Fishmonger	HGY748	Riddler Henchman	XEU824
Freeze Girl	XVK541	S.W.A.T.	HTF114
Joker Goon	UTF782	Sailor	NAV592
Joker Henchman	YUN924	Scientist	JFL786
Mad Hatter	JCA283	Security Guard	PLB946
Man-Bat	NYU942	The Joker (Tropical)	CCB199
Military Policeman	MKL382	Yeti	NJL412
Nightwing	MVY759	Zoo Sweeper	DWR243
Penguin Goon	NKA238		

VEHICLES

VEHICLE	CODE	VEHICLE	CODE
Bat-Tank	KNTT4B	Mr. Freeze's Kart	BCT229
Bruce Wayne's Private Jet	LEA664	Penguin Goon Submarine	BTN248
Catwoman's Motorcycle	HPL826	Police Bike	LJP234
Garbage Truck	DUS483	Police Boat	PLC999
Goon Helicopter	GCH328	Police Car	KJL832
Harbor Helicopter	CHP735	Police Helicopter	CWR732
Harley Quinn's Hammer Truck	RDT637	Police Van	MAC788
Mad Hatter's Glider	HS000W	Police Watercraft	VJD328
Mad Hatter's Steamboat	M4DM4N	Riddler's Jet	HAHAHA
Mr. Freeze's Iceberg	ICYICE	Robin's Submarine	TTF453
The Joker's Van	JUK657	Two-Face's Armored Truck	EFE933

CHEATS

CHEAT	CODE	CHEAT	CODE
Always Score Multiply	9LRGNB	More Batarang Targets	XWP645
Fast Batarangs	JRBDCB	Piece Detector	KHJ554
Fast Walk	ZOLM6N	Power Brick Detector	MMN786
Flame Batarang	D8NYWH	Regenerate Hearts	HJH7HJ
Freeze Batarang	XPN4NG	Score x2	N4NR3E
Extra Hearts	ML3KHP	Score x4	CX9MAT
Fast Build	EVG26J	Score x6	MLVNF2
Immune to Freeze	JXUDY6	Score x8	WCCDB9
Invincibility	WYD5CP	Score x10	18HW07
Minikit Detector	ZXGH9J		

LEGO INDIANA JONES: THE ORIGINAL ADVENTURES

CHARACTERS

Approach the blackboard in the Classsroom and enter the following codes.

CHARACTER	CODE	CHARACTER	CODE
Bandit	12N68W	Fedora	V75YSP
Bandit Swordsman	1MK4RT	First Mate	0GIN24
Barranca	04EM94	Grail Knight	NE6THI
Bazooka Trooper (Crusade)	MK83R7	Havitos Tribesman	H0V1SS
Bazooka Trooper (Raiders)	S93Y5R	Indiana Jones (Desert Disguise)	4J8S4M
Belloq	CHN3YU	Indiana Jones (Officer)	VJ850S
Belloq (Jungle)	TDR197	Jungle Guide	24PF34
Belloq (Robes)	VEO29L	Kao Kan	WM046L
British Commander	B73EUA	Kazim	NRH23J
British Officer	VJ5TI9	Kazim (Desert)	3M29TJ
British Soldier	DJ5I2W	Lao Che	2NK479
Captain Katanga	VJ3TT3	Maharajah	NFK5N2
Chatter Lal	ENW936	Major Toht	13NS01
Chatter Lal (Thuggee)	CNH4RY	Masked Bandit	N48SFO
Chen	3NK48T	Mola Ram	FJUR31
Colonel Dietrich	2K9RKS	Monkey Man	3RF6YJ
Colonel Vogel	8EAL4H	Pankot Assassin	2NKT72
Dancing Girl	C7EJ21	Pankot Guard	VN28RH
Donovan	3NFTU8	Sherpa Brawler	VJ37WJ
Elsa (Desert)	JSNRT9	Sherpa Gunner	ND762W
Elsa (Officer)	VMJ5US	Slave Child	OE3ENW
Enemy Boxer	8246RB	Thuggee	VM683E
Enemy Butler	VJ48W3	Thuggee Acolyte	T2R3F9
Enemy Guard	VJ7R51	Thuggee Slave Driver	VBS7GW
Enemy Guard (Mountains)	YR47WM	Village Dignitary	KD48TN
Enemy Officer	572E61	Village Elder	4682E1
Enemy Officer (Desert	2MK450	Willie (Dinner Suit)	VK93R7
Enemy Pilot	B84ELP	Willie (Pajamas)	MEN4IP
Enemy Radio Operator	1MF94R	Wu Han	3NSLT8
Enemy Soldier (Desert)	4NSU7Q		

EXTRAS

Approach the blackboard in the Classsroom and enter the following codes. Some cheats need to be enabled by selecting Extras from the pause menu.

CHEAT	CODE	CHEAT	CODE
Artifact Detector	VIKED7	Regenerate Hearts	MDLP69
Beep Beep	VNF59Q	Secret Characters	3X44AA
Character Treasure	VIES2R	Silhouettes	3HE85H
Disarm Enemies	VKRNS9	Super Scream	VN3R7S
Disguises	4ID1N6	Super Slap	OP1TA5
Fast Build	V83SLO	Treasure Magnet	H86LA2
Fast Dig	378RS6	Treasure x10	VI3PS8
Fast Fix	FJ59WS	Treasure x2	VM4TS9
Fertilizer	B1GW1F	Treasure x4	VLWEN3
Ice Rink	33GM7J	Treasure x6	V84RYS
Parcel Detector	VUT673	Treasure x8	A72E1M
Poo Treasure	WWQ1SA		

LEGO STAR WARS II: THE ORIGINAL TRILOGY

BEACH TROOPER

At Mos Eisley Canteena, select Enter Code and enter UCK868. You still need to select Characters and purchase this character for 20,000 studs.

BEN KENOBI (GHOST)

At Mos Eisley Canteena, select Enter Code and enter BEN917. You still need to select Characters and purchase this character for 1,100,000 studs.

BESPIN GUARD

At Mos Eisley Canteena, select Enter Code and enter VHY832. You still need to select Characters and purchase this character for 15,000 studs.

BIB FORTUNA

At Mos Eisley Canteena, select Enter Code and enter WTY721. You still need to select Characters and purchase this character for 16,000 studs.

BOBA FETT

At Mos Eisley Canteena, select Enter Code and enter HLP221. You still need to select Characters and purchase this character for 175,000 studs.

DEATH STAR TROOPER

At Mos Eisley Canteena, select Enter Code and enter BNC332. You still need to select Characters and purchase this character for 19,000 studs.

EWOK

At Mos Eisley Canteena, select Enter Code and enter TTT289. You still need to select Characters and purchase this character for 34,000 studs.

GAMORREAN GUARD

At Mos Eisley Canteena, select Enter Code and enter YZF999. You still need to select Characters and purchase this character for 40,000 studs.

GONK DROID

At Mos Eisley Canteena, select Enter Code and enter NFX582. You still need to select Characters and purchase this character for 1,550 studs.

GRAND MOFF TARKIN

At Mos Eisley Canteena, select Enter Code and enter SMG219. You still need to select Characters and purchase this character for 38,000 studs.

GREEDO

At Mos Eisley Canteena, select Enter Code and enter NAH118. You still need to select Characters and purchase this character for 60,000 studs.

HAN SOLO (HOOD)

At Mos Eisley Canteena, select Enter Code and enter YWM840. You still need to select Characters and purchase this character for 20,000 studs.

IG-88

At Mos Eisley Canteena, select Enter Code and enter NXL973. You still need to select Characters and purchase this character for 30,000 studs.

IMPERIAL GUARD

At Mos Eisley Canteena, select Enter Code and enter MMM111. You still need to select Characters and purchase this character for 45,000 studs.

IMPERIAL OFFICER

At Mos Eisley Canteena, select Enter Code and enter BBV889. You still need to select Characters and purchase this character for 28,000 studs.

IMPERIAL SHUTTLE PILOT

At Mos Eisley Canteena, select Enter Code and enter VAP664. You still need to select Characters and purchase this character for 29,000 studs.

IMPERIAL SPY

At Mos Eisley Canteena, select Enter Code and enter CVT125. You still need to select Characters and purchase this character for 13,500 studs.

JAWA

At Mos Eisley Canteena, select Enter Code and enter JAW499. You still need to select Characters and purchase this character for 24,000 studs.

LOBOT

At Mos Eisley Canteena, select Enter Code and enter UUB319. You still need to select Characters and purchase this character for 11,000 studs.

PALACE GUARD

At Mos Eisley Canteena, select Enter Code and enter SGE549. You still need to select Characters and purchase this character for 14,000 studs.

REBEL PILOT

At Mos Eisley Canteena, select Enter Code and enter CYG336. You still need to select Characters and purchase this character for 15,000 studs.

REBEL TROOPER (HOTH)

At Mos Eisley Canteena, select Enter Code and enter EKU849. You still need to select Characters and purchase this character for 16,000 studs.

SANDTROOPER

At Mos Eisley Canteena, select Enter Code and enter YDV451. You still need to select Characters and purchase this character for 14,000 studs.

SKIFF GUARD

At Mos Eisley Canteena, select Enter Code and enter GBU888. You still need to select Characters and purchase this character for 12,000 studs.

SNOWTROOPER

At Mos Eisley Canteena, select Enter Code and enter NYU989. You still need to select Characters and purchase this character for 16,000 studs.

STROMTROOPER

At Mos Eisley Canteena, select Enter Code and enter PTR345. You still need to select Characters and purchase this character for 10,000 studs.

THE EMPEROR

At Mos Eisley Canteena, select Enter Code and enter HHY382. You still need to select Characters and purchase this character for 275,000 studs.

TIE FIGHTER

At Mos Eisley Canteena, select Enter Code and enter HDY739. You still need to select Characters and purchase this character for 60,000 studs.

TIE FIGHTER PILOT

At Mos Eisley Canteena, select Enter Code and enter NNZ316. You still need to select Characters and purchase this character for 21,000 studs.

TIE INTERCEPTOR

At Mos Eisley Canteena, select Enter Code and enter QYA828. You still need to select Characters and purchase this character for 40,000 studs.

TUSKEN RAIDER

At Mos Eisley Canteena, select Enter Code and enter PEJ821. You still need to select Characters and purchase this character for 23,000 studs.

UGNAUGHT

At Mos Eisley Canteena, select Enter Code and enter UGN694. You still need to select Characters and purchase this character for 36,000 studs.

LEGO STAR WARS: THE COMPLETE SAGA

The following still need to be purchase after entering the codes.

CHARACTERS

ADMIRAL ACKBAR

At the bar in Mos Eisley Cantina, select Enter Code and enter ACK646.

BATTLE DROID (COMMANDER)

At the bar in Mos Eisley Cantina, select Enter Code and enter KPF958.

BOBA FETT (BOY)

At the bar in Mos Eisley Cantina, select Enter Code and enter GGF539.

BOSS NASS

At the bar in Mos Eisley Cantina, select Enter Code and enter HHY697.

CAPTAIN TARPALS

At the bar in Mos Eisley Cantina, select Enter Code and enter QRN714.

COUNT DOOKU

At the bar in Mos Eisley Cantina, select Enter Code and enter DDD748.

DARTH MAUL

At the bar in Mos Eisley Cantina, select Enter Code and enter EUK421.

EWOK

At the bar in Mos Eisley Cantina, select Enter Code and enter EWK785.

GENERAL GRIEVOUS

At the bar in Mos Eisley Cantina, select Enter Code and enter PMN576.

GREEDO

At the bar in Mos Eisley Cantina, select Enter Code and enter ZZR636.

IG-88

At the bar in Mos Eisley Cantina, select Enter Code and enter GIJ989.

IMPERIAL GUARD

At the bar in Mos Eisley Cantina, select Enter Code and enter GUA850.

JANGO FETT

At the bar in Mos Eisley Cantina, select Enter Code and enter KLJ897.

KI-ADI MUNDI

At the bar in Mos Eisley Cantina, select Enter Code and enter MUN486.

LUMINARA

At the bar in Mos Eisley Cantina, select Enter Code and enter LUM521.

PADMÉ

At the bar in Mos Eisley Cantina, select Enter Code and enter VBJ322.

R2-Q5

At the bar in Mos Eisley Cantina, select Enter Code and enter EVILR2.

STORMTROOPER

At the bar in Mos Eisley Cantina, select Enter Code and enter NBN431.

TAUN WE

At the bar in Mos Eisley Cantina, select Enter Code and enter PRX482.

VULTURE DROID

At the bar in Mos Eisley Cantina, select Enter Code and enter BDC866.

WATTO

At the bar in Mos Eisley Cantina, select Enter Code and enter PLL967.

ZAM WESELL

At the bar in Mos Eisley Cantina, select Enter Code and enter 584HJF.

SKILLS

DISGUISE

At the bar in Mos Eisley Cantina, select Enter Code and enter BRJ437.

FORCE GRAPPLE LEAP

At the bar in Mos Eisley Cantina, select Enter Code and enter CLZ738.

VEHICLES

DROID TRIFIGHTER

At the bar in Mos Eisley Cantina, select Enter Code and enter AAB123.

IMPERIAL SHUTTLE

At the bar in Mos Eisley Cantina, select Enter Code and enter HUT845.

TIE INTERCEPTOR

At the bar in Mos Eisley Cantina, select Enter Code and enter INT729.

TIE FIGHTER

At the bar in Mos Eisley Cantina, select Enter Code and enter DBH897.

ZAM'S AIRSPEEDER

At the bar in Mos Eisley Cantina, select Enter Code and enter UUU875.

LOONEY TUNES: ACME ARSENAL

UNLMITED AMMO

At the cheat menu, press Down, Left, Up, Right, Down, Left, Up, Right, Down.

LOST PLANET: EXTREME CONDITION

The following codes are for Single Player Mode on Easy Difficulty only.

500 THERMAL ENERGY

Pause the game and press Up, Up, Down, Down, Left, Right, Left, Right, ❌, ❤, Right Bumper + Left Bumper.

INFINITE AMMUNITION

Pause the game and press Right Trigger, Right Bumper, ❤, ❌, Right, Down, Left, Left Bumper, Left Trigger, Right Trigger, Right

Bumper, ❤, ❌, Right, Down, Left, Left Bumper, Left Trigger, Right Trigger, Left Trigger, Left Bumper, Right Bumper, ❤, Left, Down, ❌, Right Bumper + Left Bumper.

INFINITE HEALTH

Pause the game and press Down (x3), Up, ❤, Up, ❤,
Up, ❤, Up(x3), Down, ❌, Down, ❌, Down, ❌, Left, ❤, Right, ❌, –Left, ❤, Right, ❌, Right Bumper + Left Bumper.

CHANGE CAMERA ANGLE IN CUT SCENES

During a cut scene, press Ⓑ, Ⓐ, ❌, ❤, Ⓑ, Ⓐ, ❌, ❤, Ⓑ, Ⓐ, ❌, ❤.

MAJOR LEAGUE BASEBALL 2K6

UNLOCK EVERYTHING

Select Enter Cheat Code from the My 2K6 menu and enter Derek Jeter.

TOPPS 2K STARS

Select Enter Cheat Code from the My 2K6 menu and enter Dream Team.

SUPER WALL CLIMB

Select Enter Cheat Code from the My 2K6 menu and enter Last Chance. Enable the cheats by selecting My Cheats or selecting Cheat Codes from the in-game Options screen.

SUPER PITCHES

Select Enter Cheat Code from the My 2K6 menu and enter Unhittable. Enable the cheats by selecting My Cheats or selecting Cheat Codes from the in-game Options screen.

ROCKET ARMS

Select Enter Cheat Code from the My 2K6 menu and enter Gotcha. Enable the cheats by selecting My Cheats or selecting Cheat Codes from the in-game Options screen.

BOUNCY BALL

Select Enter Cheat Code from the My 2K6 menu and enter Crazy Hops. Enable the cheats by selecting My Cheats or selecting Cheat Codes from the in-game Options.

MAJOR LEAGUE BASEBALL 2K7

MICKEY MANTLE ON THE FREE AGENTS LIST

Select Enter Cheat Code from the My 2K7 menu and enter themick.

ALL CHEATS

Select Enter Cheat Code from the My 2K7 menu and enter Black Sox.

ALL EXTRAS

Select Enter Cheat Code from the My 2K7 menu and enter Game On.

UNLOCK EVERYTHING

Select Enter Cheat Code from the My 2K7 menu and enter Derek Jeter. This does not unlock the Topps cheats.

MIGHTY MICK CHEAT

Select Enter Cheat Code from the My 2K7 menu and enter mightymick.

TRIPLE CROWN CHEAT

Select Enter Cheat Code from the My 2K7 menu and enter triplecrown.

PINCH HIT MICK CHEAT

Select Enter Cheat Code from the My 2K7 menu and enter phmantle.

BIG BLAST CHEAT

Select Enter Cheat Code from the My 2K7 menu Rand enter m4murder.

MARVEL ULTIMATE ALLIANCE

UNLOCK ALL SKINS

At the Team menu, press Up, Down, Left, Right, Left, Right, Start.

UNLOCKS ALL HERO POWERS

At the Team menu, press Left, Right, Up, Down, Up, Down, Start.

ALL HEROES TO LEVEL 99

At the Team menu, press Up, Left, Up, Left, Down, Right, Down, Right, Start.

UNLOCK ALL HEROES

At the Team menu, press Up, Up, Down, Down, Left, Left, Left, Start.

UNLOCK DAREDEVIL

At the Team menu, press Left, Left, Right, Right, Up, Down, Up, Down, Start.

UNLOCK SILVER SURFER

At the Team menu, press Down, Left, Left, Up, Right, Up, Down, Left, Start.

GOD MODE

During gameplay, press Up, Down, Up, Down, Up, Left, Down, Right, Start.

TOUCH OF DEATH

During gameplay, press Left, Right, Down, Down, Right, Left, Start.

SUPER SPEED

During gameplay, press Up, Left, Up, Right, Down, Right, Start.

FILL MOMENTUM

During gameplay, press Left, Right, Right, Left, Up, Down, Down, Up, Start.

UNLOCK ALL COMICS

At the Review menu, press Left, Right, Right, Left, Up, Up, Right, Start.

UNLOCK ALL CONCEPT ART

At the Review menu, press Down, Down, Down, Right, Right, Left, Down, Start.

UNLOCK ALL CINEMATICS

At the Review menu, press Up, Left, Left, Up, Right, Right, Up, Start.

UNLOCK ALL LOAD SCREENS

At the Review menu, press Up, Down, Right, Left, Up, Up Down, Start.

UNLOCK ALL COURSES

At the Comic Missions menu, press Up, Right, Left, Down, Up, Right, Left, Down, Start.

MARVEL: ULTIMATE ALLIANCE 2

These codes will disable the ability to save.

GOD MODE

During a game, press Up, Down, Up, Down, Up, Left, Down, Right, Start.

UNLIMITED FUSION

During a game, press Right, Right, Up, Down, Up, Up, Left, Start.

UNLOCK ALL POWERS

During a game, press Left, Right, Up, Down, Up, Down, Start.

UNLOCK ALL HEROES

During a game, press Up, Up, Down, Down, Left, Left, Left, Start.

UNLOCK ALL SKINS

During a game, press Up, Down, Left, Right, Left, Right, Start.

UNLOCK JEAN GREY

During a game, press Left, Left, Right, Right, Up, Up, Down, Start.

UNLOCK HULK

During a game, press Down, Left, Left, Up, Right, Up, Down, Left, Start.

UNLOCK THOR

During a game, press Up, Right, Right, Down, Right, Down, Left, Right, Start.

UNLOCK ALL AUDIO LOGS

At the main menu, press Left, Right, Right, Left, Up, Up, Right, Start.

UNLOCK ALL DOSSIERS

At the main menu, press Down, Down, Down, Right, Right, Left, Down, Start.

UNLOCK ALL MOVIES

At the main menu, press Up, Left, Left, Up, Right, Right, Up, Start.

MONSTER MADNESS: BATTLE FOR SUBURBIA

Pause the game and press Up, Up, Down, Down, Left, Right, Left, Right, **Ⓑ**, **Ⓐ**. This brings up a screen where you can enter the following cheats. With the use of some cheats profile saving, level progression, and Xbox Live Achievements are disabled until you return to the Main menu.

EFFECT	CHEAT
Animal Sounds	patrickdugan
Disable Tracking Cameras	ihatefunkycameras
Faster Music	upthejoltcola
First Person	margythemole

EFFECT	CHEAT
Infinite Secondary Items	stevebrooks
Objects Move Away from Player	southpeak
Remove Film Grain	reverb

MOTOGP 07

ALL CHALLENGES

At the main menu, press Right, Up, **Ⓑ**, **Ⓐ**, **Ⓑ**, **Ⓐ**, Left, Down, **Ⓨ**.

ALL CHAMPIONSHIPS

At the main menu, press Right, Up, **Ⓑ**, **Ⓨ**, Right, Up, **Ⓑ**, **Ⓨ**, Right, Up, **Ⓑ**, **Ⓨ**.

ALL LIVERIES

At the main menu, press Right, **Ⓐ**, Left, Left, **Ⓨ**, Left, **Ⓐ**, Down, **Ⓨ**.

ALL RIDERS

At the main menu, press Right, Up, **Ⓑ**, **Ⓑ**, **Ⓐ**, Down, Up, **Ⓑ**, Down, Up, **Ⓑ**.

ALL TRACKS

At the main menu, press Left, **Ⓐ**, Right, Down, **Ⓨ**, **Ⓑ**, **Ⓐ**, **Ⓑ**, **Ⓨ**.

MX VS. ATV UNTAMED

ALL RIDING GEAR

Select Cheat Codes from the Options and enter crazylikea.

ALL HANDLEBARS

Select Cheat Codes from the Options and enter nohands.

27 GRAPHICS

Select Cheat Codes from the Options and enter STICKE✪.

NARUTO: THE BROKEN BOND

NINE TAILS NARUTO

At the Character Select press ✪, ✪, ✪, ✪, ✪, ✪, ✪, ✪, ✪, ✪.

NASCAR 08

ALL CHASE MODE CARS

Select Cheat Codes from the Options menu and enter checkered flag.

EA SPORTS CAR

Select Cheat Codes from the Options menu and enter ea sports car.

FANTASY DRIVERS

Select Cheat Codes from the Options menu and enter race the pack.

WALMART CAR AND TRACK

Select Cheat Codes from the Options menu and enter walmart everyday.

NASCAR 09

ALL FANTASY DRIVERS

Select EA Extras from My Nascar, choose Cheat Codes and enter CHECKERED FLAG.

WALMART TRACK AND THE WALMART CAR

Select EA Extras from My Nascar, choose Cheat Codes and enter Walmart Everyday.

NBA 2K7

MAX DURABILITY

Select Codes from the Features menu and enter ironman.

UNLIMITED STAMINA

Select Codes from the Features menu and enter norest.

+10 DEFFENSIVE AWARENESS

Select Codes from the Features menu and enter getstops.

+10 OFFENSIVE AWARENESS

Select Codes from the Features menu and enter inthezone.

TOPPS 2K SPORTS ALL-STARS

Select Codes from the Features menu and enter topps2ksports.

ABA BALL

Select Codes from the Features menu and enter payrespect.

NBA 2K8

2KSPORTS TEAM

Select Codes from the Features menu and enter 2ksports.

VISUAL CONCEPTS TEAM

Select Codes from the Features menu and enter Vcteam.

ABA BALL

Select Codes from the Features menu and enter Payrespect.

NBA 2K9

2K SPORTS TEAM

Select Codes from the Features menu and enter 2ksports.

NBA 2K TEAM

Select Codes from the Features menu and enter nba2k.

2K CHINA TEAM

Select Codes from the Features menu and enter 2kchina.

SUPERSTARS

Select Codes from the Features menu and enter llmohffaae.

VC TEAM

Select Codes from the Features menu and enter vcteam.

ABA BALL

Select Codes from the Features menu and enter payrespect.

2009 ALL-STAR UNIFORMS

Select Codes from the Features menu and enter llaveyfonus.

NBA 2K10

ABA BALL

Select Codes from Options and enter payrespect.

2K CHINA TEAM

Select Codes from Options and enter 2kchina.

NBA 2K TEAM

Select Codes from Options and enter nba2k.

2K SPORTS TEAM

Select Codes from Options and enter 2ksports.

VISUAL CONCEPTS TEAM

Select Codes from Options and enter vcteam.

NBA LIVE 07

ADIDAS ARTILLERY II BLACK AND THE RBK ANSWER 9 VIDEO

Select NBA Codes from My NBA Live and enter 99B6356HAN.

ADIDAS ARTILLERY II

Select NBA Codes and enter NTGNFUE87H.

ADIDAS BTB LOW AND THE MESSAGE FROM ALLEN IVERSON VIDEO

Select NBA Codes and enter 7FB3KS9JQ0.

ADIDAS C-BILLUPS

Select NBA Codes and enter BV6877HB9N.

ADIDAS C-BILLUPS BLACK

Select NBA Codes and enter 85NVLDMWS5.

ADIDAS CAMPUS LT

Select NBA Codes and enter CLT2983NC8.

ADIDAS CRAZY 8

Select NBA Codes and enter CC98KKL814.

ADIDAS EQUIPMENT BBALL
Select NBA Codes and enter 22OIUJKMDR.

ADIDAS GARNETT BOUNCE
Select NBA Codes and enter HYIOUHCAAN.

ADIDAS GARNETT BOUNCE BLACK
Select NBA Codes and enter KDZ2MQL17W.

ADIDAS GIL-ZERO
Select NBA Codes and enter 23DN1PPOG4.

ADIDAS GIL-ZERO BLACK
Select NBA Codes and enter QQQ3JCUYQ7.

ADIDAS GIL-ZERO MID
Select NBA Codes and enter 1GSJC8JWRL.

ADIDAS GIL-ZERO MID BLACK
Select NBA Codes and enter 369V6RVU3G.

ADIDAS STEALTH
Select NBA Codes and enter FE454DFJCC.

ADIDAS T-MAC 6
Select NBA Codes and enter MCJK843NNC.

ADIDAS T-MAC 6 WHITE
Select NBA Codes and enter 84GF7EJG8V.

CHARLOTTE BOBCATS 2006-2007 ALTERNATE JERSEY
Select NBA Codes and enter WEDX671H7S.

UTAH JAZZ 2006-2007 ALTERNATE JERSEY
Select NBA Codes and enter VCBI89FK83.

NEW JERSEY NETS 2006-2007 ALTERNATE JERSEY
Select NBA Codes and enter D4SAA98U5H.

WASHINGTON WIZARDS 2006-2007 ALTERNATE JERSEY
Select NBA Codes and enter QV93NLKXQC.

EASTERN ALL-STARS 2006-2007 AWAY JERSEY
Select NBA Codes and enter WOCNW4KL7L.

EASTERN ALL-STARS 2006-2007 HOME JERSEY
Select NBA Codes and enter 5654ND43N6.

WESTERN ALL-STARS 2006-2007 AWAY JERSEY
Select NBA Codes and enter XX93BVL20U.

WESTERN ALL-STARS 2006-2007 HOME JERSEY
Select NBA Codes and enter 993NSKL199.

NBA LIVE 09

SUPER DUNKS MODE
Use the Sprite vending machine in the practice area and enter spriteslam.

NBA STREET HOMECOURT

ALL TEAMS
At the Main menu, hold Right Bumper + Left Bumper and press Left, Right, Left, Right.

ALL COURTS
At the Main menu, hold Right Bumper + Left Bumper and press Up, Right, Down, Left.

BLACK/RED BALL
At the Main menu, hold Right Bumper + Left Bumper and press Up, Down, Left, Right.

NCAA FOOTBALL 07

#16 BAYLOR
Select Pennant Collection from My NCAA. Press Select and enter Sic Em.

#16 NIKE SPEED TD
Select Pennant Collection from My NCAA. Press Select and enter Light Speed.

#63 ILLINOIS
Select Pennant Collection from My NCAA. Press Select and enter Oskee Wow.

#160 TEXAS TECH
Select Pennant Collection from My NCAA. Press Select and enter Fight.

#200 FIRST AND FIFTEEN
Select Pennant Collection from My NCAA. Press Select and enter Thanks.

#201 BLINK
Select Pennant Collection from My NCAA. Press Select and enter For.

#202 BOING
Select Pennant Collection from My NCAA. Press Select and enter Registering.

#204 BUTTER FINGERS
Select Pennant Collection from My NCAA. Press Select and enter With EA.

#205 CROSSED THE LINE
Select Pennant Collection from My NCAA. Press Select and enter Tiburon.

#206 CUFFED
Select Pennant Collection from My NCAA. Press Select and enter EA Sports.

#207 EXTRA CREDIT
Select Pennant Collection from My NCAA. Press Select and enter Touchdown.

#208 HELIUM
Select Pennant Collection from My NCAA. Press Select and enter In The Zone.

#209 HURRICANE

Select Pennant Collection from My NCAA. Press Select and enter Turnover.

#210 INSTANT FREPLAY

Select Pennant Collection from My NCAA. Press Select and enter Impact.

#211 JUMBALAYA

Select Pennant Collection from My NCAA. Press Select and enter Heisman.

#212 MOLASSES

Select Pennant Collection from My NCAA. Press Select and enter Game Time.

#213 NIKE FREE

Select Pennant Collection from My NCAA. Press Select and enter Break Free.

#214 NIKE MAGNIGRIP

Select Pennant Collection from My NCAA. Press Select and enter Hand Picked.

#215 NIKE PRO

Select Pennant Collection from My NCAA. Press Select and enter No Sweat.

#219 QB DUD

Select Pennant Collection from My NCAA. Press Select and enter Elite 11.

#221 STEEL TOE

Select Pennant Collection from My NCAA. Press Select and enter Gridiron.

#222 STIFFED

Select Pennant Collection from My NCAA. Press Select and enter NCAA.

#223 SUPER DIVE

Select Pennant Collection from My NCAA. Press Select and enter Upset.

#224 TAKE YOUR TIME

Select Pennant Collection from My NCAA. Press Select and enter Football.

#225 THREAD & NEEDLE

Select Pennant Collection from My NCAA. Press Select and enter 06.

#226 TOUGH AS NAILS

Select Pennant Collection from My NCAA. Press Select and enter Offense.

#227 TRIP

Select Pennant Collection from My NCAA. Press Select and enter Defense.

#228 WHAT A HIT

Select Pennant Collection from My NCAA. Press Select and enter Blitz.

#229 KICKER HEX

Select Pennant Collection from My NCAA. Press Select and enter Sideline.

#273 2004 ALL-AMERICANS

Select Pennant Collection from My NCAA. Press Select and enter Fumble.

#274 ALL-ALABAMA

Select Pennant Collection from My NCAA. Press Select and enter Roll Tide.

#276 ALL-ARKANSAS

Select Pennant Collection from My NCAA. Press Select and enter Woopigsooie.

#277 ALL-AUBURN

Select Pennant Collection from My NCAA. Press Select and enter War Eagle.

#278 ALL-CLEMSON
Select Pennant Collection from My NCAA. Press Select and enter Death Valley.

#279 ALL-COLORADO
Select Pennant Collection from My NCAA. Press Select and enter Glory.

#280 ALL-FLORIDA
Select Pennant Collection from My NCAA. Press Select and enter Great To Be.

#281 ALL-FSU
Select Pennant Collection from My NCAA. Press Select and enter Uprising.

#282 ALL-GEORGIA
Select Pennant Collection from My NCAA. Press Select and enter Hunker Down.

#283 ALL-IOWA
Select Pennant Collection from My NCAA. Press Select and enter On Iowa.

#284 ALL-KANSAS STATE
Select Pennant Collection from My NCAA. Press Select and enter Victory.

#285 ALL-LSU
Select Pennant Collection from My NCAA. Press Select and enter Geaux Tigers.

#286 ALL-MIAMI
Select Pennant Collection from My NCAA. Press Select and enter Raising Cane.

#287 ALL-MICHIGAN
Select Pennant Collection from My NCAA. Press Select and enter Go Blue.

#288 ALL-MISSISSIPPI STATE
Select Pennant Collection from My NCAA. Press Select and enter Hail State.

#289 ALL-NEBRASKA
Select Pennant Collection from My NCAA. Press Select and enter Go Big Red.

#290 ALL-NORTH CAROLINA
Select Pennant Collection from My NCAA. Press Select and enter Rah Rah.

#291 ALL-NOTRE DAME
Select Pennant Collection from My NCAA. Press Select and enter Golden Domer.

#292 ALL-OHIO STATE
Select Pennant Collection from My NCAA. Press Select and enter Killer Nuts.

#293 ALL-OKLAHOMA
Select Pennant Collection from My NCAA. Press Select and enter Boomer.

#294 ALL-OKLAHOMA STATE
Select Pennant Collection from My NCAA. Press Select and enter Go Pokes.

#295 ALL-OREGON
Select Pennant Collection from My NCAA. Press Select and enter Quack Attack.

#296 ALL-PENN STATE
Select Pennant Collection from My NCAA. Press Select and enter We Are.

#297 ALL-PITTSBURGH
Select Pennant Collection from My NCAA. Press Select and enter Lets Go Pitt.

#298 ALL-PURDUE
Select Pennant Collection from My NCAA. Press Select and enter Boiler Up.

#299 ALL-SYRACUSE

Select Pennant Collection from My NCAA. Press Select and enter Orange Crush.

#300 ALL-TENNESSEE

Select Pennant Collection from My NCAA. Press Select and enter Big Orange.

#301 ALL-TEXAS

Select Pennant Collection from My NCAA. Press Select and enter Hook Em.

#302 ALL-TEXAS A&M

Select Pennant Collection from My NCAA. Press Select and enter Gig Em.

#303 ALL-UCLA

Select Pennant Collection from My NCAA. Press Select and enter MIGHTY.

#304 ALL-USC

Select Pennant Collection from My NCAA. Press Select and enter Fight On.

#305 ALL-VIRGINIA

Select Pennant Collection from My NCAA. Press Select and enter Wahoos.

#306 ALL-VIRGINIA TECH

Select Pennant Collection from My NCAA. Press Select and enter Tech Triumph.

#307 ALL-WASHINGTON

Select Pennant Collection from My NCAA. Press Select and enter Bow Down.

#308 ALL-WISCONSIN

Select Pennant Collection from My NCAA. Press Select and enter U Rah Rah.

#311 ARK MASCOT

Select Pennant Collection from My NCAA. Press Select and enter Bear Down.

#329 GT MASCOT

Select Pennant Collection from My NCAA. Press Select and enter RamblinWreck.

#333 ISU MASCOT

Select Pennant Collection from My NCAA. Press Select and enter Red And Gold.

#335 KU MASCOT

Select Pennant Collection from My NCAA. Press Select and enter Rock Chalk.

#341 MINN MASCOT

Select Pennant Collection from My NCAA. Press Select and enter Rah Rah Rah.

#344 MIZZOU MASCOT

Select Pennant Collection from My NCAA. Press Select and enter Mizzou Rah.

#346 MSU MASCOT

Select Pennant Collection from My NCAA. Press Select and enter Go Green.

#349 NCSU MASCOT

Select Pennant Collection from My NCAA. Press Select and enter Go Pack.

#352 NU MASCOT

Select Pennant Collection from My NCAA. Press Select and enter Go Cats.

#360 S CAR MASCOT

Select Pennant Collection from My NCAA. Press Select and enter Go Carolina.

#371 UK MASCOT

Select Pennant Collection from My NCAA. Press Select and enter On On UK.

#382 WAKE FOREST

Select Pennant Collection from My NCAA. Press Select and enter Go Deacs Go.

#385 WSU MASCOT

Select Pennant Collection from My NCAA. Press Select and enter All Hail.

#386 WVU MASCOT

Select Pennant Collection from My NCAA. Press Select and enter Hail WV.

NEED FOR SPEED CARBON

CASTROL CASH

At the Main menu, press Down, Up, Left, Down, Right, Up, ❌, ⓑ. This will give you 10,000 extra cash.

INFINITE CREW CHARGE

At the Main menu, press Down, Up, Up, Right, Left, Left, Right, ❌.

INFINITE NITROUS

At the Main menu, press Left, Up, Left, Down, Left, Down, Right, ❌.

INFINITE SPEEDBREAKER

At the Main menu, press Down, Right, Right, Left, Right, Up, Down, ❌.

NEED FOR SPEED CARBON LOGO VINYLS

At the Main menu, press Right, Up, Down, Up, Down, Left, Right, ❌.

NEED FOR SPEED CARBON SPECIAL LOGO VINYLS

At the Main menu, press Up, Up, Down, Down, Down, Down, Up, ❌.

NEED FOR SPEED PROSTREET

$2,000

Select Career and then choose Code Entry. Enter 1MA9X99.

$4,000

Select Career and then choose Code Entry. Enter W2IOLLO1.

$8,000

Select Career and then choose Code Entry. Enter L1IS97A1.

$10,000

Select Career and then choose Code Entry. Enter 1MI9K7E1.

$10,000

Select Career and then choose Code Entry. Enter CASHMONEY.

$10,000

Select Career and then choose Code Entry. Enter REGGAME.

AUDI TT

Select Career and then choose Code Entry. Enter ITSABOUTYOU.

CHEVELLE SS

Select Career and then choose Code Entry. Enter HO✪EPOWER.

COKE ZERO GOLF GTI

Select Career and then choose Code Entry. Enter COKEZERO.

DODGE VIPER

Select Career and then choose Code Entry. Enter WORLDSLONGESTLASTING.

MITSUBISHI LANCER EVOLUTION

Select Career and then choose Code Entry. Enter MITSUBISHIGOFAR.

UNLOCK ALL BONUSES

Select Career and then choose Code Entry. Enter UNLOCKALLTHINGS.

5 REPAIR MARKERS

Select Career and then choose Code Entry. Enter SAFETYNET.

ENERGIZER VINYL

Select Career and then choose Code Entry. Enter ENERGIZERLITHIUM.

CASTROL SYNTEC VINYL

Select Career and then choose Code Entry. Enter CASTRO ⬤ YNTEC. This also gives you $10,000.

NEED FOR SPEED UNDERCOVER

$10,000

Select Secret Codes from the Options menu and enter SEDSOC.

DIE-CAST BMW M3 E92

Select Secret Codes from the Options menu and enter)B7@B=.

DIE-CAST LEXUS IS F

Select Secret Codes from the Options menu and enter 0;5M2;.

NEEDFORSPEED.COM LOTUS ELISE

Select Secret Codes from the Options menu and enter -KJ3=E.

DIE-CAST NISSAN 240SX (S13)

Select Secret Codes from the Options menu and enter ?P:COL.

DIE-CAST PORSCHE 911 TURBO

Select Secret Codes from the Options menu and enter >8P:I;.

SHELBY TERLINGUA

Select Secret Codes from the Options menu and enter NeedForSpeedShelbyTerlingua.

DIE-CAST VOLKSWAGEN R32

Select Secret Codes from the Options menu and enter!2ODBJ:.

NHL 08

ALL RBK EDGE JERSEYS

At the ⬛ K Edge Code option, enter h3oyxpwksf8ibcgt.

NHL 2K8

2007-2008 NHL REEBOK EDGE JERSEYS

From the Features menu, select Unlock 2007-2008/Enter Password. Enter S6j83RMk01.

NHL 2K9

3RD JERSEYS

From the Features menu, enter R6y34bsH52 as a code.

NPPL CHAMPIONSHIP PAINTBALL 2009

TIPPMANN X-7 AK-47 SCENARIO PAINTBALL MARKER

Select Field Gear and press Up, Up, Right, Right, Down, Down, Left, Left.

PETER JACKSON'S KING KONG: THE OFFICIAL GAME OF THE MOVIE

At the Main menu hold Left Bumper + Right Bumper + Left Trigger + Right Trigger and press Down, Up, **Y**, **X**, Down, Down, **Y**, **Y**. Release the buttons to access the Cheat option. The Cheat option will also be available on the pause menu. You cannot record your scores using cheat codes.

GOD MODE

Select Cheat and enter 8wonder.

ALL CHAPTERS

Select Cheat and enter KKst0ry.

AMMO 999

Select Cheat and enter KK 999 mun.

MACHINE GUN

Select Cheat and enter KKcapone.

REVOLVER

Select Cheat and enter KKtigun.

SNIPER RIFLE

Select Cheat and enter KKsn1per.

INFINITE SPEARS

Select Cheat and enter lance 1nf.

ONE-HIT KILLS

Select Cheat and enter GrosBras.

EXTRAS

Select Cheat and enter KKmuseum.

PRINCE OF PERSIA

SANDS OF TIME PRINCE/FARAH SKINS

Select Skin Manager from the Extras menu. Press ❤ and enter 52585854. This gives you the Sands of Time skin for the Prince and Farah from Sands of Time for the Princess. Access them from the Skin Manager

PRINCE ALTAIR IBN LA-AHAD SKIN

At the main menu, press Y for Exclusive Content. Create an Ubisoft account. Then select "Altair Skin for Prince" to unlock.

RATATOUILLE

UNLIMITED RUNNING

At the Cheat Code screen, enter SPEEDY.

ALL MULTIPLAYER AND SINGLE PLAYER MINI GAMES

At the Cheat Code screen, enter MATTELME.

ROCKSTAR GAMES PRESENTS TABLE TENNIS

Use of the following codes will disable achievements.

SWEATY CHARACTER VIEWER

After loading the map and before accepting the match, press Right Trigger, Up, Down, Left Trigger, Left, Right, ❤, ✖, ✖, ❤.

SMALL CROWD AUDIO

After loading the map and before accepting the match, press Down, Down, Down, Left Bumper, Left Trigger, Left Bumper, Left Trigger.

BIG BALL

After loading the map and before accepting the match, press Left, Right, Left, Right, Up, Up, Up, ❌.

COLORBLIND SPINDICATOR (ONLY IN NEWER PATCH)

After loading the map and before accepting the match, press Up, Down, ❌, ❌, ❓, ❓.

SILHOUETTE MODE

After loading the map and before accepting the match, press Up, Down, ❓, ❓, Left Bumper, Left Trigger, Right Trigger, Right Bumper.

BIG PADDLES CHEAT (ONLY IN NEWER PATCH)

After loading the map and before accepting the match, press Up, Left, Up, Right, Up, Down, Up, Up, ❌, ❌.

UNLOCK ALL

After loading the map and before accepting the match, press Up, Right, Down, Left, Left Bumper, Right, Up, Left, Down, Right Bumper.

VINTAGE AUDIO

After loading the map and before accepting the match, press Up, Up, Down, Down, Left, Right, Left, Right, Left Bumper, Right Bumper.

BIG CROWD AUDIO

After loading the map and before accepting the match, press Up, Up, Up, Right Bumper, Right Trigger, Right Bumper, Right Trigger.

OFFLINE GAMERTAGS

After loading the map and before accepting the match, press ❌, ❓, ❌, ❓, ❌, ❓, Left Trigger, Right Trigger, Down, Down, Down.

SAMURAI SHODOWN 2

PLAY AS KUROKO IN 2-PLAYER

At the character select, press Up, Down, Left, Up, Down, Right + ❌.

SEGA SUPERSTARS TENNIS

UNLOCK CHARACTERS

Complete the following missions to unlock the corresponding character.

CHARACTER	MISSION TO COMPLETE
Alex Kidd	Mission 1 of Alex Kidd's World
Amy Rose	Mission 2 of Sonic the Hedgehog's World
Gilius	Mission 1 of Golden Axe's World
Gum	Mission 12 of Jet Grind Radio's World
Meemee	Mission 8 of Super Monkey Ball's World
Pudding	Mission 1 of Space Channel 5's World
Reala	Mission 2 of NiGHTs' World
Shadow The Hedgehog	Mission 14 of Sonic the Hedgehog's World

SHREK THE THIRD

10,000 GOLD COINS

At the gift shop, press Up, Up, Down, Up, Right, Left.

THE SIMPSONS GAME

After unlocking the following, the outfits can be changed at the downstairs closet in the Simpson's house. The Trophies can be viewed at different locations in the house: Bart's room, Lisa's room, Marge's room, and the garage.

BART'S OUTFITS AND TROPHIES (POSTER COLLECTION)

At the main menu, press Right, Left, ✪, ✪, ✪, Right Thumb Stick.

HOMER'S OUTFITS AND TROPHIES (BEER BOTTLE COLLECTION)

At the main menu, press Left, Right, ✪, ✪, ✪, Left Thumb Stick.

LISA'S OUTFITS AND TROPHIES (DOLLS)

At the main menu, press ✪, ✪, ✪, ✪, ✪, Left Thumb Stick.

MARGE'S OUTFITS AND TROPHIES (HAIR PRODUCTS)

At the main menu, press ✪, ✪, ✪, ✪, ✪, Right Thumb Stick.

SKATE

EXCLUSIVE BEST BUY CLOTHES

At the Main Menu, press Up, Down, Left, Right, ✗, Right Bumper, Ⓨ, Left Bumper. You can get the clothes at Reg's or Slappy's Skate Shop. Find it under Skate.

DEM BONES CHARACTER

Break each bone in your body at least 3 times.

SKATE 2

BIG BLACK

Select Enter Cheat from the Extras menu and enter letsdowork.

3D MODE

Select Enter Cheat from the Extras menu and enter strangeloops. Use glasses to view in 3D.

SPIDER-MAN: FRIEND OR FOE

NEW GREEN GOBLIN AS A SIDEKICK

While standing in the Helicarrier between levels, press Left, Down, Right, Right, Down, Left.

SANDMAN AS A SIDEKICK

While standing in the Helicarrier between levels, press Right, Right, Right, Up, Down, Left.

VENOM AS A SIDEKICK

While standing in the Helicarrier between levels, press Left, Left, Right, Up, Down, Down.

5000 TECH TOKENS

While standing in the Helicarrier between levels, press Up, Up, Down, Down, Left, Right.

STAR TREK: D-A-C

KOBAYASHI MARU CHEAT AND ACHIEVEMENT

Once a match begins, pause the game, and press Left Trigger, Ⓨ, ✗, ✗, Ⓨ, Right Trigger. This increases your rate of fire and regeneration. This also gives you the Kobayashi Maru achievement.

STAR WARS: THE FORCE UNLEASHED

CHEAT CODES

Pause the game and select Input Code. Here you can enter the following codes. Activating any of the following cheat codes will disable some unlockables, and you will be unable to save your progress.

CHEAT	CODE	CHEAT	CODE
All Force Powers at Max Power	KATARN	All Saber Crystals	HURRIKANE
All Force Push Ranks	EXARKUN	All Talents	JOCASTA
All Saber Throw Ranks	ADEGAN	Deadly Saber	LIGHTSABER
All Repulse Ranks	DATHOMIR		

COMBOS

Pause the game and select Input Code. Here you can enter the following codes. Activating any of the following cheat codes will disable some unlockables, and you will be unable to save your progress.

COMBO	CODE	COMBO	CODE
All Combos	MOLDYCROW	Saber Slam	PLOKOON
Aerial Ambush	VENTRESS	Saber Sling	KITFISTO
Aerial Assault	EETHKOTH	Sith Saber Flurry	LUMIYA
Aerial Blast	YADDLE	Sith Slash	DARAGON
Impale	BRUTALSTAB	Sith Throw	SAZEN
Lightning Bomb	MASSASSI	New Combo	FREEDON
Lightning Grenade	RAGNOS	New Combo	MARAJADE

ALL DATABANK ENTRIES

Pause the game and select Input Code. Enter OSSUS.

MIRRORED LEVEL

Pause the game and select Input Code. Enter MINDTRICK. Re-enter the code to return level to normal.

SITH MASTER DIFFICULTY

Pause the game and select Input Code. Enter SITHSPAWN.

COSTUMES

Pause the game and select Input Code. Here you can enter the following codes.

COSTUME	CODE	COSTUME	CODE
All Costumes	SOHNDANN	Master Kento	WOOKIEE
Bail Organa	VICEROY	Proxy	PROTOTYPE
Ceremonial Jedi Robes	DANTOOINE	Scout Trooper	FERRAL
Drunken Kota	HARDBOILED	Shadow Trooper	BLACKHOLE
Emperor	MASTERMIND	Sith Stalker Armor	KORRIBAN
Incinerator Trooper	PHOENIX	Snowtrooper	SNOWMAN
Jedi Adventure Robe	HOLOCRON	Stormtrooper	TK421WHITE
Kashyyyk Trooper	TK421GREEN	Stormtrooper Commander	TK421BLUE
Kota	MANDALORE		

STAR WARS THE CLONE WARS: REPUBLIC HEROES

ULTIMATE LIGHTSABER

Pause the game, select Cheats from the Shop, and press Right, Down, Down, Up, Left, Up, Up, Down.

STUNTMAN IGNITION

3 PROPS IN STUNT CREATOR MODE

Select Cheats from Extras and enter COOLPROP.

ALL ITEMS UNLOCKED FOR CONSTRUCTION MODE

Select Cheats from Extras and enter NOBLEMAN.

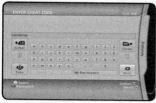 

MVX SPARTAN

Select Cheats from Extras and enter fastride.

ALL CHEATS

Select Cheats from Extras and enter Wearefrozen. This unlocks the following cheats: Slo-mo Cool, Thrill Cam, Vision Switcher, Nitro Addiction, Freaky Fast, and Ice Wheels.

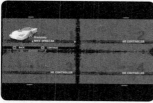 

ALL CHEATS

Select Cheats from Extras and enter Kungfoopete.

ICE WHEELS CHEAT

Select Cheats from Extras and enter IceAge.

NITRO ADDICTION CHEAT

Select Cheats from Extras and enter TheDuke.

VISION SWITCHER CHEAT

Select Cheats from Extras and enter GFXMODES.

SUPER CONTRA

UNLIMITED LIVES AND SUPER MACHINEGUN

At the Main menu, select Arcade Game, and then press Up, Up, Down, Down, Left, Right, Left, Right, **B**, **A**. Achievements and the Leaderboard are disabled with this code.

SUPERMAN RETURNS: THE VIDEOGAME

GOD MODE
Pause the game, select Options and press Up, Up, Down, Down, Left, Right, Left, Right, **Ⓨ**, **Ⓧ**.

INFINITE CITY HEALTH
Pause the game, select Options and press **Ⓨ**, Right, **Ⓨ**, Right, Up, Left, Right, **Ⓨ**.

ALL POWER-UPS
Pause the game, select Options and press Left, **Ⓨ**, Right, **Ⓧ**, Down, **Ⓨ**, Up, Down, **Ⓧ**, **Ⓨ**, **Ⓧ**.

ALL UNLOCKABLES
Pause the game, select Options and press Left, Up, Right, Down, **Ⓨ**, **Ⓧ**, **Ⓨ** Up, Right, **Ⓧ**.

FREE ROAM AS BIZARRO
Pause the game, select Options and press Up, Right, Down, Right, Up, Left, Down, Right, Up.

SUPER PUZZLE FIGHTER II TURBO HD REMIX

PLAY AS AKUMA
At the Character Select screen, highlight Hsien-Ko and press Down.

PLAY AS DAN
At the Character Select screen, highlight Donovan and press Down.

PLAY AS DEVILOT
At the Character Select screen, highlight Morrigan and press Down.

PLAY AS ANITA
At the Character Select screen, hold Left Bumper + Right Bumper and choose Donovan.

PLAY AS HSIEN-KO'S TALISMAN
At the Character Select screen, hold Left Bumper + Right Bumper and choose Hsien-Ko.

PLAY AS MORRIGAN AS A BAT
At the Character Select screen, hold Left Bumper + Right Bumper and choose Morrigan.

SURF'S UP

ALL CHAMPIONSHIP LOCATIONS
Select Cheat Codes from the Extras menu and enter FREEVISIT.

ALL LEAF SLIDE STAGES
Select Cheat Codes from the Extras menu and enter GOINGDOWN.

ALL MULTIPLAYER LEVELS
Select Cheat Codes from the Extras menu and enter MULTIPASS.

ALL BOARDS
Select Cheat Codes from the Extras menu and enter MYPRECIOUS.

ASTRAL BOARD
Select Cheat Codes from the Extras menu and enter ASTRAL.

MONSOON BOARD
Select Cheat Codes from the Extras menu and enter MONSOON.

TINE SHOCKWAVE BOARD
Select Cheat Codes from the Extras menu and enter TINYSHOCKWAVE.

ALL CHARACTER CUSTOMIZATIONS

Select Cheat Codes from the Extras menu and enter TOPFASHION.

PLAY AS ARNOLD

Select Cheat Codes from the Extras menu and enter TINYBUTSTRONG.

PLAY AS ELLIOT

Select Cheat Codes from the Extras menu and enter SURPRISEGUEST.

PLAY AS GEEK

Select Cheat Codes from the Extras menu and enter SLOWANDSTEADY.

PLAY AS TANK EVANS

Select Cheat Codes from the Extras menu and enter IMTHEBEST.

PLAY AS TATSUHI KOBAYASHI

Select Cheat Codes from the Extras menu and enter KOBAYASHI.

PLAY AS ZEKE TOPANGA

Select Cheat Codes from the Extras menu and enter THELEGEND.

ALL VIDEOS AND SPEN GALLERY

Select Cheat Codes from the Extras menu and enter WATCHAMOVIE.

ART GALLERY

Select Cheat Codes from the Extras menu and enter NICEPLACE.

THRILLVILLE: OFF THE RAILS

$50,000

While in a park, press ❌, 🅱, 🆈, ❌, 🅱, 🆈, 🅰.

500 THRILL POINTS

While in a park, press 🅱, ❌, 🆈, 🅱, ❌, 🆈, ❌.

ALL PARKS

While in a park, press ❌, 🅱, 🆈, ❌, 🅱, 🆈, ❌.

ALL RIDES IN CURRENT PARK

While in a park, press ❌, 🅱, 🆈, ❌, 🅱, 🆈, 🆈.

MISSION UNLOCK

While in a park, press ❌, 🅱, 🆈, ❌, 🅱, 🆈, 🅱.

ALL MINI-GAMES IN PARTY PLAY

While in a park, press ❌, 🅱, 🆈, ❌, 🅱, 🆈, Right.

TIGER WOODS PGA TOUR 07

BIG HEAD MODE FOR CROWDS

Select Password and enter tengallonhat.

TIGER WOODS PGA TOUR 08

ALL COURSES

Select Password from EA Sports Extras and enter greensfees.

ALL GOLFERS

Select Password from EA Sports Extras and enter allstars.

WAYNE ROONEY

Select Password from EA Sports Extras and enter playfifa08.

INFINITE MONEY

Select Password from EA Sports Extras and enter cream.

TIGER WOODS PGA TOUR 09

SPECTATORS BIG HEAD MODE

Select EA SPORTS Extras from My Tiger '09, choose Password and enter cephalus.

TMNT

CHALLENGE MAP 2

At the Main menu, hold the Left Bumper and press Ⓐ, Ⓐ, Ⓑ, Ⓐ.

DON'S BIG HEAD GOODIE

At the Main menu, hold the Left Bumper and press Ⓑ, Ⓨ, Ⓐ, Ⓧ.

TOMB RAIDER: LEGEND

The following codes must be unlocked in the game before using them.

BULLETPROOF

During a game, hold Left Trigger and press Ⓐ, Right Trigger, Ⓨ, Right Trigger, Ⓧ, Left Bumper.

DRAIN ENEMY HEALTH

During a game, hold Left Trigger and press Ⓧ, Ⓑ, Ⓐ, Left Bumper, Right Trigger, Ⓨ.

INFINITE ASSAULT RIFLE AMMO

During a game, hold Left Bumper and press Ⓐ, Ⓑ, Ⓐ, Left Trigger, Ⓧ, Ⓨ.

INFINITE GRENADE LAUNCHER AMMO

During a game, hold Left Bumper and press Left Trigger, Ⓨ, Right Trigger, Ⓑ, Left Trigger, Ⓧ

INFINITE SHOTGUN AMMO

During a game, hold Left Bumper and press Right Trigger, Ⓑ, Ⓧ, Left Trigger, Ⓧ, Ⓐ.

INFINITE SMG AMMO

During a game, hold Left Bumper and press Ⓑ, Ⓨ, Left Trigger, Right Trigger, Ⓐ, Ⓑ.

EXCALIBUR

During a game, hold Left Bumper and press Ⓨ, Ⓐ, Ⓑ, Right Trigger, Ⓨ, Left Trigger.

SOUL REAVER

During a game, hold Left Bumper and press Ⓐ, Right Trigger, Ⓑ, Right Trigger, Left Trigger, Ⓧ.

ONE-SHOT KILL

During a game, hold Left Trigger and press Ⓨ, Ⓐ, Ⓨ, Ⓧ, Left Bumper, Ⓑ.

TEXTURELESS MODE

During a game, hold Left Trigger and press Left Bumper, Ⓐ, Ⓑ, Ⓐ, Ⓨ, Right Trigger.

CHEAT CODE EXPLOSION FOR CONSOLES

TOM CLANCY'S GHOST RECON ADVANCED WARFIGHTER

ALL MISSIONS

At the Mission Select screen, hold Back + Left Trigger + Right Trigger and press **Y**, Right Bumper, **Y**, Right Bumper, **X**.

FULL HEALTH

Pause the game, hold Back + Left Trigger + Right Trigger and press Left Bumper, Left Bumper, Right Bumper, **X**, Right Bumper, **Y**.

INVINCIBLE

Pause the game, hold Back + Left Trigger + Right Trigger and press **Y**, **Y**, **X**, Right Bumper, **X**, Left Bumper.

TEAM INVINCIBLE

Pause the game, hold Back + Left Trigger + Right Trigger and press **X**, **X**, **Y**, Right Bumper, **Y**, Left Bumper.

UNLIMITED AMMO

Pause the game, hold Back + Left Trigger + Right Trigger and press Right Bumper, Right Bumper, Left Bumper, **X**, Left Bumper, **Y**.

TOM CLANCY'S HAWX

A-12 AVENGER II

At the hangar, hold Left Trigger and press **X**, **LB**, **X**, **RB**, **Y**, **X**.

F-18 HARV

At the hangar, hold Left Trigger and press **LB**, **Y**, **LB**, **Y**, **LB**, **X**.

FB-22 STRIKE RAPTOR

At the hangar, hold Left Trigger and press **RB**, **X**, **RB**, **X**, **RB**, **Y**.

TONY HAWK'S PROJECT 8

SPONSOR ITEMS

As you progress through Career mode and move up the rankings, you gain sponsors and each comes with its own Create-a-skater item.

RANK REQUIRED	CAS ITEM UNLOCKED
Rank 040	Adio Kenny V2 Shoes
Rank 050	Quiksilver Hoody 3
Rank 060	Birdhouse Tony Hawk Deck
Rank 080	Vans No Skool Gothic Shoes
Rank 100	Volcom Scallero Jacket
Rank 110	eS Square One Shoes
Rank 120	Almost Watch What You Say Deck
Rank 140	DVS Adage Shoe
Rank 150	Element Illuminate Deck
Rank 160	Etnies Sheckler White Lavender Shoes
Complete Skateshop Goal	Stereo Soundwave Deck

SKATERS

All of the skaters, except for Tony Hawk, must be unlocked by completing challenges in the Career Mode. They are useable in Free Skate and 2 Player modes.

SKATER	HOW THEY ARE UNLOCKED
Tony Hawk	Always UnlocOked
Lyn-z Adams Hawkins	Complete Pro Challenge
Bob Burquist	Complete Pro Challenge
Dustin Dollin	Complete Pro Challenge
Nyjah Huston	Complete Pro Challenge
Bam Margera	Complete Pro Challenge
Rodney Mullen	Complete Pro Challenge
Paul Rodriguez	Complete Pro Challenge
Ryan Sheckler	Complete Pro Challenge
Daewon Song	Complete Pro Challenge
Mike Vallely	Complete Pro Challenge
Stevie Willams	Complete Pro Challenge
Travis Barker	Complete Pro Challenge
Kevin Staab	Complete Pro Challenge
Zombie	Complete Pro Challenge
Christaian Hosoi	Rank #1
Jason Lee	Complete Final Tony Hawk Goal
Photographer	Unlock Shops
Security Guard	Unlock School
Bum	Unlock Car Factory
Beaver Mascot	Unlock High School
Real Estate Agent	Unlock Downtown
Filmer	Unlock High School
Skate Jam Kid	Rank #4
Dad	Rank #1
Colonel	All Gaps
Nerd	Complete School Spirit Goal

CHEAT CODES

Select Cheat Codes from the Options and enter the following codes. In game you can access some codes from the Options menu.

CHEAT CODE	RESULTS
plus44	Unlocks Travis Barker
hohohosoi	Unlocks Christian Hosoi
notmono	Unlocks Jason Lee
mixitup	Unlocks Kevin Staab
strangefellows	Unlocks Dad & Skater Jam Kid
themedia	Unlocks Photog Girl & Filmer
militarymen	Unlocks Colonel & Security Guard
jammypack	Unlocks Always Special
balancegalore	Unlocks Perfect Rail
frontandback	Unlocks Perect Manual
shellshock	Unlocks Unlimited Focus
shescaresme	Unlocks Big Realtor
birdhouse	Unlocks Inkblot deck
allthebest	Full Stats
needaride	All Decks unlocked and free, except for inkblot deck and gamestop deck
yougotitall	All specials unlocked and in player's special list and set as owned in skate shop
wearelosers	Unlocks Nerd and a Bum
manineedadate	Unlocks Beaver Mascot
suckstobedead	Unlocks Officer Dick
HATEDANDPROUD	Unlocks the Vans unlockable item

TONY HAWK'S PROVING GROUND

Select Cheat Codes from the Options and enter the following cheats. Some codes need to be enabled by selecting Cheats from the Options during a game.

UNLOCK	CHEAT
Unlocks Boneman	CRAZYBONEMAN
Unlocks Bosco	MOREMILK
Unlocks Cam	NOTACAMERA
Unlocks Cooper	THECOOP
Unlocks Eddie X	SKETCHY
Unlocks El Patinador	PILEDRIVER
Unlocks Eric	FLYAWAY
Unlocks Mad Dog	RABBIES
Unlocks MCA	INTERGALACTIC
Unlocks Mel	NOTADUDE
Unlocks Rube	LOOKSSMELLY
Unlocks Spence	DAPPER
Unlocks Shayne	MOVERS
Unlocks TV Producer	SHAKER
Unlock FDR	THEPREZPARK
Unlock Lansdowne	THELOCALPARK
Unlock Air & Space Museum	THEINDOORPARK
Unlocks all Fun Items	OVERTHETOP
Unlocks all CAS items	GIVEMESTUFF
Unlocks all Decks	LETSGOSKATE
Unlock all Game Movies	WATCHTHIS
Unlock all Lounge Bling Items	SWEETSTUFF
Unlock all Lounge Themes	LAIDBACKLOUNGE
Unlock all Rigger Pieces	IMGONNABUILD
Unlock all Video Editor Effects	TRIPPY
Unlock all Video Editor Overlays	PUTEMONTOP
All specials unlocked and in player's special list	LOTSOFTRICKS
Full Stats	BEEFEDUP
Give player +50 skill points	NEEDSHELP

The following cheats lock you out of the Leaderboards:

UNLOCK	CHEAT
Unlocks Perfect Manual	STILLAINTFALLIN
Unlocks Perfect Rail	AINTFALLIN
Unlock Super Check	BOOYAH
Unlocks Unlimited Focus	MYOPIC
Unlock Unlimited Slash Grind	SUPERSLASHIN
Unlocks 100% branch completion in NTT	FOREVERNAILED
No Bails	ANDAINTFALLIN

You can not use the Video Editor with the following cheats:

UNLOCK	CHEAT
Invisible Man	THEMISSING
Mini Skater	TINYTATER
No Board	MAGICMAN

TRANSFORMERS: THE GAME

The following cheats disable saving and achievements:

INFINITE HEALTH
At the Main menu, press Left, Left, Up, Left, Right, Down, Right.

INFINITE AMMO
At the Main menu, press Up, Down, Left, Right, Up, Up, Down.

NO MILITARY OR POLICE
At the Main menu, press Right, Left, Right, Left, Right, Left, Right.

ALL MISSIONS
At the Main menu, press Down, Up, Left, Right, Right, Right, Up, Down.

BONUS CYBERTRON MISSIONS
At the Main menu, press Right, Up, Up, Down, Right, Left, Left.

GENERATION 1 SKIN: JAZZ
At the Main menu, press Left, Up, Down, Down, Left, Up, Right.

GENERATION 1 SKIN: MEGATRON
At the Main menu, press Down, Left, Left, Down, Right, Down, Up.

GENERATION 1 SKIN: OPTIMUS PRIME
At the Main menu, press Down, Right, Left, Up, Down, Down, Left.

GENERATION 1 SKIN: ROBOVISION OPTIMUS PRIME
At the Main menu, press Down, Down, Up, Up, Right, Right, Right.

GENERATION 1 SKIN: STARSCREAM
At the Main menu, press Right, Down, Left, Left, Down, Up, Up.

TRANSFORMERS REVENGE OF THE FALLEN

LOW GRAVITY MODE
Select Cheat Code and enter Ⓐ, ❌, Ⓨ, ⓔ, Ⓨ, ⓔ.

NO WEAPON OVERHEAT
Select Cheat Code and enter ⓔ, ❌, Ⓐ, ⓔ, Ⓨ, ⓛⓑ.

ALWAYS IN OVERDRIVE MODE
Select Cheat Code and enter ⓛⓑ, Ⓑ, ⓛⓑ, Ⓐ, ❌, ⓡ.

UNLIMITED TURBO
Select Cheat Code and enter Ⓑ, ⓔ, ❌, ⓡ, Ⓐ, Ⓨ.

NO SPECIAL COOLDOWN TIME
Select Cheat Code and enter ⓡ, ❌, ⓡ, ⓡ, ❌, Ⓐ.

INVINCIBILITY
Select Cheat Code and enter ⓡ, Ⓐ, ❌, ⓔ, ❌, ❌.

4X ENERGON FROM DEFEATED ENEMIES
Select Cheat Code and enter ⓨ, ⓧ, ⓑ, ✦, ⓐ, ⓨ.

INCREASED WEAPON DAMAGE IN ROBOT FORM
Select Cheat Code and enter ⓨ, ⓨ, ✦, ⓐ, ⓛⓑ, ⓨ.

INCREASED WEAPON DAMAGE IN VEHICLE FORM
Select Cheat Code and enter ⓨ, ⓑ, ⓡⓑ, ⓧ, ✦, ●.

MELEE INSTANT KILLS
Select Cheat Code and enter ✦, ⓐ, ⓛⓑ, ⓑ, ✦, ⓛⓑ.

LOWER ENEMY ACCURACY
Select Cheat Code and enter ⓧ, ●, ✦, ●, ✦, ⓡⓑ.

INCREASED ENEMY HEALTH
Select Cheat Code and enter ⓑ, ⓧ, ⓛⓑ, ⓑ, ✦, ⓨ.

INCREASED ENEMY DAMAGE
Select Cheat Code and enter ⓛⓑ, ⓨ, ⓐ, ⓨ, ✦, ✦.

INCREASED ENEMY ACCURACY
Select Cheat Code and enter ⓨ, ⓨ, ⓑ, ⓐ, ⓧ, ⓛⓑ.

SPECIAL KILLS ONLY MODE
Select Cheat Code and enter ⓑ, ⓑ, ⓡⓑ, ⓑ, ⓐ, ●.

UNLOCK ALL SHANGHAI MISSIONS AND ZONES
Select Cheat Code and enter ⓨ, ●, ✦, ⓛⓑ, ⓨ, ⓐ.

UNLOCK ALL WEST COAST MISSIONS AND ZONES
Select Cheat Code and enter ⓛⓑ, ⓡⓑ, ✦, ⓨ, ✦, ⓑ.

UNLOCK ALL DEEP SIX MISSIONS AND ZONES
Select Cheat Code and enter ⓧ, ⓡⓑ, ⓨ, ⓑ, ⓐ, ⓛⓑ.

UNLOCK ALL EAST COAST MISSIONS AND ZONES
Select Cheat Code and enter ✦, ●, ⓡⓑ, ⓐ, ⓑ, ⓧ.

UNLOCK ALL CAIRO MISSIONS AND ZONES
Select Cheat Code and enter ✦, ⓨ, ⓐ, ⓨ, ●, ⓛⓑ.

UNLOCK AND ACTIVATE ALL UPGRADES
Select Cheat Code and enter ⓛⓑ, ⓨ, ⓛⓑ, ⓑ, ⓧ, ⓧ.

UNDERTOW

GAMER PIC 1 – SCUBA DIVER
Total 100 kills.

GAMER PIC 2 – ATLANTIS MAN
Total 10,000 kills.

VIRTUA TENNIS 3

KING & DUKE

At the Main menu, press Up, Up, Down, Down, Left, Right, Left, Right, **LB**, **RB**.

ALL GEAR

At the Main menu, press Left, Right, **B**, Left, Right, **B**, Up, Down.

ALL COURTS

At the Main menu, press Up, Up, Down, Down, Left, Right, Left, Right.

WIN ONE MATCH TO WIN TOURNAMENT

At the Main menu, press **B**, Left, **B**, Right, **B**, Up, **B**, Down.

VIVA PINATA

NEW ITEMS IN PET STORE

Select New Garden and enter chewnicorn as the name.

NEW ITEMS IN PET STORE

Select New Garden and enter bullseye as the name.

NEW ITEMS IN PET STORE

Select New Garden and enter goobaa as the name.

NEW ITEMS IN PET STORE

Select New Garden and enter kittyfloss as the name.

VIVA PINATA: PARTY ANIMALS

CLASSIC GAMER AWARD ACHIEVEMENT

At the START screen, press Up, Up, Down, Down, Left, Right, Left, Right, **B**, **A**. This earns you 10 points toward your Gamerscore.

VIVA PINATA: TROUBLE IN PARADISE

CREDITS

Select Play Garden and name your garden Piñata People. This unlocks the ability to view the credits on the main menu.

WALL-E

The following cheats will disable saving. The five possible characters starting with Wall-E and going down are: Wall-E, Auto, EVE, M-O, GEL-A Steward.

ALL BONUS FEATURES UNLOCKED

Select Cheats from the Bonus Features menu and enter Wall-E, Auto, EVE, GEL-A Steward.

ALL GAME CONTENT UNLOCKED

Select Cheats from the Bonus Features menu and enter M-O, Auto, GEL-A Steward, EVE.

ALL SINGLE-PLAYER LEVELS UNLOCKED

Select Cheats from the Bonus Features menu and enter Auto, GEL-A Steward, M-O, Wall-E.

ALL MULTIPLAYER MAPS UNLOCKED

Select Cheats from the Bonus Features menu and enter EVE, M-O, Wall-E, Auto.

ALL HOLIDAY COSTUMES UNLOCKED

Select Cheats from the Bonus Features menu and enter Auto, Auto, GEL-A Steward, GEL-A Steward.

ALL MULTIPLAYER COSTUMES UNLOCKED

Select Cheats from the Bonus Features menu and enter GEL-A Steward, Wall-E, M-O, Auto.

UNLIMITED HEALTH UNLOCKED

Select Cheats from the Bonus Features menu and enter Wall-E, M-O, Auto, M-O.

WALL-E: MAKE ANY CUBE AT ANY TIME

Select Cheats from the Bonus Features menu and enter Auto, M-O, Auto, M-O.

WALL-EVE: MAKE ANY CUBE AT ANY TIME

Select Cheats from the Bonus Features menu and enter M-O, GEL-A Steward, EVE, EVE.

WALL-E WITH A LASER GUN AT ANY TIME

Select Cheats from the Bonus Features menu and enter Wall-E, EVE, EVE, Wall-E.

WALL-EVE WITH A LASER GUN AT ANY TIME

Select Cheats from the Bonus Features menu and enter GEL-A Steward, EVE, M-O, Wall-E.

WALL-E: PERMANENT SUPER LASER UPGRADE

Select Cheats from the Bonus Features menu and enter Wall-E, Auto, EVE, M-O.

EVE: PERMANENT SUPER LASER UPGRADE

Select Cheats from the Bonus Features menu and enter EVE, Wall-E, Wall-E, Auto.

CREDITS

Select Cheats from the Bonus Features menu and enter Auto, Wall-E, GEL-A Steward, M-O.

WWE SMACKDOWN! VS. RAW 2008

HBK AND HHH'S DX OUTFIT

Select Cheat Codes from the Options and enter DXCostume69K2.

KELLY KELLY'S ALTERNATE OUTFIT

Select Cheat Codes from the Options and enter KellyKG12R.

BRET HART

Complete the March 31, 1996 Hall of Fame challenge by defeating Bret Hart with Shawn Michaels in a One-On-One 30-Minute Iron Man Match on Legend difficulty. Purchase from WWE Shop for $210,000.

MICK FOLEY

Complete the June 28, 1998 Hall of Fame challenge by defeating Mick Foley with The Undertaker in a H*** In a Cell Match on Legend difficulty. Purchase from WWE Shop for $210,000.

MR. MCMAHON

Win or successfully defend a championship (WWE or World Heavyweight) at WrestleMania in WWE 24/7 GM Mode. Purchase from WWE Shop for $110,000.

THE ROCK

Complete the April 1, 2001 Hall of Fame challenge by defeating The Rock with Steve Austin in a Single Match on Legend Difficulty. Purchase from WWE Shop for $210,000.

STEVE AUSTIN

Complete the March 23, 1997 Hall of Fame challenge by defeating Steve Austin with Bret Hart in a Submission Match on Legend Difficulty. Purchase from WWE Shop for $210,000.

TERRY FUNK

Complete the April 13, 1997 Hall of Fame challenge by defeating Tommy Dreamer, Sabu and Sandman with any Superstar in an ECW Extreme Rules 4-Way Match on Legend difficulty. Purchase from WWE Shop for $210,000.

MR. MCMAHON BALD

Must unlock Mr. McMahon as a playable character first. Purchase from WWE Shop for $60,000.

WWE SMACKDOWN VS. RAW 2009

BOOGEYMAN

Select Cheat Codes from My WWE and enter BoogeymanEatsWorms!!.

GENE SNITSKY

Select Cheat Codes from My WWE and enter UnlockSnitskySvR2009.

HAWKINS & RYDER

Select Cheat Codes from My WWE and enter Ryder&HawkinsTagTeam.

JILLIAN HALL

Select Cheat Codes from My WWE and enter PlayAsJillianHallSvR.

LAYLA

Select Cheat Codes from My WWE and enter UnlockECWDivaLayla09.

RIC FLAIR

Select Cheat Codes from My WWE and enter FlairWoooooooooooooo.

TAZZ

Select Cheat Codes from My WWE and enter UnlockECWTazzSvR2009.

VINCENT MCMAHON

Select Cheat Codes from My WWE and enter VinceMcMahonNoChance.

HORNSWOGGLE AS MANAGER

Select Cheat Codes from My WWE and enter HornswoggleAsManager.

CHRIS JERICHO COSTUME B

Select Cheat Codes from My WWE and enter AltJerichoModelSvR09.

CM PUNK COSTUME B

Select Cheat Codes from My WWE and enter CMPunkAltCostumeSvR!.

REY MYSTERIO COSTUME B

Select Cheat Codes from My WWE and enter BooyakaBooyaka619SvR.

SATURDAY NIGHT'S MAIN EVENT ARENA

Select Cheat Codes from My WWE and enter SatNightMainEventSvR.

WWE SMACKDOWN VS. RAW 2010

THE ROCK

Select Cheat Codes from the Options menu and enter The Great One.

DIRT SHEET BRAWL AND OFFICE STAGE BRAWL

Select Cheat Codes from the Options menu and enter BonusBrawl.

SHAWN MICHAELS' NEW COSTUME

Select Cheat Codes from the Options menu and enter Bow Down.

RANDY ORTON'S NEW COSTUME

Select Cheat Codes from the Options menu and enter ViperRKO.

TRIPLE H'S NEW COSTUME

Select Cheat Codes from the Options menu and enter Suck IT!.

YOU'RE IN THE MOVIES

ALL TRAILERS AND DIRECTOR'S MODE

At the options screen, press Left Bumper, Right Bumper, Left Bumper, Right Bumper, ⓨ.

PLAYSTATION® 2

CONTENTS

ASTRO BOY: THE VIDEO GAME

INVULNERABLE
Pause the game and press Up, Down, Down, Up, L1, R1.

MAX STATS
Pause the game and press Left, Left, R1, Down, Down, L1.

INFINITE SUPERS
Pause the game and press Left, L1, Right, L1, Up, Down.

INFINITE DASHES
Pause the game and press R1, R1, L1, R1, Left, Up.

DISABLE SUPERS
Pause the game and press L1, L1, R1, R1, L1, Left.

COSTUME SWAP (ARENA AND CLASSIC COSTUMES)
Pause the game and press R1, Up, L1, Up, Down, R1.

UNLOCK LEVELS
Pause the game and press Up, L1, Right, L1, Down, L1. This allows you to travel to any level from the Story menu.

AVATAR: THE LAST AIRBENDER-THE BURNING EARTH

1 HIT DISHONOR
At the Main menu, press **L1** and select Code Entry. Enter 28260.

ALL BONUS GAME
At the Main menu, press **L1** and select Code Entry. Enter 99801.

ALL GALLERY ITEMS
At the Main menu, press **L1** and select Code Entry. Enter 85061.

DOUBLE DAMAGE
At the Main menu, press **L1** and select Code Entry. Enter 90210.

INFINITE HEALTH
At the Main menu, press **L1** and select Code Entry. Enter 65049.

MAX LEVEL
At the Main menu, press **L1** and select Code Entry. Enter 89121.

UNLIMITED SPECIAL ATTACKS
At the Main menu, press **L1** and select Code Entry. Enter 66206.

AVATAR - THE LAST AIRBENDER: INTO THE INFERNO

ALL CHAPTERS
Select Game Secrets at Ember Islands and enter 52993833.

MAX COINS
Select Game Secrets at Ember Islands and enter 66639224.

ALL ITEMS AVAILABLE AT SHOP
Select Game Secrets at Ember Islands and enter 34737253.

ALL CONCEPT ART
Select Game Secrets at Ember Islands and enter 27858343.

BEN 10: ALIEN FORCE THE GAME

LEVEL LORD
Enter Gwen, Kevin, Big Chill, Gwen as a code.

INVINCIBILITY
Enter Kevin, Big Chill, Swampfire, Kevin as a code.

ALL COMBOS
Enter Swampfire, Gwen, Kevin, Ben as a code.

INFINITE ALIENS
Enter Ben, Swampfire, Gwen, Big Chill as a code.

BEN 10: PROTECTOR OF EARTH

INVINCIBILITY
Select a game from the Continue option. Go to the Map Selection screen, press Start and choose Extras. Select Enter Secret Code and enter XLR8, Heatblast, Wildvine, Fourarms.

ALL COMBOS
Select a game from the Continue option. Go to the Map Selection screen, press Start and choose Extras. Select Enter Secret Code and enter Cannonblot, Heatblast, Fourarms, Heatblast.

ALL LOCATIONS
Select a game from the Continue option. Go to the Map Selection screen, press Start and choose Extras. Select Enter Secret Code and enter Heatblast, XLR8, XLR8, Cannonblot.

DNA FORCE SKINS
Select a game from the Continue option. Go to the Map Selection screen, press Start and choose Extras. Select Enter Secret Code and enter Wildvine, Fourarms, Heatblast, Cannonbolt.

DARK HEROES SKINS
Select a game from the Continue option. Go to the Map Selection screen, press Start and choose Extras. Select Enter Secret Code and enter Cannonbolt, Cannonbolt, Fourarms, Heatblast.

ALL ALIEN FORMS
Select a game from the Continue option. Go to the Map Selection screen, press Start and choose Extras. Select Enter Secret Code and enter Wildvine, Fourarms, Heatblast, Wildvine.

MASTER CONTROL
Select a game from the Continue option. Go to the Map Selection screen, press Start and choose Extras. Select Enter Secret Code and enter Cannonbolt, Heatblast, Wildvine, Fourarms.

BOLT

Some of the following cheats can be toggled on/off by selecting Cheats from the pause menu.

ALL GAME LEVELS
Select Cheats from the Extras menu and enter Right, Up, Left, Right, Up, Right.

ALL MINI GAMES
Select Cheats from the Extras menu and enter Right, Up, Right, Right.

ENCHANCED VISION
Select Cheats from the Extras menu and enter Left, Right, Up, Down.

UNLIMITED GAS MINES
Select Cheats from the Extras menu and enter Right, Left, Left, Up, Down, Right.

UNLIMITED GROUND POUND
Select Cheats from the Extras menu and enter Right, Up, Right, Up, Left, Down.

UNLIMITED INVULNERABILITY

Select Cheats from the Extras menu and enter Down, Down, Up, Left.

UNLIMITED LASER EYES

Select Cheats from the Extras menu and enter Left, Left, Up, Right.

UNLIMITED STEALTH CAMO

Select Cheats from the Extras menu and enter Left, Down, Down, Down.

UNLIMITED SUPERBARK

Select Cheats from the Extras menu and enter Right, Left -Left, Up, Down, Up.

BRATZ: THE MOVIE

FEELIN' PRETTY CLOTHING LINE

In the Bratz office at the laptop computer, enter PRETTY.

HIGH SCHOOL CLOTHING LINE

In the Bratz office at the laptop computer, enter SCHOOL.

PASSION 4 FASHION CLOTHING LINE

In the Bratz office at the laptop computer, enter ANGELZ.

SWEETZ CLOTHING LINE

In the Bratz office at the laptop computer, enter SWEETZ.

CAPCOM CLASSICS COLLECTION VOL. 2

UNLOCK EVERYTHING

At the Title screen, press Left, Right, Up, Down, **L1**, **R1**, **L1**, **R1**. This code unlocks Cheats, Tips, Art, and Sound Tests.

CARS

UNLOCK EVERYTHING

Select Cheat Codes from the Options and enter IF900HP.

ALL CHARACTERS

Select Cheat Codes from the Options and enter YAYCARS.

ALL CHARACTER SKINS

Select Cheat Codes from the Options and enter R4MONE.

ALL MINI-GAMES AND COURSES

Select Cheat Codes from the Options and enter MATTL66.

MATER'S COUNTDOWN CLEAN-UP MINI-GAME AND MATER'S SPEEDY CIRCUIT

Select Cheat Codes from the Options and enter TRGTEXC.

FAST START

Select Cheat Codes from the Options and enter IMSPEED.

INFINITE BOOST

Select Cheat Codes from the Options and enter VROOOOM.

ART

Select Cheat Codes from the Options and enter CONC3PT.

VIDEOS

Select Cheat Codes from the Options and enter WATCHIT.

CARS MATER-NATIONAL

ALL ARCADE RACES, MINI-GAMES, AND WORLDS

Select Codes/Cheats from the options and enter PLAYALL.

ALL CARS

Select Codes/Cheats from the options and enter MATTEL07.

ALTERNATE LIGHTNING MCQUEEN COLORS

Select Codes/Cheats from the options and enter NCEDUDZ.

ALL COLORS FOR OTHERS

Select Codes/Cheats from the options and enter PAINTIT.

UNLIMITED TURBO

Select Codes/Cheats from the options and enter ZZOOOOM.

EXTREME ACCELERATION

Select Codes/Cheats from the options and enter 0TO200X.

EXPERT MODE

Select Codes/Cheats from the options and enter VRYFAST.

ALL BONUS ART

Select Codes/Cheats from the options and enter BUYTALL.

CARS RACE-O-RAMA

ALL ARCADE MODE EVENTS

Select Cheats from the Options menu and enter SLVRKEY.

ALL STORY MODE EVENTS

Select Cheats from the Options menu and enter GOLDKEY.

ALL OF LIGHTNING MCQUEEN'S FRIENDS

Select Cheats from the Options menu and enter EVRYBDY.

ALL LIGHTNING MCQUEEN CUSTOM KIT PARTS

Select Cheats from the Options menu and enter GR8MODS.

ALL PAINT JOBS FOR ALL NON-LIGHTNING MCQUEEN CHARACTERS

Select Cheats from the Options menu and enter CARSHOW.

CORALINE

BUTTON EYE CORALINE

Select Cheats from Options and enter Cheese.

CRASH OF THE TITANS

BIG HEAD CRASH

Pause the game, hold **R1**, and press ●, ●, ▲, ✕. Re-enter the code to disable.

SHADOW CRASH

Pause the game, hold **R1**, and press ▲, ●, ▲, ●. Re-enter the code to disable.

THE DA VINCI CODE

GOD MODE

Select Codes from the Options and enter
VITRUVIAN MAN.

EXTRA HEALTH

Select Codes from the Options and
enter SACRED FEMININE.

MISSION SELECT

Select Codes from the Options and
enter CLOS LUCE 1519.

ONE-HIT FIST KILL

Select Codes from the Options and
enter PHILLIPS EXETER.

ONE-HIT WEAPON KILL

Select Codes from the Options and enter
ROYAL HOLLOWAY.

ALL VISUAL DATABASE

Select Codes from the Options and enter APOCRYPHA.

ALL VISUAL DATABASE AND
CONCEPT ART

Select Codes from the Options and
enter ET IN ARCADIA EGO.

DISNEY PRINCESS: ENCHANTED JOURNEY

BELLE'S KINGDOM
Select Secrets and enter GASTON.

GOLDEN SET
Select Secrets and enter BLUEBIRD.

FLOWER WAND
Select Secrets and enter SLEEPY.

HEART WAND
Select Secrets and enter BASHFUL.

SHELL WAND
Select Secrets and enter RAJAH.

SHIELD WAND
Select Secrets and enter CHIP.

STAR WAND
Select Secrets and enter SNEEZY.

FLATOUT 2

ALL CARS AND 1,000,000 CREDITS
Select Enter Code from the Extras and enter GIEVEPIX.

1,000,000 CREDITS
Select Enter Code from the Extras and enter GIVECASH.

PIMPSTER CAR
Select Enter Code from the Extras and enter RUTTO.

FLATMOBILE CAR
Select Enter Code from the Extras and enter WOTKINS.

MOB CAR
Select Enter Code from the Extras and enter BIGTRUCK.

SCHOOL BUS
Select Enter Code from the Extras and enter GIEVCARPLZ.

ROCKET CAR

Select Enter Code from the Extras and enter KALJAKOPPA.

TRUCK

Select Enter Code from the Extras and enter ELPUEBLO.

G.I. JOE: THE RISE OF COBRA

CLASSIC DUKE

At the main menu, press Left, Up, X, Up, Right, ▲.

CLASSIC SCARLETT

At the main menu, press Right, Up, Down, Down, ▲.

THE GOLDEN COMPASS

The following codes are entered in the order of top/left, bottom/left, top/right. The Featurettes can then be accessed through the Extras menu.

VOICE SESSION 1 FETUREETE

In Extras, select Enter Code from the Game Secrets menu and enter Compass, Sun, Madonna.

VOICE SESSION 2 FEATURETTE

In Extras, select Enter Code from the Game Secrets menu and enter Compass, Moon, Wild Man.

BEHIND THE SCENES FEATURETTE

In Extras, select Enter Code from the Game Secrets menu and enter Alpha/Omega, Alpha/Omega, Compass.

WILDLIFE WAYSTATION FEATURETTE

In Extras, select Enter Code from the Game Secrets menu and enter Griffin, Elephant, Owl.

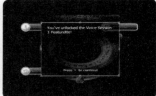

POLAR BEARS IN MOTION FEATURETTE

In Extras, select Enter Code from the Game Secrets menu and enter Sun, Moon, Wild Man.

HARRY POTTER AND THE HALF-BLOOD PRINCE

CASTLE GATES ARENA

At the rewards menu, press Right, Right, Down, Down, Left, Right, Left, Right, Left, Right, Start.

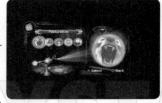

ICE AGE 2: THE MELTDOWN

INFINITE PEBBLES

Pause the game and press Down, Down, Left, Up, Up, Right, Up, Down.

INFINITE ENERGY

Pause the game and press Down, Left, Right, Down, Down, Right, Left, Down.

INFINITE HEALTH

Pause the game and press Up, Right, Down, Up, Left, Down, Right, Left.

IRON MAN

ARMOR SELECTION

Iron Man's different armor suits are unlocked by completing certain missions. Refer to the following tables for when each is unlocked. After selecting a mission to play, you can pick the armor you wish to use.

COMPLETE MISSION	SUIT UNLOCKED
1: Escape	Mark I
2: First Flight	Mark II
3: Fight Back	Mark III
6: Flying Fortress	Comic Tin Can
9: Home Front	Classic
13: Showdown	Silver Centurion

CONCEPT ART

Concept Art is unlocked after finding certain numbers of Weapon Crates.

CONCEPT ART UNLOCKED	NUMBER OF WEAPON CRATES FOUND
Environments Set 1	6
Environments Set 2	12
Iron Man	18
Environments Set 3	24
Enemies	30
Environments Set 4	36
Villains	42
Vehicles	48
Covers	50

JUICED 2: HOT IMPORT NIGHTS

ASCARI KZ1

Select Cheats and Codes from the DNA Lab menu and enter KNOX. Defeat the challenge to earn the car.

NISSAN SKYLINE R34 GT-R

Select Cheats and Codes from the DNA Lab menu and enter JWRS. Defeat the challenge to earn the car.

KUNG FU PANDA

INVULNERABILITY

Select Cheats from the Extras menu and enter Down, Down, Right, Up, Left.

INFINITE CHI

Select Cheats from the Extras menu and enter Down, Right, Left, Up, Down.

BIG HEAD MODE

Select Cheats from the Extras menu and enter Down, Up, Left, Right, Right.

ALL MULTIPLAYER CHARACTERS

Select Cheats from the Extras menu and enter Left, Down, Left, Right, Down.

DRAGON WARRIOR OUTFIT IN MULTIPLAYER

Select Cheats from the Extras menu and enter Left, Down, Right, Left, Up.

THE LEGEND OF SPYRO: THE ETERNAL NIGHT

INFINITE MAGIC

Pause the game and press Up, Up, Down, Down, Left, Right, Left, Right, L1, R1, L1, R1.

THE LEGEND OF SPYRO: DAWN OF THE DRAGON

INFINITE HEALTH

Pause the game, hold L1 and press Right, Right, Down, Down, Left with the Left Analog Stick.

INFINITE MANA

Pause the game, hold L1 and press Up, Right, Up, Left, Down with the Left Analog Stick.

MAX XP

Pause the game, hold L1 and press Up, Left, Left, Down, Up with the Left Analog Stick.

ALL ELEMENTAL UPGRADES

Pause the game, hold L1 and press Left, Up, Down, Up, Right with the Left Analog Stick.

LEGO BATMAN

BATCAVE CODES

Using the computer in the Batcave, select Enter Code and enter the following codes.

CHARACTERS

CHARACTER	CODE	CHARACTER	CODE
Alfred	ZAQ637	Penguin Henchman	BJH782
Batgirl	JKR331	Penguin Minion	KJP748
Bruce Wayne	BDJ327	Poison Ivy Goon	GTB899
Catwoman (Classic)	M1AAWW	Police Marksman	HKG984
Clown Goon	HJK327	Police Officer	JRY983
Commissioner Gordon	DDP967	Riddler Goon	CRY928
Fishmonger	HGY748	Riddler Henchman	XEU824
Freeze Girl	XVK541	S.W.A.T.	HTF114
Joker Goon	UTF782	Sailor	NAV592
Joker Henchman	YUN924	Scientist	JFL786
Mad Hatter	JCA283	Security Guard	PLB946
Man-Bat	NYU942	The Joker (Tropical)	CCB199
Military Policeman	MKL382	Yeti	NJL412
Nightwing	MVY759	Zoo Sweeper	DWR243
Penguin Goon	NKA238		

VEHICLES

VEHICLE	CODE	VEHICLE	CODE
Bat-Tank	KNTT4B	Mr. Freeze's Kart	BCT229
Bruce Wayne's Private Jet	LEA664	Penguin Goon Submarine	BTN248
Catwoman's Motorcycle	HPL826	Police Bike	LJP234
Garbage Truck	DUS483	Police Boat	PLC999
Goon Helicopter	GCH328	Police Car	KJL832
Harbor Helicopter	CHP735	Police Helicopter	CWR732
Harley Quinn's Hammer Truck	RDT637	Police Van	MAC788
Mad Hatter's Glider	HS000W	Police Watercraft	VJD328
Mad Hatter's Steamboat	M4DM4N	Riddler's Jet	HAHAHA
Mr. Freeze's Iceberg	ICYICE	Robin's Submarine	TTF453
The Joker's Van	JUK657	Two-Face's Armored Truck	EFE933

CHEATS

CHEAT	CODE	CHEAT	CODE
Always Score Multiply	9LRGNB	More Batarang Targets	XWP645
Fast Batarangs	JRBDCB	Piece Detector	KHJ554
Fast Walk	ZOLM6N	Power Brick Detector	MMN786
Flame Batarang	D8NYWH	Regenerate Hearts	HJH7HJ
Freeze Batarang	XPN4NG	Score x2	N4NR3E
Extra Hearts	ML3KHP	Score x4	CX9MAT
Fast Build	EVG26J	Score x6	MLVNF2
Immune to Freeze	JXUDY6	Score x8	WCCDB9
Invincibility	WYD5CP	Score x10	18HW07
Minikit Detector	ZXGH9J		

LEGO STAR WARS II: THE ORIGINAL TRILOGY

BEACH TROOPER

At Mos Eisley Canteena, select Enter Code and enter UCK868. You still need to select Characters and purchase this character for 20,000 studs.

 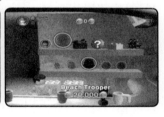

BEN KENOBI (GHOST)

At Mos Eisley Canteena, select Enter Code and enter BEN917. You still need to select Characters and purchase this character for 1,100,000 studs.

BESPIN GUARD

At Mos Eisley Canteena, select Enter Code and enter VHY832. You still need to select Characters and purchase this character for 15,000 studs.

BIB FORTUNA

At Mos Eisley Canteena, select Enter Code and enter WTY721. You still need to select Characters and purchase this character for 16,000 studs.

BOBA FETT

At Mos Eisley Canteena, select Enter Code and enter HLP221. You still need to select Characters and purchase this character for 175,000 studs.

DEATH STAR TROOPER

At Mos Eisley Canteena, select Enter Code and enter BNC332. You still need to select Characters and purchase this character for 19,000 studs.

EWOK

At Mos Eisley Canteena, select Enter Code and enter TTT289. You still need to select Characters and purchase this character for 34,000 studs.

GAMORREAN GUARD

At Mos Eisley Canteena, select Enter Code and enter YZF999. You still need to select Characters and purchase this character for 40,000 studs.

GONK DROID

At Mos Eisley Canteena, select Enter Code and enter NFX582. You still need to select Characters and purchase this character for 1,550 studs.

GRAND MOFF TARKIN

At Mos Eisley Canteena, select Enter Code and enter SMG219. You still need to select Characters and purchase this character for 38,000 studs.

GREEDO

At Mos Eisley Canteena, select Enter Code and enter NAH118. You still need to select Characters and purchase this character for 60,000 studs.

HAN SOLO (HOOD)

At Mos Eisley Canteena, select Enter Code and enter YWM840. You still need to select Characters and purchase this character for 20,000 studs.

IG-88

At Mos Eisley Canteena, select Enter Code and enter NXL973. You still need to select Characters and purchase this character for 30,000 studs.

IMPERIAL GUARD

At Mos Eisley Canteena, select Enter Code and enter MMM111. You still need to select Characters and purchase this character for 45,000 studs.

IMPERIAL OFFICER

At Mos Eisley Canteena, select Enter Code and enter BBV889. You still need to select Characters and purchase this character for 28,000 studs.

IMPERIAL SHUTTLE PILOT

At Mos Eisley Canteena, select Enter Code and enter VAP664. You still need to select Characters and purchase this character for 29,000 studs.

IMPERIAL SPY

At Mos Eisley Canteena, select Enter Code and enter CVT125. You still need to select Characters and purchase this character for 13,500 studs.

JAWA

At Mos Eisley Canteena, select Enter Code and enter JAW499. You still need to select Characters and purchase this character for 24,000 studs.

LOBOT
At Mos Eisley Canteena, select Enter Code and enter UUB319. You still need to select Characters and purchase this character for 11,000 studs.

PALACE GUARD
At Mos Eisley Canteena, select Enter Code and enter SGE549. You still need to select Characters and purchase this character for 14,000 studs.

REBEL PILOT
At Mos Eisley Canteena, select Enter Code and enter CYG336. You still need to select Characters and purchase this character for 15,000 studs.

REBEL TROOPER (HOTH)
At Mos Eisley Canteena, select Enter Code and enter EKU849. You still need to select Characters and purchase this character for 16,000 studs.

SANDTROOPER
At Mos Eisley Canteena, select Enter Code and enter YDV451. You still need to select Characters and purchase this character for 14,000 studs.

SKIFF GUARD
At Mos Eisley Canteena, select Enter Code and enter GBU888. You still need to select Characters and purchase this character for 12,000 studs.

SNOWTROOPER
At Mos Eisley Canteena, select Enter Code and enter NYU989. You still need to select Characters and purchase this character for 16,000 studs.

STROMTROOPER
At Mos Eisley Canteena, select Enter Code and enter PTR345. You still need to select Characters and purchase this character for 10,000 studs.

THE EMPEROR
At Mos Eisley Canteena, select Enter Code and enter HHY382. You still need to select Characters and purchase this character for 275,000 studs.

TIE FIGHTER
At Mos Eisley Canteena, select Enter Code and enter HDY739. You still need to select Characters and purchase this character for 60,000 studs.

TIE FIGHTER PILOT
At Mos Eisley Canteena, select Enter Code and enter NNZ316. You still need to select Characters and purchase this character for 21,000 studs.

TIE INTERCEPTOR
At Mos Eisley Canteena, select Enter Code and enter QYA828. You still need to select Characters and purchase this character for 40,000 studs.

TUSKEN RAIDER
At Mos Eisley Canteena, select Enter Code and enter PEJ821. You still need to select Characters and purchase this character for 23,000 studs.

UGNAUGHT
At Mos Eisley Canteena, select Enter Code and enter UGN694. You still need to select Characters and purchase this character for 36,000 studs.

LOONEY TUNES: ACME ARSENAL

UNLIMITED AMMUNITION

At the cheats menu, enter Down, Left, Up, Right, Down, Left, Up, Right, Down.

MAJOR LEAGUE BASEBALL 2K8

BIG HEAD MODE

Select Enter Cheat Code from the My 2K8 menu and enter Black Sox. This unlocks the Smart Choice cheat. Go to My Cheats to toggle the cheat on and off.

MAJOR LEAGUE BASEBALL 2K9

BIG HEADS

At the cheats menu, enter Black Sox.

MARVEL SUPER HERO SQUAD

IRON MAN BONUS COSTUMES
Select Enter Code from the Options and enter 111111.

HULK BONUS COSTUMES
Select Enter Code from the Options and enter 222222.

WOLVERINE BONUS COSTUMES
Select Enter Code from the Options and enter 333333.

THOR BONUS COSTUMES
Select Enter Code from the Options and enter 444444.

SILVER SURFER BONUS COSTUMES
Select Enter Code from the Options and enter 555555.

FALCON BONUS COSTUMES
Select Enter Code from the Options and enter 666666.

CHEAT SUPER KNOCKBACK
Select Enter Code from the Options and enter 777777.

CHEAT NO BLOCK MODE
Select Enter Code from the Options and enter 888888.

DR. DOOM BONUS COSTUMES
Select Enter Code from the Options and enter 999999.

MARVEL ULTIMATE ALLIANCE

UNLOCK ALL SKINS
At the Team Menu, press Up, Down, Left, Right, Left, Right, Start.

UNLOCKS ALL HERO POWERS
At the Team Menu, press Left, Right, Up, Down, Up, Down, Start.

UNLOCK ALL HEROES
At the Team Menu, press Up, Up, Down, Down, Left, Left, Left, Start.

UNLOCK DAREDEVIL
At the Team Menu, press Left, Left, Right, Right, Up, Down, Up, Down, Start.

UNLOCK SILVER SURFER
At the Team Menu, press Down, Left, Left, Up, Right, Up, Down, Left, Start.

GOD MODE
During gameplay, press Up, Down, Up, Down, Up, Left, Down, Right, Start.

TOUCH OF DEATH
During gameplay, press Left, Right, Down, Down, Right, Left, Start.

SUPER SPEED
During gameplay, press Up, Left, Up, Right, Down, Right, Start.

FILL MOMENTUM
During gameplay, press Left, Right, Right, Left, Up, Down, Down, Up, Start.

UNLOCK ALL COMICS
At the Review menu, press Left, Right, Right, Left, Up, Up, Right, Start.

UNLOCK ALL CONCEPT ART
At the Review menu, press Down, Down, Down, Right, Right, Left, Down, Start.

UNLOCK ALL MOVIES
At the Review menu, press Up, Left, Left, Up, Right, Right, Up, Start.

UNLOCK ALL LOAD SCREENS

At the Review menu, press Up, Down, Right, Left, Up, Up Down, Start.

UNLOCK ALL COURSES

At the Comic Missions menu, press Up, Right, Left, Down, Up, Right, Left, Down, Start.

MARVEL: ULTIMATE ALLIANCE 2

GOD MODE

At any point during a game, press Up, Up, Down, Down, Left, Right, Down.

GIVE MONEY

At the Team Select or Hero Details screen press Up, Up, Down, Down, Up, Up, Up, Down.

UNLOCK ALL POWERS

At the Team Select or Hero Details screen press Up, Up, Down, Down, Left, Right, Right, Left.

ADVANCE ALL CHARACTERS TO L99

At the Hero Details screen press Down, Up, Left, Up, Right, Up, Left, Down.

UNLOCK ALL BONUS MISSIONS

While using the Bonus Mission Simulator, press Up, Right, Down, Left, Left, Right, Up, Up.

ADD 1 CHARACTER LEVEL

During a game, press Down, Up, Right, Up, Right, Up, Right, Down.

ADD 10 CHARACTER LEVELS

During a game, press Down, Up, Left, Up, Left, Up, Left, Down.

MLB 07: THE SHOW

CLASSIC STADIUMS

At the Main menu, press Down, Up, Right, Down, Up, Left, Down, Up.

GOLDEN/SLIVER ERA PLAYERS

At the Main menu, press Left, Up, Right, Down, Down, Left, Up, Down.

MLB 08: THE SHOW

ALL CLASSIC STADIUMS

At the main menu, press Down, Right, ⊙, ⊕, Left, ▲, Up, L1. The controller will vibrate if entered correctly.

ALL GOLDEN & SILVER ERA PLAYERS IN EXHIBITION

At the main menu, press L1, L2, ⊕, ⊕, ▲, ⊙, Down. The controller will vibrate if entered correctly.

MLB POWER PROS

VIEW MLB PLAYERS AT CREATED PLAYERS MENU

Select View or Delete Custom Players/Password Display from the My Data menu. Press Up, Up, Down, Down, Left, Right, Left Right, L1, R1.

ALVIN LOCKHART'S BATTING STANCE AND PITCHING FORM

At the main menu, press Right, Left, Up, Down, Down, Right, Right, Up, Up, Left, Down, Left. These will be available at the shop.

MVP 07 NCAA BASEBALL

ALL CHALLENGE ITEMS

In Dynasty Mode, create a player with the name David Hamel.

MX VS. ATV UNTAMED

EVERYTHING

Select Cheat Codes from the options menu and enter YOUGOTIT.

1,000,000 STORE POINTS

Select Cheat Codes from the options menu and enter MANYZEROS.

50CC BIKE CLASS

Select Cheat Codes from the options menu and enter LITTLEGUY.

ALL BIKES

Select Cheat Codes from the options menu and enter ONRAILS.

ALL CHALLENGES

Select Cheat Codes from the options menu and enter MORESTUFF.

ALL FREESTYLE TRACKS

Select Cheat Codes from the options menu and enter ALLSTYLE.

ALL GEAR

Select Cheat Codes from the options menu and enter WELLDRESSED.

ALL MACHINES

Select Cheat Codes from the options menu and enter MCREWHEELS.

ALL RIDERS

Select Cheat Codes from the options menu and enter WHOSTHAT.

ALL TRACKS

Select Cheat Codes from the options menu and enter FREETICKET.

MONSTER TRUCK

Select Cheat Codes from the options menu and enter PWNAGE.

NARUTO: ULTIMATE NINJA 2

In Naruto's house, select Input Password. This is where you can enter an element, then three signs. Enter the following here:

1,000 RYO

Water, Hare, Monkey, Monkey
Water, Ram, Horse, Dog
Water, Horse, Horse, Horse
Water, Rat, Rooster, Boar
Water, Rat, Monkey, Rooster
Fire, Rat, Dragon, Dog

5,000 RYO

Water, Tiger, Dragon, Tiger
Water, Snake, Rooster, Horse

10,000 RYO

Fire, Tiger, Tiger, Rooster
Fire, Tiger, Dragon, Hare

NASCAR 08

ALL CHASE MODE CARS

Select Cheat Codes from the Options menu and enter checkered flag.

EA SPORTS CAR

Select Cheat Codes from the Options menu and enter ea sports car.

FANTASY DRIVERS

Select Cheat Codes from the Options menu and enter race the pack.

WALMART CAR AND TRACK

Select Cheat Codes from the Options menu and enter walmart everyday.

NASCAR 09

WALMART TRACK AND THE WALMART CAR

In Chase for the Sprint Cup, enter the driver's name as WalMart EveryDay.

NBA 09 THE INSIDE

ALL-STAR 09 EAST

Select Trophy Room from the Options. Press L1, then ●, and enter SHPNV2K699.

ALL-STAR 09 WEST

Select Trophy Room from the Options. Press L1, then ●, and enter K8AV6YMLNF.

ALL TROPHIES

Select Trophy Room from the Options. Press L1, then ●, and enter K@ZZ@@M!.

LA LAKERS LATIN NIGHTS

Select Trophy Room from the Options. Press L1, then ●, and enter NMTWCTC84S.

MIAMI HEAT LATIN NIGHTS

Select Trophy Room from the Options. Press L1, then ●, and enter WCTGSA8SPD.

PHOENIX SUNS LATIN NIGHTS

Select Trophy Room from the Options. Press L1, then ●, and enter LKUTSENFJH.

SAN ANTONIO LATIN NIGHTS

Select Trophy Room from the Options. Press L1, then ●, and enter JFHSY73MYD.

NBA 2K8

2K SPORTS TEAM

Select Codes from the Features menu and enter 2ksports.

NBA DEVELOPMENT TEAM

Select Codes from the Features menu and enter nba2k.

VISUAL CONCEPTS TEAM

Select Codes from the Features menu and enter vcteam.

ABA BALL

Select Codes from the Features menu and enter payrespect.

NBA 2K10

ABA BALL

Select Codes from Options and enter payrespect.

2K SPORTS TEAM

Select Codes from Options and enter 2ksports.

NBA 2K TEAM

Select Codes from Options and enter nba2k.

VISUAL CONCEPTS TEAM

Select Codes from Options and enter vcteam.

NBA LIVE 08

ADIDAS GIL II ZERO SHOE CODES

Select NBA Codes from My NBA Live and enter the following:

SHOES	CODE
Agent Zero	ADGILLIT6BE
Black President	ADGILLIT7BF
Cuba	ADGILLIT4BC
Cust0mize Shoe	ADGILLIT5BD
GilWood	ADGILLIT1B9
TS Lightswitch Away	ADGILLIT0B8
TS Lightswitch Home	ADGILLIT2BA

NCAA FOOTBALL 08

PENNANT CODES

Go to My Shrine and select Pennants. Press Select and enter the following:

PENNANT	CODE	PENNANT	CODE
#200 1st & 15 Cheat	Thanks	#278 All-Clemson Team	Death Valley
#201 Blink Cheat	For	#279 All-Colorado Team	Glory
#202 Boing Cheat	Registering	#281 All-FSU Team.	Uprising
#204 Butter Fingers Cheat	With EA	#282 All-Georgia Team	Hunker Down
#205 Crossed The Line Cheat	Tiburon	#283 All-Iowa Team	On Iowa
#206 Cuffed Cheat	EA Sports	#285 All-LSU Team	Geaux Tigers
#207 Extra Credit Cheat	Touchdown	#287 All-Michigan Team	Go Blue
#208 Helium Cheat	In The Zone	#288 All-Mississippi State Team	Hail State
#209 Hurricane Cheat	Turnover	#289 All-Nebraska Team	Go Big Red
#210 Instant FrePlay Cheat	Impact	#291 All-Notre Dame Team	Golden Domer
#211 Jumbalaya Cheat	Heisman	#292 All-Ohio State Team	Killer Nuts
#212 Molasses Cheat	Game Time	#293 All-Oklahoma Team	Boomer
#213 Nike Free Cheat	Break Free	#294 All-Oklahoma State Team	Go Pokes
#214 Nike Magnigrip Cheat	Hand Picked	#296 All-Penn State Team	We Are
#215 Nike Pro Cheat	No Sweat	#298 All-Purdue Team	Boiler Up
#219 QB Dud Cheat	Elite 11	#300 All-Tennessee Team	Big Orange
#221 Steel Toe Cheat	Gridiron	#301 All-Texas Team	Hook Em
#222 Stiffed Cheat	NCAA	#302 All-Texas A&M Team	Gig Em
#223 Super Dive Cheat	Upset	#303 All-UCLA Team	Mighty
#226 Tough As Nail Cheat	Offense	#304 All-USC Team	Fight On
#228 What A Hit Cheat	Blitz	#305 All-Virginia Team	Wahoos
#229 Kicker Hex Cheat	Sideline	#307 All-Washington Team	Bow Down
#273 2004 All-American Team	Fumble	#308 All-Wisconsin Team	U Rah Rah
#274 All-Alabama Team	Roll Tide	#344 MSU Mascot Team	Mizzou Rah
#276 All-Arkansas Team	Woopigsooie	#385 Wyo Mascot	All Hail
#277 All-Auburn Team	War Eagle	#386 Zips Mascot	Hail WV

NEED FOR SPEED PROSTREET

$2,000
Select Career and then choose Code Entry. Enter 1MA9X99.

$4,000
Select Career and then choose Code Entry. Enter W2IOLLO1.

$8,000
Select Career and then choose Code Entry. Enter L1IS97A1.

$10,000
Select Career and then choose Code Entry. Enter 1MI9K7E1.

$10,000
Select Career and then choose Code Entry. Enter CASHMONEY.

$10,000
Select Career and then choose Code Entry. Enter REGGAME.

AUDI TT
Select Career and then choose Code Entry. Enter ITSABOUTYOU.

CHEVELLE SS
Select Career and then choose Code Entry. Enter HORSEPOWER.

COKE ZERO GOLF GTI
Select Career and then choose Code Entry. Enter COKEZERO.

DODGE VIPER
Select Career and then choose Code Entry. Enter WORLDSLONGESTLASTING.

MITSUBISHI LANCER EVOLUTION
Select Career and then choose Code Entry. Enter MITSUBISHIGOFAR.

UNLOCK ALL BONUSES
Select Career and then choose Code Entry. Enter UNLOCKALLTHINGS.

5 REPAIR MARKERS
Select Career and then choose Code Entry. Enter SAFETYNET.

ENERGIZER VINYL
Select Career and then choose Code Entry. Enter ENERGIZERLITHIUM.

CASTROL SYNTEC VINYL
Select Career and then choose Code Entry. Enter CASTROLSYNTEC. This also gives you $10,000.

NHL 08

ALL RBK EDGE JERSEYS
At the RBK Edge Code option, enter h3oyxpwksf8ibcgt.

NHL 09

UNLOCK 3RD JERSEYS
At the cheat menu, enter xe6377uyrwm48frf.

NICKTOONS: ATTACK OF THE TOYBOTS

DAMAGE BOOST
Select Cheats from the Extras menu. Choose Enter Cheat Code and enter 456645.

INVULNERABILITY
Select Cheats from the Extras menu. Choose Enter Cheat Code and enter 313456.

UNLOCK EXO-HUGGLES 9000
Select Cheats from the Extras menu. Choose Enter Cheat Code and enter 691427.

UNLOCK MR. HUGGLES
Select Cheats from the Extras menu. Choose Enter Cheat Code and enter 654168.

UNLIMITED LOBBER GOO
Select Cheats from the Extras menu. Choose Enter Cheat Code and enter 118147.

UNLIMITED SCATTER GOO
Select Cheats from the Extras menu. Choose Enter Cheat Code and enter 971238.

UNLIMITED SPLITTER GOO
Select Cheats from the Extras menu. Choose Enter Cheat Code and enter 854511.

RATATOUILLE

Select Gusteau's Shop from the Extras menu. Choose Secrets, select the appropriate code number, and then enter the code. Once the code is entered, select the cheat you want to activate it.

 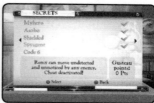

CODE NUMBER	CODE	EFFECT
1	Pieceocake	Very Easy difficulty mode
2	Myhero	No impact and no damage from enemies
3	Asobo	Plays the Asobo logo
4	Shielded	No damage from enemies
5	Spyagent	Move undetected by any enemy
6	Ilikeonions	Release air every time Remy jumps
7	Hardfeelings	Head butt when attacking instead of tailswipe
8	Slumberparty	Multiplayer mode
9	Gusteauart	All Concept Art
10	Gusteauship	All four championship modes
11	Mattelme	All single player and multiplayer mini-games
12	Gusteauvid	All Videos
13	Gusteaures	All Bonus Artworks
14	Gusteaudream	All Dream Worlds in Gusteau's Shop
15	Gusteauslide	All Slides in Gusteau's Shop
16	Gusteaulevel	All single player mini-games
17	Gusteaucombo	All items in Gusteau's Shop
18	Gusteaupot	5,000 Gusteau points
19	Gusteaujack	10,000 Gusteau points
20	Gusteauomni	50,000 Gusteau points

SCOOBY-DOO! FIRST FRIGHTS

DAPHNE'S SECRET COSTUME
Select Codes from the Extras menu and enter 2839.

FRED'S SECRET COSTUME
Select Codes from the Extras menu and enter 4826.

SCOOBY DOO'S SECRET COSTUME
Select Codes from the Extras menu and enter 1585.

SHAGGY'S SECRET COSTUME
Select Codes from the Extras menu and enter 3726.

VELMA'S SECRET COSTUME
Select Codes from the Extras menu and enter 6588.

SEGA SUPERSTARS TENNIS

UNLOCK CHARACTERS
Complete the following missions to unlock the corresponding character.

CHARACTER	MISSION TO COMPLETE
Alex Kidd	Mission 1 of Alex Kidd's World
Amy Rose	Mission 2 of Sonic the Hedgehog's World
Gilius	Mission 1 of Golden Axe's World
Gum	Mission 12 of Jet Grind Radio's World
Meemee	Mission 8 of Super Monkey Ball's World
Pudding	Mission 1 of Space Channel 5's World
Reala	Mission 2 of NiGHTs' World
Shadow The Hedgehog	Mission 14 of Sonic the Hedgehog's World

SHREK THE THIRD

10,000 GOLD COINS
At the gift shop, press Up, Up, Down, Up, Right, Left.

THE SIMPSONS GAME

UNLIMITED POWER FOR ALL CHARACTERS
At the Extras menu, press ●, Left, Right, ●, ●, L1.

ALL CLICHÉS.
At the Extras menu, press Left, ●, Right, ●, Right, L1.

ALL MOVIES
At the Extras menu, press ●, Left, ●, Right, ●, R1.

THE SIMS 2: CASTAWAY

CHEAT GNOME
During a game, press R1, L1, Down, ●, R2. You can now use this Gnome to get the following:

MAX ALL MOTIVES
During a game, press R2, Up, X, ●, L1.

MAX CURRENT INVENTORY
During a game, press Left, Right, ●, R2, ●.

MAX RELATIONSHIPS
During a game, press L1, Up, R2, Left, ▲.

ALL RESOURCES
During a game, press ●, ▲, Down, X, Left.

CHEAT CODE EXPLOSION FOR CONSOLES

ALL CRAFTING PLANS

During a game, press X, ⬆, L2, ⬤, R1.

ADD 1 TO SKILL

During a game, press ⬆, L1, L1, Left, ⬆.

EXCLUSIVE VEST AND TANKTOP

Pause the game and go to Fashion and Grooming. Press ⬤, R2, R2, ⬆, Down.

THE SIMS 2: PETS

CHEAT GNOME

During a game, press L1, L1, R1, ⊗, ⊗, Up.

GIVE SIM PET POINTS

After activating the Cheat Gnome, press ⬆, ⬤, ⊗, ⬤, L1, R1 during a game. Select the Gnome to access the cheat.

ADVANCE 6 HOURS

After activating the Cheat Gnome, press Up, Left, Down, Right, R1 during a game. Select the Gnome to access the cheat.

GIVE SIM SIMOLEONS

After activating the Cheat Gnome, enter the Advance 6 Hours cheat. Access the Gnome and exit. Enter the cheat again. Now, Give Sim Simoleons should be available from the Gnome.

CAT AND DOG CODES

When creating a family, press ⬤ to Enter Unlock Code. Enter the following for new fur patterns.

FUR PATTERN/CAT OR DOG	UNLOCK CODE
Bandit Mask Cats	EEGJ2YRQZZAIZ9QHA64
Bandit Mask Dogs	EEGJ2YRQZQARQ9QHA64
Black Dot Cats	EEGJ2YRZQQ1IQ9QHA64
Black Dot Dogs	EEGJ2YRQZZ1IQ9QHA64
Black Smiley Cats	EEGJ2YRQQZ1RQ9QHA64
Black Smiley Dogs	EEGJ2YRZQQARQ9QHA64

FUR PATTERN/CAT OR DOG	UNLOCK CODE
Blue Bones Cats	EEGJ2YRQZZARQ9QHA64
Blue Bones Dogs	EEGJ2YRZZZ1IZ9QHA64
Blue Camouflage Cats	EEGJ2YRZZZQ1IQ9QHA64
Blue Camouflage Dogs	EEGJ2YRZZZ1RQ9QHA64
Blue Cats	EEGJ2YRQZZAIQ9QHA64
Blue Dogs	EEGJ2YRQQQ1IZ9QHA64
Blue Star Cats	EEGJ2YRQQZ1IZ9QHA64
Blue Star Dogs	EEGJ2YRQZQ1IQ9QHA64
Deep Red Cats	EEGJ2YRQQQAIQ9QHA64
Deep Red Dogs	EEGJ2YRQZQ1RQ9QHA64
Goofy Cats	EEGJ2YRQZQ1IZ9QHA64
Goofy Dogs	EEGJ2YRZZZARQ9QHA64
Green Cats	EEGJ2YRZQQAIZ9QHA64
Green Dogs	EEGJ2YRQZQAIQ9QHA64
Green Flower Cats	EEGJ2YRZQZAIQ9QHA64
Green Flower Dogs	EEGJ2YRZQZZ1R09QHA64
Light Green Cats	EEGJ2YRZZQ1RQ9QHA64
Light Green Dogs	EEGJ2YRZQQ1RQ9QHA64
Navy Hearts Cats	EEGJ2YRZQZ1IQ9QHA64
Navy Hearts Dogs	EEGJ2YRQQZ1IQ9QHA64
Neon Green Cats	EEGJ2YRZZQAIQ9QHA64
Neon Green Dogs	EEGJ2YRZQQAIQ9QHA64
Neon Yellow Cats	EEGJ2YRZZQARQ9QHA64
Neon Yellow Dogs	EEGJ2YRQQQAIZ9QHA64
Orange Diagonal Cats	EEGJ2YRQQZAIQ9QHA64
Orange Diagonal Dogs	EEGJ2YRZQZQT1IZ9QHA64
Panda Cats	EEGJ2YRQZQAIZ9QHA64
Pink Cats	EEGJ2YRQZZ1IZ9QHA64
Pink Dogs	EEGJ2YRZQZ1RQ9QHA64
Pink Vertical Strip Cats	EEGJ2YRQQQARQ9QHA64
Pink Vertical Strip Dogs	EEGJ2YRZZZAIQ9QHA64
Purple Cats	EEGJ2YRQQZARQ9QHA64
Purple Dogs	EEGJ2YRQQZAIZ9QHA64
Star Cats	EEGJ2YRZQZARQ9QHA64
Star Dogs	EEGJ2YRZQZAIZ9QHA64
White Paws Cats	EEGJ2YRQQQ1RQ9QHA64
White Paws Dogs	EEGJ2YRZQQ1IZ9QHA64
White Zebra Stripe Cats	EEGJ2YRZZQ1IZ9QHA64
White Zebra Stripe Dogs	EEGJ2YRZZZ1IQ9QHA64
Zebra Stripes Dogs	EEGJ2YRZZQAIZ9QHA64

SLY 3: HONOR AMONG THIEVES

TOONAMI PLANE

While flying the regular plane, pause the game and press **R1**, **R1**, Right, Down, Down, Right.

RESTART EPISODES

Pause the game during the Episode and enter the following codes to restart that Episode. You must first complete that part of the Episode to use the code.

EPISODE	CODE
Episode 1, Day 1	Left, R2, Right, L1, R2, L1
Episode 1, Day 2	Down, L2, Up, Left, R2, L2
Episode 2, Day 1	Right, L2, Left, Up, Right, Down
Episode 2, Day 2	Down, Up, R1, Up, R2, L2
Episode 3, Day 1	R2, R1, L1, Left, L1, Down
Episode 3, Day 2	L2, R1, R2, L2, L1, Up

EPISODE	CODE
Episode 4, Day 1	Left, Right, L1, R2, Right, R2
Episode 4, Day 2	L1, Left, L2, Left, Up, L1
Episode 5, Day 1	Left, R2, Right, Up, L1, R2
Episode 5, Day 2	R2, R1, L1, R1, R2, R1
Operation Laptop Retrieval	L2, Left, R1, L2, L1, Down
Operation Moon Crash	L2, Up, Left, L1, L2, L1
Operation Reverse Double Cross	Right, Left, Up, Left, R2, Left
Operation Tar Be-Gone	Down, L2, R1, L2, R1, Right
Operation Turbo Dominant Eagle	Down, Right, Left, L2, R1, Right
Operation Wedding Crasher	L2, R2, Right, Down, L1, R2

SPIDER-MAN: FRIEND OR FOE

NEW GREEN GOBLIN AS A SIDEKICK

While standing in the Helicarrier between levels, press Left, Down, Right, Right, Down, Left.

SANDMAN AS A SIDEKICK

While standing in the Helicarrier between levels, press Right, Right, Right, Up, Down, Left.

VENOM AS A SIDEKICK

While standing in the Helicarrier between levels, press Left, Left, Right, Up, Down, Down.

5000 TECH TOKENS

While standing in the Helicarrier between levels, press Up, Up, Down, Down, Left, Right.

THE SPIDERWICK CHRONICLES

INVULNERABILITY

During the game, hold L1 + R1 and press ▲, ▲, ▲, ▲, ✕, ✕, ▲, ▲.

HEAL

During the game, hold L1 + R1 and press ▲, ■, ✕, ●, ▲, ■, ✕, ●.

COMBAT LOADOUT

During the game, hold L1 + R1 and press ▲, ▲, ✕, ✕, ■, ●, ▲, ▲.

INFINITE AMMO

During the game, hold L1 + R1 and press ■, ■, ●, ●, ✕, ✕, ✕, ▲.

FIELD GUIDE UNLOCKED

During the game, hold L1 + R1 and press ●, ●, ●, ■, ▲, ▲, ▲, ✕.

SPRITE A

During the game, hold L2 + R2 and press ▲, ✕, ●, ■, ✕, ▲, ■, ●.

SPRITE B

During the game, hold L2 + R2 and press ✕, ✕, ▲, ■, ●, ●, ▲, ✕.

SPRITE C

During the game, hold L2 + R2 and press ●, ▲, ■, ✕, ●, ▲, ■, ✕.

SPONGEBOB SQUAREPANTS FEATURING NICKTOONS: GLOBS OF DOOM

When entering the following codes, the order of the characters going down is: SpongeBob SquarePants, Nicolai Technus, Danny Phantom, Dib, Zim, Tlaloc, Tak, Beautiful Gorgeous, Jimmy Neutron, Plankton. These names are shortened to the first name in the following.

163

ATTRACT COINS

Using the Upgrade Machine on the bottom level of the lair, select "Input cheat codes here". Enter Tlaloc, Plankton, Danny, Plankton, Tak. Coins are attracted to you making them much easier to collect.

DON'T LOSE COINS

Using the Upgrade Machine on the bottom level of the lair, select "Input cheat codes here". Enter Plankton, Jimmy, Beautiful, Jimmy, Plankton. You don't lose coins when you get knocked out.

GOO HAS NO EFFECT

Using the Upgrade Machine on the bottom level of the lair, select "Input cheat codes here". Enter Danny, Danny, Danny, Nicolai, Nicolai. Goo does not slow you down.

MORE GADGET COMBO TIME

Using the Upgrade Machine on the bottom level of the lair, select "Input cheat codes here". Enter SpongeBob, Beautiful, Danny, Plankton, Nicolai. You have more time to perform gadget combos.

STAR WARS: THE FORCE UNLEASHED

CHEATS

Once you have accessed the Rogue Shadow, select Enter Code from the Extras menu. Now you can enter the following codes:

CHEAT	CODE	CHEAT	CODE
Invincibility	CORTOSIS	Max Force Power Level	KATARN
Unlimited Force	VERGENCE	Max Combo Level	COUNTDOOKU
1,000,000 Force Points	SPEEDER	Stronger Lightsaber	LIGHTSABER
All Force Powers	TYRANUS		

COSTUMES

Once you have accessed the Rogue Shadow, select Enter Code from the Extras menu. Now you can enter the following codes:

COSTUME	CODE	COSTUME	CODE
All Costumes	GRANDMOFF	Juno Eclipse	ECLIPSE
501st Legion	LEGION	Kento's Robe	WOOKIEE
Aayla Secura	AAYLA	Kleef	KLEEF
Admiral Ackbar	ITSATWAP	Lando Calrissian	SCOUNDREL
Anakin Skywalker	CHOSENONE	Luke Skywalker	T16WOMPRAT
Asajj Ventress	ACOLYTE	Luke Skywalker (Yavin)	YELLOWJCKT
Ceremonial Jedi Robes	DANTOOINE	Mace Windu	JEDIMASTER
Chop'aa Notimo	NOTIMO	Mara Jade	MARAJADE
Classic stormtrooper	TK421	Maris Brook	MARISBROOD
Count Dooku	SERENNO	Navy commando	STORMTROOP
Darth Desolous	PAUAN	Obi Wan Kenobi	BENKENOBI
Darth Maul	ZABRAK	Proxy	HOLOGRAM
Darth Phobos	HIDDENFEAR	Qui Gon Jinn	MAVERICK
Darth Vader	SITHLORD	Shaak Ti	TOGRUTA
Drexl Roosh	DREXLROOSH	Shadow trooper	INTHEDARK
Emperor Palpatine	PALPATINE	Sith Robes	HOLOCRON
General Rahm Kota	MANDALORE	Sith Stalker Armor	KORRIBAN
Han Solo	NERFHERDER	Twi'lek	SECURA
Heavy trooper	SHOCKTROOP		

STREET FIGHTER ALPHA

PLAY AS DAN

At the Character Select screen in Arcade Mode, hold the Start button and place the cursor on the Random Select space then input one of the following commands within 1 second:

LP LK MK HK HP MP

HP HK MK LK LP MP

LK LP MP HP HK MK

HK HP MP LP LK HK

PLAY AS M.BISON

At the Character Select screen, hold the Start button, place the cursor on the random select box, and input:

1P side: Down, Down, Back, Back, Down, Back, Back + LP + HP

2P side: Down, Down, Forward, Forward, Down, Forward, Forward + LP + HP

PLAY AS AKUMA

At the Character Select screen, hold the Start button, place the cursor on the random select box, and input:

1P side: Down, Down, Down, Back, Back, Back + LP + HP

2P side: Down, Down, Down, Forward, Forward, Forward + LP + HP

AKUMA MODE

Select your character in Arcade mode, then press and hold Start + MP + MK as the Character Selection screen ends.

RYU AND KEN VS. M.BISON

On both the 1p and 2p side in Arcade mode, press and hold Start, then:

1P side: place the cursor on Ryu and input Up, Up, release Start, Up, Up + LP

2P side: place the cursor on Ken and input Up, Up, release Start, Up, Up + HP

LAST BOSS MODE

Select Arcade mode while holding ⬤, ✖, and **R1**.

DRAMATIC BATTLE MODE

Select Dramatic Battle mode while holding ⬤, ✖, and **R2**.

RANDOM BATTLE MODE

Select Versus mode while holding ⬤, ✖, and **R2**.

STREET FIGHTER ALPHA 2

PLAY AS ORIGINAL CHUN-LI

Highlight Chun-Li on the Character Select screen, hold the Start button for 3 seconds, then select Chun-Li normally.

PLAY AS SHIN AKUMA

Highlight Akuma on the Character Select screen, hold the Start button for 3 seconds, then select Akuma normally.

PLAY AS EVIL RYU

Highlight Ryu on the Character Select screen, hold the Start button, input Forward, Up, Down, Back, then select Ryu normally.

165

PLAY AS EX DHALSIM

Highlight Dhalsim on the Character Select screen, hold the Start button, input Back, Down, Forward, Up, then select Dhalsim normally.

PLAY AS EX ZANGIEF

Highlight Zangief on the Character Select screen, hold the Start button, input Down, Back, Back, Back, Back, Up, Up, Forward, Forward, Forward, Forward, Down, then select Zangief normally.

LAST BOSS MODE

Select Arcade mode while holding the ⬤, ⬤, and **R1** buttons.

DRAMATIC BATTLE MODE

Select Dramatic Battle mode while holding the ⬤ + ✖ + **R2**.

SELECT SPECIAL ROUTE IN SURVIVAL MODE

Select Survival Battle while holding the **R1** or **R2**.

RANDOM BATTLE MODE

Select Versus mode while holding the ⬤ + ✖ + **R2**.

STREET FIGHTER ALPHA 2 GOLD

PLAY AS EX RYU

Highlight Ryu and press the Start button once before selecting normally.

PLAY AS EVIL RYU

Highlight Ryu and press the Start button twice before selecting normally.

PLAY AS ORIGINAL CHUN-LI

Highlight Chun-Li and press the Start button once before selecting normally.

PLAY AS EX CHUN-LI

Highlight Chun-Li and press the Start button twice before selecting normally.

PLAY AS EX KEN

Highlight Ken and press the Start button once before selecting normally.

PLAY AS EX DHALSIM

Highlight Dhalsim and press the Start button once before selecting normally.

PLAY AS EX ZANGIEF

Highlight Zangief and press the Start button once before selecting normally.

PLAY AS EX SAGAT

Highlight Sagat and press the Start button once before selecting normally.

PLAY AS EX M.BISON

Highlight M.Bison and press the Start button once before selecting normally.

PLAY USING SAKURA'S ALTERNATE COLORS

Highlight Sakura and press the Start button five times before selecting normally.

PLAY AS SHIN AKUMA

Highlight Akuma and press the Start button five times before selecting normally.

PLAY AS CAMMY

Highlight M.Bison and press the Start button twice before selecting normally.

LAST BOSS MODE

Select Arcade mode while holding ⬤ + ⬤ + **R1**.

SELECT SPECIAL ROUTE IN SURVIVAL MODE

Select Survival Battle while holding the **R1** or **R2**.

DRAMATIC BATTLE MODE

Select Dramatic Battle mode while holding ● + ⊗ + **R2**.

RANDOM BATTLE MODE

Select Versus mode while holding ● + ⊗ + **R2**.

STREET FIGHTER ALPHA 3

PLAY AS BALROG

Highlight Karin for one second, then move the cursor to the random select box and hold Start before selecting normally.

PLAY AS JULI

Highlight Karin for one second, then move the cursor to the random select box and press Up, or Down, while selecting normally.

PLAY AS JUNI

Highlight Karin for one second, then move the cursor to the random select box and press Back, or Forward, while selecting normally.

CLASSICAL MODE

Press and hold HP + HK while starting game.

SPIRITED MODE

Press and hold MP + MK while starting game.

SAIKYO MODE

Press and hold LP + LK while starting game.

SHADALOO MODE

Press and hold LK + MK + HK while starting game.

SELECT SPECIAL ROUTE IN SURVIVAL MODE

Select Survival mode while holding **R1** or **R2**.

DRAMATIC BATTLE MODE

Select Dramatic Battle mode while holding ● + ⊗ + **R2**.

RANDOM BATTLE MODE

Select Versus mode while holding ● + ⊗ + **R2**.

STUNTMAN IGNITION

3 PROPS IN STUNT CREATOR MODE

Select Cheats from Extras and enter COOLPROP.

ALL ITEMS UNLOCKED FOR CONSTRUCTION MODE

Select Cheats from Extras and enter NOBLEMAN.

MVX SPARTAN

Select Cheats from Extras and enter fastride.

ALL CHEATS

Select Cheats from Extras and enter Wearefrozen. This unlocks the following cheats: Slo-mo Cool, Thrill Cam, Vision Switcher, Nitro Addiction, Freaky Fast, and Ice Wheels.

ALL CHEATS

Select Cheats from Extras and enter Kungfoopete.

ICE WHEELS CHEAT

Select Cheats from Extras and enter IceAge.

NITRO ADDICTION CHEAT

Select Cheats from Extras and enter TheDuke.

VISION SWITCHER CHEAT

Select Cheats from Extras and enter GFXMODES.

TAK AND THE GUARDIANS OF GROSS

INVULNERABILITY

Select Cheat Codes from the Extras menu and enter KRUNKIN.

INFINITE NOVA

Select Cheat Codes from the Extras menu and enter CAKEDAY.

WEAK ENEMIES

Select Cheat Codes from the Extras menu and enter CODMODE.

ALL LEVELS

Select Cheat Codes from the Extras menu and enter GUDGEON.

ALL MINI GAMES

Select Cheat Codes from the Extras menu and enter CURLING.

ALL AWARDS

Select Cheat Codes from the Extras menu and enter SNEAKER.

ALL CONCEPT ART

Select Cheat Codes from the Extras menu and enter FRIVERS.

RAINBOW TRAIL

Select Cheat Codes from the Extras menu and enter UNICORN.

TEENAGE MUTANT NINJA TURTLES: SMASH-UP

CYBER SHREDDER

At the Bonus Content menu, press Up, Down, Right, Up, Down, Right, Left, Up, Right, Down.

4 NINJA TURTLES' ALTERNATE COSTUMES

At the Bonus Content menu, press Up, Left, Down, Right, Up, Down, Left, Up, Left, Left.

TIGER WOODS PGA TOUR 08

ALL GOLFERS

Select Passwords from the Options and enter GAMEFACE.

BRIDGESTONE ITEMS

Select Passwords from the Options and enter SHOJIRO.

COBRA ITEMS

Select Passwords from the Options and enter SNAKEKING.

GRAFALLOY ITEMS

Select Passwords from the Options and enter JUSTSHAFTS.

MACGREGOR ITEMS

Select Passwords from the Options and enter MACTEC.

MIZUNO ITEMS

Select Passwords from the Options and enter RIHACHINRIZO.

NIKE ITEMS

Select Passwords from the Options and enter JUSTDOIT.

OAKLEY ITEMS

Select Passwords from the Options and enter JANNARD.

PING ITEMS

Select Passwords from the Options and enter SOLHEIM.

PRECEPT ITEMS

Select Passwords from the Options and enter GUYSAREGOOD.

TAYLORMADE ITEMS

Select Passwords from the Options and enter MRADAMS.

TIGER WOODS PGA TOUR 09

$1,000,000

Select Passwords from the Extras menu and enter JACKPOT.

MAX SKILL POINTS

Select Passwords from the Extras menu and enter IAMRUBBISH.

ALL CLOTHING & EQUIPMENT

Select Passwords from the Extras menu and enter SHOP2DROP.

ALL PGA TOUR EVENTS

Select Passwords from the Extras menu and enter BEATIT.

ALL COVER STORIES

Select Passwords from the Extras menu and enter HEADLINER.

TONY HAWK'S PROVING GROUND

CHEAT CODES

Select Cheat Codes from the Options and enter the following cheats. Some codes need to be enabled by selecting Cheats from the Options during a game.

UNLOCK	CHEAT
Unlocks Bosco	MOREMILK
Unlocks Cam	NOTACAMERA
Unlocks Cooper	THECOOP
Unlocks Eddie X	SKETCHY
Unlocks El Patinador	PILEDRIVER
Unlocks Eric	FLYAWAY
Unlocks Judy Nails	LOVEROCKNROLL
Unlocks Mad Dog	RABBIES
Unlocks MCA	INTERGALACTIC
Unlocks Mel	NOTADUDE
Unlocks Rube	LOOKSSMELLY
Unlocks Spence	DAPPER
Unlocks Shayne	MOVERS
Unlocks TV Producer	SHAKER
Unlock FDR	THEPREZPARK
Unlock Lansdowne	THELOCALPARK
Unlock Air & Space Museum	THEINDOORPARK
Unlocks all Fun Items	OVERTHETOP
Unlock all Game Movies	WATCHTHIS
Unlock all Rigger Pieces	IMGONNABUILD

UNLOCK	CHEAT
All specials unlocked and in player's special list	LOTSOFTRICKS
Full Stats	BEEFEDUP
Give player +50 skill points	NEEDSHELP
Unlocks Perfect Manual	STILLAINTFALLIN
Unlocks Perfect Rail	AINTFALLIN
Unlocks Unlimited Focus	MYOPIC
Invisible Man	THEMISSING
Mini Skater	TINYTATER

TRANSFORMERS: THE GAME

INFINITE HEALTH

At the Main menu, press Left, Left, Up, Left, Right, Down, Right.

INFINITE AMMO

At the Main menu, press Up, Down, Left, Right, Up, Up, Down.

NO MILITARY OR POLICE

At the Main menu, press Right, Left, Right, Left, Right, Left, Right.

ALL MISSIONS

At the Main menu, press Down, Up, Left, Right, Right, Right, Up, Down.

BONUS CYBERTRON MISSIONS

At the Main menu, press Right, Up, Up, Down, Right, Left, Left.

GENERATION 1 SKIN: JAZZ

At the Main menu, press Left, Up, Down, Down, Left, Up, Right.

GENERATION 1 SKIN: MEGATRON

At the Main menu, press Down, Left, Left, Down, Right, Right, Up.

GENERATION 1 SKIN: OPTIMUS PRIME

At the Main menu, press Down, Right, Left, Up, Down, Down, Left.

GENERATION 1 SKIN: ROBOVISION OPTIMUS PRIME

At the Main menu, press Down, Down, Up, Up, Right, Right, Right.

GENERATION 1 SKIN: STARSCREAM

At the Main menu, press Right, Down, Left, Left, Down, Up, Up.

ALL COVERS

Pause the game and select Controller Setup from the Options. Press Left, Left, Right, Left, Up, Left, Left, Down.

ALL CONCEPT ART

Pause the game and select Controller Setup from the Options. Press Down, Down, Down, Up, Down, Up, Left, Left.

ALL LANDMARKS

Pause the game and select Controller Setup from the Options. Press Up, Right, Down, Left, Down, Up, Right, Left.

UP

You will need to activate the following cheats at the pause menu after entering them.

RUSSELL ATTRACTS ALL BUTTERFLIES

Select Cheats from the Bonuses menu and enter BUTTERFLY.

MUNTZ'S AVIATOR GOGGLES FOR CARL

Select Cheats from the Bonuses menu and enter AVIATORGOGGLES.

CARL JUMPS FROM TEETER TOTTER TO LIFT RUSSEL

Select Cheats from the Bonuses menu and enter CARLHEAVYWEIGHT.

BALLOONS WHEN CARL JUMPS

Select Cheats from the Bonuses menu and enter BALLOONPARTY.

WWE SMACKDOWN VS. RAW 2009

BOOGEYMAN

Select Cheat Codes from My WWE and enter BoogeymanEatsWorms!!.

GENE SNITSKY

Select Cheat Codes from My WWE and enter UnlockSnitskySvR2009.

HAWKINS & RYDER

Select Cheat Codes from My WWE and enter Ryder&HawkinsTagTeam.

JILLIAN HALL

Select Cheat Codes from My WWE and enter PlayAsJillianHallSvR.

LAYLA

Select Cheat Codes from My WWE and enter UnlockECWDivaLayla09.

RIC FLAIR

Select Cheat Codes from My WWE and enter FlairWoooooooooooooo.

TAZZ

Select Cheat Codes from My WWE and enter UnlockECWTazzSvR2009.

VINCENT MCMAHON

Select Cheat Codes from My WWE and enter VinceMcMahonNoChance.

HORNSWOGGLE AS MANAGER

Select Cheat Codes from My WWE and enter HornswoggleAsManager.

CHRIS JERICHO COSTUME B

Select Cheat Codes from My WWE and enter AltJerichoModelSvR09.

CM PUNK COSTUME B

Select Cheat Codes from My WWE and enter CMPunkAltCostumeSvR!.

REY MYSTERIO COSTUME B

Select Cheat Codes from My WWE and enter BooyakaBooyaka619SvR.

SATURDAY NIGHT'S MAIN EVENT ARENA

Select Cheat Codes from My WWE and enter SatNightMainEventSvR.

WWE SMACKDOWN VS. RAW 2010

THE ROCK

Select Cheat Codes from the Options and enter The Great One.

VINCE'S OFFICE AND DIRT SHEET FOR BACKSTAGE BRAWL

Select Cheat Codes from the Options menu and enter BonusBrawl.

SHAWN MICHAELS' NEW COSTUME

Select Cheat Codes from the Options menu and enter Bow Down.

RANDY ORTON'S NEW COSTUME

Select Cheat Codes from the Options menu and enter ViperRKO.

TRIPLE H'S NEW COSTUME

Select Cheat Codes from the Options menu and enter Suck IT!.

X-MEN: THE OFFICIAL GAME

DANGER ROOM ICEMAN

At the Cerebro Files menu, press Right, Right, Left, Left, Down, Up, Down, Up, Start.

DANGER ROOM NIGHTCRAWLER

At the Cerebro Files menu, press Up, Up, Down, Down, Left, Right, Left, Right, Start.

DANGER ROOM WOLVERINE

At the Cerebro Files menu, press Down, Down, Up, Up, Right, Left, Right, Left, Start.

CHEAT CODE EXPLOSION

FOR HANDHELDS

◆ DANGER ◆ COMBUSTIBLE

FLIP THIS BOOK OVER FOR HOME CONSOLES

PlayStation®3
Nintendo Wii™
Xbox 360™
PlayStation®2

LOOK FOR CODEY
When you see Codey's face, you've found the newest and coolest codes!

CHEAT CODE EXPLOSION

EXCLUSIVE SCHOLASTIC EDITION

DK/BradyGames, a division of Penguin Group (USA) Inc.
800 East 96th Street, 3rd Floor
Indianapolis, IN 46240

ISBN: 978-0-7440-1187-6

Printing Code: The rightmost double-digit number is the year of the book's printing; the rightmost single-digit number is the number of the book's printing. For example, 08-1 shows that the first printing of the book occurred in 2008.

11 10   4 3

Printed in the USA.

CREDITS

Senior Development Editor
Ken Schmidt

Cheat Code and Screenshot Editor
Michael Owen

Book Designer
Doug Wilkins

Production Designer
Wil Cruz

BRADYGAMES STAFF

Publisher
David Waybright

Editor-In-Chief
H. Leigh Davis

Licensing Director
Mike Degler

Marketing Director
Debby Neubauer

International Translations
Brian Saliba

NINTENDO DS™

TABLE OF CONTENTS

CHEAT CODE EXPLOSION FOR HANDHELDS

ADVANCE WARS: DAYS OF RUIN

UNLOCK COS

Complete the following missions to unlock the corresponding CO.

COMPLETE MISSION	CO UNLOCKED
12	Tasha
13	Gage
14	Forthsythe
20	Waylon
21	Greyfield
24	Penny
25	Tabitha
26	Caulder

ADVANCE WARS: DUAL STRIKE

ADVANCE WARS MAP

Select Map from the Design Room menu and immediately press and hold L + R. You will get a map that spells out Advance Wars. By having old versions of advance wars inserted in your DS at the same time as Dual Strike, you can unlock new buyables at the the Battle Maps Shop!

ADVANCE WARPAPER

Insert Advance Wars in the GBA slot of your Nintendo DS. Start Advance Wars: Dual Strike. Select Battle Maps and purchase Advance Warpaper. Select Display from the Design Room and choose Classic 1.

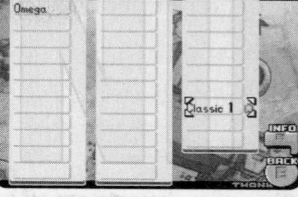

HACHI'S LAND

Insert Advance Wars in the GBA slot of your Nintendo DS. Start Advance Wars: Dual Strike.
Select Battle Maps and purchase Hachi's Land for 1.

NELL'S LAND

Insert Advance Wars in the GBA slot of your Nintendo DS. Start Advance Wars: Dual Strike.
Select Battle Maps and purchase Nell's Land for 1.

ADVANCE WARPAPER 2

Insert Advance Wars 2: Black Hole Rising in the GBA slot of your Nintendo DS. Start Advance
Wars: Dual Strike. Select Battle Maps and purchase Advance Warpaper 2. Select Display from
the Design Room and choose Classic 2.

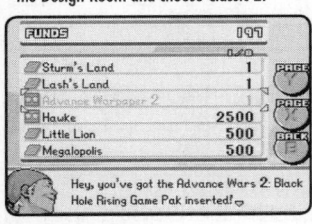

LASH'S LAND

Insert Advance Wars 2: Black Hole Rising in the GBA slot of your Nintendo DS. Start Advance
Wars: Dual Strike. Select Battle Maps and purchase Lash's Land for 1.

STRUM'S LAND

Insert Advance Wars 2: Black Hole Rising in the GBA slot of your Nintendo DS. Start Advance
Wars: Dual Strike. Select Battle Maps and purchase Strum's Land for 1.

BAKUGAN BATTLE BRAWLERS

1000 BP

Start a new game and enter the name as 180978772269.

5000 BP

Start a new game and enter the name as 332044292925.

10,000 BP

Start a new game and enter the name as 423482942968.

BRONZE WARIUS

Start a new game and enter the name as 449824934071.

BATTLE OF GIANTS - DRAGONS

Select Unlock Gold Gems from the Extras Menu and enter the following passwords:

BREATH ATTACK GOLD GEMS

LEVEL	ATTACK	PASSWORD
1	NAMGILIMA	ISAM SKNF DKTD
2	NIGHHALAMA	ZNBN QOKS THGO
3	KUGDIM	AWBF CRSL HGAT
4	KUZEN	ACLC SCRS VOSK
5	SUGZAG	XSPC LLSL KJLP

CLAW ATTACK GOLD GEMS

LEVEL	ATTACK	PASSWORD
1	USUD	NAKF HLAP SDSP
2	ULUH	SAPO RLNM VUSD
3	NIGHZU	POZX MJDR GJSA
4	GHIDRU	GPGE SMEC TDTB
5	MUDRU	ABLP CGPG SGAM

HEAD ATTACK GOLD GEMS

LEVEL	ATTACK	PASSWORD
1	MEN	PQTM AONV UTNA
2	SAGHMEN	TNAP CTJS LDUF
3	KINGAL	FHSK EUFV KALP
4	DALLA	EPWB MPOR TRTA
5	AGA	GPKT BBWT SGNR

TAIL ATTACK GOLD GEMS

LEVEL	ATTACK	PASSWORD
1	A'ASH	LSSN GOAJ READ
2	ASH	FUTY HVNS LNVS
3	ASH SAR	LPAQ KOYH TGDS
4	AHS BALA	VLQL QELB IYDS
5	NAMTAGTAG	VLDB DDSL NCJA

WING ATTACK GOLD GEMS

LEVEL	ATTACK	PASSWORD
1	NIM	SGHJ VLPO QEIK
2	NIMSAHARA	QPLA OKFC NBUS
3	BARASH	IQUW ENPC SRGA
4	A'SHUM	LRYV LCJC MEBT
5	ATUKU	ALVN HRSF MSEP

BEN 10: PROTECTOR OF EARTH

GWEN 10 SKINS
At the level select, press Left, Right, Left, Right, L, R, Select.

GALACTIC ENFORCER SKINS
At the level select, press A, B, X, Y, L, R, Select.

ULTRA BEN SKINS
At the level select, press Up, Right, Down, Left, A, B, Select.

BRAIN AGE: TRAIN YOUR BRAIN IN MINUTES A DAY

BRAIN AGE CHECK SELECTION MENU
At the Daily Training Menu, hold Select while choosing Brain Age Check.

TOP 3 LISTS
At the Daily Training Menu, hold Select while choosing Graph.

BRAIN VOYAGE

ALL GOLD MEDALS
At the World Map, press A, B, Up, L, L, Y.

INFINITE COINS
At the World Tour Mode, press L, Up, X, Up, R, Y.

BUBBLE BOBBLE REVOLUTION

BONUS LEVELS IN CLASSIC MODE
At the Classic mode Title screen, press L, R, L, R, L, R, Right, Select. Touch the door at Level 20.

POWER UP! MODE IN CLASSIC VERSION
At the Classic mode Title screen, press Select, R, L, Left, Right, R, Select, Right.

SUPER BUBBLE BOBBLE IN CLASSIC VERSION
You must first defeat the boss with two players. At the Classic mode Title screen, press Left, R, Left, Select, Left, L, Left, Select.

BUILD-A-BEAR WORKSHOP

At the Select a Slot screen, press Up, Up, Down, Down, Left, Right, Left, Right, B, A. Now you can enter the following codes:

ALL LEVELS
At the level select, hold L + R.

ALL ACTIVITIES
At the workshop screen, press R.

ALL MOVES
At the garden screen, press L.

BUST-A-MOVE DS

DARK WORLD
First you must complete the game. At the Title screen, press A Left Right A.

SOUND TEST
At the Main menu, press Select, A, B, Left, Right, A, Select, Right.

DINOSAUR KING

STONE CIRCLE PASSWORDS
Defeat the game to unlock the Stone Circle in South Euro. Now you can enter the following passwords to unlock dinosaurs. Find the level 1 dinosaur in a chest at the shrine.

009 DASPLETEOSARUS
Enter Grass, Water, Ligthning, Lightning, Earth, Earth, Water, Wind.

012 SIAMOTYRRANUS
Enter Fire, Wind, Fire, Water, Wind, Grass, Fire, Water.

025 JOBARIA
Enter Water, Lightning, Lightning, Earth, Fire, Earth, Fire, Wind.

029 TRICERATOPS
Enter Lightning, Fire, Lightning, Fire, Water, Lightning, Grass, Earth.

038 MONOCLONIUS
Enter Lightning, Earth, Water, Water, Grass, Fire, Earth, Wind.

046 EUOPLOCEPHALUS
Enter Earth, Earth, Grass, Water, Wind, Earth, Wind, Fire.

058 ALTIRHINUS

Enter Wind, Fire, Fire, Fire, Lightning, Earth, Water, Grass.

061 CARNOTAURUS

Enter Earth, Wind, Water, Lightning, Fire, Wind, Wind, Water.

EX ACE/EX CHOMP

Enter Lightning, Grass, Fire, Earth, Water, Water, Lightning, Fire. This gives you Ace if you are playing as Rex and Chomp as Max.

EX MINI-KING

Enter Lightning, Wind, Earth, Lightning, Grass, Wind, Fire, Water.

EX PARIS

Enter Grass, Water, Water, Earth, Wind, Grass, Lightning, Lightning.

EX SAUROPHAGANAX

Enter Fire, Water, Earth, Grass, Wind, Lightning, Fire, Water.

EX SPINY

Enter Water, Earth, Fire, Water, Fire, Grass, Wind, Earth.

EX TANK

Enter Earth, Grass, Earth, Water, Wind, Water, Grass, Fire.

EX TERRY

Enter Fire, Lightning, Wind, Wind, Water, Fire, Fire, Earth.

DISNEY FAIRIES: TINKER BELL

TINKERBELL MAGIC BOOK CODES

Talk to Queen Clarion about the Magic Book and enter the following codes.

EFFECCT	CODE
Augustus	5318 3479 7972
Baden	1199 2780 8802
Blair	6899 6003 4480
Cera	1297 0195 5747
Chipper	7980 9298 9818
Dewberry	0241 4491 0630
Elwood	3527 5660 3684
Fawn	9556 0047 1043
Idalia	2998 8832 2673
Iridessa	0724 0213 6136
Luminaria	8046 5868 5678
Magnolia	1697 4780 6430
Mariana	5138 8216 9240
Minister Autumn	2294 0281 6332
Minister Spring	2492 1155 4907
Minister Summer	2582 7972 6926
Minister Winter	2618 8587 2083
Nollie	5905 2346 9329
Olwen	7629 0545 7105
One Black Shell	1234 5678 9012
One Blue Dewdrop	0987 6543 2109
One Fairy Medal	1111 1111 1111
One Green Leaf	4444 4444 4444
One Pink Petal	2222 2222 2222
One Red Leaf	5555 5555 5555

EFFECCT	CODE
One Snow Grain	7777 7777 7777
One Weak Thread	9999 9999 9999
One White Feather	8888 8888 8888
One Yellow Leaf	6666 6666 6666
One Yellow Petal	3333 3333 3333
Party Shoes	1390 5107 4096
Party Skirt	6572 4809 6680
Party Tiara	8469 7886 7938
Party Top	0977 4584 3869
Queen Clarion	1486 4214 8147
Rosetta	8610 2523 6122
Rune	3020 5768 5351
Silvermist	0513 4563 6800
Terence	8606 6039 6383
Tinkerbell	2495 7761 9313
Vidia	3294 3220 0349

DRAGLADE

CHARACTERS

CHARACTER	TO UNLOCK
Asuka	Defeat Daichi's story
Gyamon	Defeat Guy's story
Koki	Defeat Hibito's story
Shura	Defeat Kairu's story

HIDDEN QUEST: SHADOW OF DARKNESS

Defeat Story Mode with all of the main characters. This unlocks the hidden quest in Synethesia.

ZEKE

Complete all of the quests including Shadow of Darkness to unlock Zeke in wireless battle.

DRAGON QUEST HEROES: ROCKET SLIME

KNIGHTRO TANK IN MULTIPLAYER

While in the church, press Y, L, L, Y, R, R, Y, Up, Down, Select.

THE NEMESIS TANK IN MULTIPLAYER

While in the church, press Y, R, R, up, L, L, Y, Down, Down, Down, Y, Select.

DRAGON QUEST MONSTERS: JOKER

CAPTAIN CROW

As you travel between the islands on the sea scooters, you are occasionally attacked by pirates. Discover the route on which the pirates are located at the bulletin board in any scoutpost den. When you face them between Infant Isle and Celeste Isle, Captain Crow makes an appearance. Defeat him and he forces himself into your team.

SOLITAIRE'S CHALLENGE

After completing the main game, load your game again for a new endeavor. The hero is in Solitaire's office, where she proposes a new nonstop challenge known as Solitaire's Challenge.

METAL KING SLIME

Acquire 100 different skills for your library and talk to the woman in Solitaire's office.

METAL KAISER SLIME

Acquire 150 different skills for your library and talk to the woman in Solitaire's office.

LEOPOLD

Acquire all of the skills for your library and talk to the woman in Solitaire's office.

LIQUID METAL SLIME

Collect 100 monsters in your library and talk to the man in Solitaire's office.

GRANDPA SLIME

Collect 200 monsters in your library and talk to the man in Solitaire's office.

EMPYREA

Collect all of the monsters in your library and talk to the man in Solitaire's office.

TRODE AND ROBBIN' HOOD

Complete both the skills and monster libraries and talk to both the man and woman in Solitaire's office.

DRAWN TO LIFE

HEAL ALL DAMAGE

During a game, press Start, hold L and press Y, X, Y, X, Y, X, A.

INVINCIBLITY

During a game, press Start, hold L and press A, X, B, B, Y.

ALIEN TEMPLATES

During a game, press Start, hold L and press X, Y, B, A, A.

ANIMAL TEMPLATES

During a game, press Start, hold L and press B, B, A, A, X.

ROBOT TEMPLATES

During a game, press Start, hold L and press Y, X, Y, X, A.

SPORTS TEMPLATES

During a game, press Start, hold L and press Y, A, B, A, X.

DRAWN TO LIFE: SPONGEBOB SQUAREPANTS EDITION

EXTRA REWARD COINS

Select Cheat Entry and enter Down, Down, B, B, Down, Left, Up, Right, A.

ELEBITS: THE ADVENTURES OF KAI & ZERO

BIG RED BONUS OMEGA

Select Download Additional Omegas from the Extra menu. Choose Download Data and press B, Y, Up, L, Right, R, Down, Left, X, A.

FINAL FANTASY FABLES: CHOCOBO TALES

OMEGA—WAVE CANNON CARD

Select Send from the Main menu and then choose Download Pop-Up Card. Press L, L, Up, B, B, Left.

GODZILLA UNLEASHED: DOUBLE SMASH

ANGUIRUS

Defeat Hedorah Terrorizes San Francisco.

DESTOROYAH

Defeat Monster Island, The Final Battle.

FIRE RODAN

Defeat Biollante Attacks Paris.

KING GHIDORAH

Defeat Mecha King Ghidorah Ravages Bangkok.

GRID

UNLOCK ALL

Select Cheat Codes from the Options and enter 233558.

INVULNERABILITY

Select Cheat Codes from the Options and enter 161650.

DRIFT MASTER

Select Cheat Codes from the Options and enter 789520.

PERFECT GRIP

Select Cheat Codes from the Options and enter 831782.

HIGH ROLLER

Select Cheat Codes from the Options and enter 401134.

GHOST CAR

Select Cheat Codes from the Options and enter 657346.

TOY CARS

Select Cheat Codes from the Options and enter 592014.

MM MODE

Select Cheat Codes from the Options and enter 800813.

IZUNA: LEGEND OF THE UNEMPLOYED NINJA

PATH OF TRAILS BONUS DUNGEON

After completing the game, touch the crystal from the beginning.

TM

JAKE HUNTER: DETECTIVE CHRONICLES

PASSWORDS

Select Password from the main menu and enter the following:

UNLOCKABLE	PASSWORD
1 Password Info	AAAA
2 Visuals	LEET
3 Visuals	GONG
4 Visuals	CARS
5 Movies	ROSE
6 Jukebox	BIKE
7 Hints	HINT

JAKE HUNTER DETECTIVE STORY: MEMORIES OF THE PAST

JAKE HUNTER QUIZ

Select Password and enter NEET.

JAKE HUNTER SERIES

Select Password and enter MISS.

JAKE HUNTER UNLEASHED 01 BONUS

Select Password and enter NONE.

JAKE HUNTER UNLEASHED 02 BONUS

Select Password and enter ANGL.

JAKE HUNTER UNLEASHED 03 BONUS

Select Password and enter SNAP.

JAKE HUNTER UNLEASHED 04 BONUS

Select Password and enter DOOR.

JAKE HUNTER UNLEASHED 05 BONUS

Select Password and enter STOP.

JAKE HUNTER UNLEASHED DS1 BONUS

Select Password and enter KING.

JAKE HUNTER VISUALS 1

Select Password and enter LEET.

JAKE HUNTER VISUALS 2

Select Password and enter GONG.

JAKE HUNTER VISUALS 3

Select Password and enter CARS.

JAKE HUNTER VISUALS 4

Select Password and enter TREE.

JAKE HUNTER VISUALS 5

Select Password and enter PAPA.

JUKEBOX

Select Password and enter BIKE.

MOVIE GALLERY

Select Password and enter ROSE.

PASSWORD HINTS

Select Password and enter HINT.

SIDE CHARACTER'S BONUS STORY

Select Password and enter MINU.

STAFF COMMENTS 1

Select Password and enter AQUA.

STAFF COMMENTS 2

Select Password and enter MOTO.

WHAT IS A PASSWORD?

Select Password and enter AAAA.

JAM SESSIONS

BONUS SONGS

At the Free Play menu, press Up, Up, Down, Down, Left, Right, Left, Right. This unlocks I'm Gonna Miss Her by Brad Paisley, Needles and Pins by Tom Petty, and Wild Thing by Jimi Hendrix.

JUMBLE MADNESS

FEBRUARY 31 PUZZLE

For Daily Jumble and Jumble Crosswords, select the square under February 28, 2009.

KONAMI CLASSICS SERIES: ARCADE HITS

GRADIUS

ALL POWER-UPS EXCEPT SPEED

At the Gradius title screen, press Up, Up, Down, Down, Left, Right, Left, Right, B, A. After starting a game, press Start to get every power-up except Speed. This code can be entered only once.

LEGO BATMAN

ALFRED PENNYWORTH

Use the computer in the Batcave, select Enter Code and enter ZAQ637.

BATGIRL

Use the computer in the Batcave, select Enter Code and enter JKR331.

BRUCE WAYNE

Use the computer in the Batcave, select Enter Code and enter BDJ327.

CLASSIC CATWOMAN

Use the computer in the Batcave, select Enter Code and enter M1AAWW.

CLOWN GOON

Use the computer in the Batcave, select Enter Code and enter HJK327.

COMMISSIONER GORDON

Use the computer in the Batcave, select Enter Code and enter DDP967.

FISHMONGER

Use the computer in the Batcave, select Enter Code and enter HGY748.

FREEZE GIRL

Use the computer in the Batcave, select Enter Code and enter XVK541.

FREEZE HENCHMAN

Use the computer in the Batcave, select Enter Code and enter NJL412.

JOKER GOON

Use the computer in the Batcave, select Enter Code and enter UTF782.

JOKER HENCHMAN

Use the computer in the Batcave, select Enter Code and enter YUN924.

NIGHTWING

Use the computer in the Batcave, select Enter Code and enter MVY759.

TROPICAL JOKER

Use the computer in the Batcave, select Enter Code and enter CCB199.

1 MILLION STUDS

At the main menu, press X, Y, B, B, Y, X, L, L, R, R, Up, Down, Left, Right, Start, Select.

3 MILLION STUDS

At the main menu, press Up, Up, B, Down, Down, X, Left, Left, Y, L, R, L, R, B, Y, X, Start, Select.

ALL CHARACTERS

At the main menu, press X, Up, B, Down, Y, Left, Start, Right, R, R, L, R, R, Down, Down, Up, Y, Y, Y, Start, Select.

ALL EPISODES AND FREE PLAY MODE

At the main menu, press Right, Up, R, L, X, Y, Right, Left, B, L, R, L, Down, Down, Up, Y, Y, X, X, B, B, Up, Up, L, R, Start, Select.

ALL EXTRAS

At the main menu, press Up, Down, L, R, L, R, L, Left, Right, X, X, Y, Y, B, B, L, Up, Down, L, R, L, R, Up, Up, Down, Start, Select.

LEGO BATTLES

INVINCIBLE HERO

At the Lego Store, tap the Red Brick and enter HJCRAWK.

REGENERATING HEALTH

At the Lego Store, tap the Red Brick and enter ABABLRX.

ONE HIT KILL (HEROES)

At the Lego Store, tap the Red Brick and enter AVMPWHK.

LONG RANGE MAGIC

At the Lego Store, tap the Red Brick and enter ZPWJFUQ.

SUPER MAGIC

At the Lego Store, tap the Red Brick and enter DWFTBNS.

DOUBLE LEGO BRICKS

At the Lego Store, tap the Red Brick and enter BGQOYRT.

FAST BUILDING

At the Lego Store, tap the Red Brick and enter QMSLPOE.

FAST HARVESTING

At the Lego Store, tap the Red Brick and enter PQZLJOB.

FAST MAGIC

At the Lego Store, tap the Red Brick and enter JRTPASX.

FAST MINING

At the Lego Store, tap the Red Brick and enter KVBPQRJ.

FULL UNIT CAP

At the Lego Store, tap the Red Brick and enter UMSXIRQ.

SUPER EXPLOSIONS

At the Lego Store, tap the Red Brick and enter THNBGRE.

UPGRADED TOWERS

At the Lego Store, tap the Red Brick and enter EDRFTGY.

SHOW ENEMIES

At the Lego Store, tap the Red Brick and enter IBGOFWX.

SHOW LEGO STUDS

At the Lego Store, tap the Red Brick and enter CPLYREK.

SHOW MINIKIT

At the Lego Store, tap the Red Brick and enter LJYQRAC.

SHOW RED BRICKS

At the Lego Store, tap the Red Brick and enter RTGYPKC.

REVEAL MAP

At the Lego Store, tap the Red Brick and enter SKQMXPL.

UNLOCK ISLANDER

At the Lego Store, tap the Red Brick and enter UGDRSQP.

UNLOCK NINJA MASTER

At the Lego Store, tap the Red Brick and enter SHWSDGU.

UNLOCK SPACE CRIMINAL LEADER

At the Lego Store, tap the Red Brick and enter ZVDNJSU.

UNLOCK TROLL KING

At the Lego Store, tap the Red Brick and enter XRCTVYB.

LEGO INDIANA JONES: THE ORIGINAL ADVENTURES

You should hear a confirmation sound after the following codes are entered.

ALL CHARACTERS

At the title screen, press X, Up, B, Down, Y, Left, Start, Right, R, R, L, R, R, Down, Down, Up, Y, Y, Y, Start, Select.

ALL EPISODES AND FREE PLAY MODE

Right, Up, R, L, X, Y, Right, Left, B, L, R, L, Down, Down, Up, Y, Y, X, X, B, B, Up, Up, L, R, Start, Select.

ALL EXTRAS

Up, Down, L, R, L, R, L, Left, Right, X, X, Y, Y, B, B, L, Up, Down, L, R, L, R, Up, Up, Down, Start, Select.

1,000,000 STUDS

At the title screen, press X, Y, B, B, Y, X, L, L, R, R, Up, Down, Left, Right, Start, Select.

3,000,000 STUDS

At the title screen, press Up, Up, B, Down, Down, X, Left, Left, Y, L, R, L, R, B, Y, X, Start, Select.

LEGO STAR WARS II: THE ORIGINAL TRILOGY

10 STUDS

At the Mos Eisley cantina, enter 4PR28U.

OBI WAN GHOST

At the Mos Eisley cantina, enter BEN917.

LEGO STAR WARS: THE COMPLETE SAGA

3,000,000 STUDS

At the main menu, press Start, Start, Down, Down, Left, Left, Up, Up, Select. This cheat can only be used once.

DEBUG MENUS

At the main menu, press Up, Left, Down, Right, Up, Left, Down, Right, Up, Left, Down, Right, R, L, Start, Select.

BONUS TOUCH GAME 1

At the main menu, press Up, Up, Down, L, L, R, R.

LITTLEST PET SHOP: GARDEN

GIRAFFE PET

Select Passwords from the Options and enter LPSTRU. It is available in the Meow Market.

LITTLEST PET SHOP: JUNGLE

GIRAFFE PET

Select Passwords from the Options and enter LPSTRU. It is available in the Meow Market.

LOCK'S QUEST

REPLACE CLOCKWORKS WITH KINGDOM FORCE

After completing the game, hold R and select your profile.

ENDING STORY

After completing the game, hold L and select your profile.

MARIO PARTY DS

BOSS BASH

Complete Story Mode.

EXPERT CPU DIFFICULTY LEVEL

Complete Story Mode.

MUSIC AND VOICE ROOM

Complete Story Mode.

SCORE SCUFFLE

Complete Story Mode.

TRIANGLE TWISTER PUZZLE MODE

Complete Story Mode.

MEGA MAN STAR FORCE 3: BLACK ACE

STARS ON NEW GAME/CONTINUE SCREEN

Do the following to earn each star on the New Game/Continue screen.

STAR	HOW TO EARN
Black Ace	Defeat the game
G Comp	Collect all Giga cards
M Comp	Collect all Mega cards
S Comp	Collect all Standard cards
SS	Defeat Sirius

RANDOM SIGMA BOSSES

At the New Game/Continue screen, hold L and tap S Comp Star, G Comp Star, S Comp Star, M Comp Star, SS Star, SS Star, Black Ace Star.

FIGHT ROGUEZZ

At the New Game/Continue screen, hold L and tap G Comp Star, M Comp Star, M Comp Star, SS Star, G Comp Star, S Comp Star, Black Ace Star. RogueZZ appears in Meteor G Control CC.

MEGA MAN STAR FORCE 3: RED JOKER

STARS ON NEW GAME/CONTINUE SCREEN

Star	How to earn
DO THE FOLLOWING TO EARN EACH STAR ON THE NEW GAME/CONTINUE SCREEN.	
Red Joker	Defeat the game
G Comp	Collect all Giga cards
M Comp	Collect all Mega cards
S Comp	Collect all Standard cards
SS	Defeat Sirius

RANDOM SIGMA BOSSES

At the New Game/Continue screen, hold L and tap S Comp Star, G Comp Star, S Comp Star, M Comp Star, SS Star, SS Star, Red Joker Star.

FIGHT ROGUEZZ

At the New Game/Continue screen, hold L and tap G Comp Star, M Comp Star, M Comp Star, SS Star, G Comp Star, S Comp Star, Red Joker Star. RogueZZ appears in Meteor G Control CC.

METROID PRIME PINBALL

PHAZON MINES

Complete Omega Pirate in Multi Mission mode.

PHENDRANA DRIFTS

Complete Thardus in Multi Mission mode.

MY JAPANESE COACH

UNLOCK LESSONS

Look up the word cheat in the dictionary. Touch the V next to the verb to open the conjugation chart. Hold L + R for a few seconds. You should hear the word cheat in Japanese. Return to the main menu, go to Options, then Sound. Pressing R will advance you 1 lesson, and pressing L will advance you to the beginning of the next lesson group.

MY WORD COACH

WORD POPPERS MINIGAME

After reaching 200 word successes, at the options menu, press A, B, X, Y, A, B.

MYSIMS KINGDOM

SAMURAI ARMOR

Pause the game and press Y, X, Right, Left, L, R, Down, Up.

SAMURAI HELMET

Pause the game and press X, Y, R, L, X, Y, R, L.

DETECTIVE OUTFIT

Pause the game and press Left, Right, Left, Right, Left, Right.

PUNK BOTTOM

Pause the game and press Left, R, L, Right, Y, Y, X, X.

PUNK TOP

Pause the game and press Up, X, Down, Y, Left, L, Right, R.

N+

ATARI BONUS LEVELS

Select Unlockables from the main menu, hold L + R and press A, B, A, B, A, A, B.

NAMCO MUSEUM DS

DIG-DUG 2 OLD VERSION

From the Dig Dug 2 menu, select Hardcore Options from the Settings. Change New Version to Old.

SECRET GAME: SUPER XEVIOUS

From the Xevious menu, select Hardcore Options from the Settings. Change the version to Super Xevious.

NARUTO: PATH OF THE NINJA

After defeating the game, talk to Knohamaru on the roof of the Ninja Academy. He allows you go get certain cheats by tapping four successive spots on the touch screen in order. There are 12 different spots on the screen. We have numbered them from left to right, top to bottom, as follows:

1	2	3	4
5	6	7	8
9	10	11	12

Enter the following codes by touching the four spots in the order listed.

UNLOCK	CODE
4th Hokage's Sword	4, 7, 11, 5
Fuji Fan	8, 11, 2, 5
Jiraiya	11, 3, 1, 6
Rajin's Sword	7, 6, 5, 11
Rasengan	9, 2, 12, 7

NARUTO: PATH OF THE NINJA 2

CHARACTER PASSWORDS

Talk to Konohamaru at the school to enter the following passwords. You must first complete the game for the passwords to work.

CHARACTER	PASSWORD
Gaara	D K F I A B J L
Gai	I K A G D E F L
Iruka	J G D L K A I B
Itachi Uchiha	G B E I D A L F
Jiraiya	E B J D A G F L
Kankuro	A L J K B E D G
Kyuubi Naruto	G J H L B F D E
Orochimaru	A H F B L E J G
Temari	H F I C L K B G
The Third Hokage	C G H A J B E L

MISSION PASSWORDS

Talk to Konohamaru at the school to enter the following passwords. You must first complete the game for the passwords to work.

MISSION	PASSWORD
An Extreme Battle!	H L B A K G C D
The Legendary Haze Ninja!	F G E H I D A L
The Legendary Sannin!	B C E G K F H L

NEED FOR SPEED CARBON: OWN THE CITY

INFINITE NITROUS
At the Main menu, press Up, Up, Down, Left, A, B, B, A.

NEW SUPER MARIO BROS.

PLAY AS LUIGI IN SINGLE PLAYER
At the Select a File screen, hold L + R while selecting a saved game.

SECRET CHALLENGE MODE
On the map, pause the game and press L, R, L, R, X, X, Y, Y.

THE NEW YORK TIMES CROSSWORDS

BLACK & WHITE
At the Main menu, press Up, Up, Down, Down, B, B, Y, Y.

NICKTOONS: ATTACK OF THE TOYBOTS

DANNY PHANTOM 2
Select Unlock Code from the Options and enter Tak, Jimmy, Zim, El Tigre.

SPONGEBOB 2
Select Unlock Code from the Options and enter Patrick, Jenny, Timmy, Tak.

NICKTOONS: BATTLE FOR VOLCANO ISLAND

FRUIT BECOMES TOYS IN FRUIT COLLECTING MINI-GAME
Select Unlock Codes from the Options and enter Spongebob, Danny, Timmy, Cosmo.

NIGHT AT THE MUSEUM: BATTLE OF THE SMITHSONIAN

SUPER LARRY
During a game, hold L + R, and press Left, A, Right, Right, Y.

PEGGLE: DUAL SHOT

Q LEVEL 10
Send the trial game to another DS.

PHINEAS AND FERB

STOP CANDACE
At the title screen, press X, Y, L, R, Select.

DOUBLE SPEED
At the title screen, press A, B, L, R, Select.

PIRATES OF THE CARIBBEAN: DEAD MAN'S CHEST

10 GOLD
During a game, press Right, X, X, Right, Left.

INVINCIBILITY
During a game, press Up, Down, Left, Right (x5), Left, Right, Up, Down, Left, Right, Up (x5), Left.

UNLIMITED POWER
During a game, press Up, Up, Down, Down, Left, Right, Left, Right, L, R.

RESTORE HEALTH
During a game, press Y, Y, Select, Left, Right, Left, Right, Left.

RESTORE SAVVY
During a game, press X, X, Select, Up, Down, Up, Down, Up.

GHOST FORM MODE
During a game, press Y, X, Y, X, Y, X.

SEASICKNESS MODE
During a game, press X, X, Y, X, X, Y.

SILLY WEAPONS
During a game, press Y, Y, X, Y (x3).

AXE
During a game, press Left, L, L, Down, Down, Left, Up, Up, Down, Down.

BLUNDERBUSS
During a game, press Down, L, L, Down (x3).

CHICKEN
During a game, press Right, L, L, Up, Down, Down.

EXECUTIONER AXE
During a game, press Right, L, L, Up, Down, Up, Right, Right, Left(x2).

PIG
During a game, press Right, R, R, Down, Up, Up.

PISTOL
During a game, press Down, L, L, Down, Down, Right.

RIFLE
During a game, press Left, L, L, Up (x3).

FAST MUSIC
During a game, press Y, Select, Y (x4).

SLOW MUSIC
During a game, press Y, Select, X (x4).

DISABLE CHEATS
During a game, press X (x6).

RACE DRIVER: CREATE & RACE

ALL CHALLENGES
Select Cheat Codes from Extras and enter 942785.

ALL CHAMPIONSHIPS
Select Cheat Codes from Extras and enter 761492.

ALL REWARDS
Select Cheat Codes from Extras and enter 112337.

FREE DRIVE
Select Cheat Codes from Extras and enter 171923.

NO DAMAGE
Select Cheat Codes from Extras and enter 505303.

EASY STEERING
Select Cheat Codes from Extras and enter 611334.

MINIATURE CARS
Select Cheat Codes from Extras and enter 374288.

MM VIEW
Select Cheat Codes from Extras and enter 467348.

RETRO GAME CHALLENGE

COSMIC GATE

HARD MODE
At the title screen, press Down, Down, B, B, A, A, Start.

POWERED-UP INFINITY
Pause the game and press Up, Up, A, B. This cheat can only be used once per game.

SKIP POWER-UP
Pause the game and press Up, Up, A, A, B, B.

CONTINUE GAME
At the Game Over screen, press Left + Start. You will continue the game with a score of 000.

INFINITE TIME
Before a level, hold Up/Left and press A + B.

HAGGLE MAN CODES

FULL HEALTH
Pause the game and press Down, Right, Up, Left, B, B, B, A, A, A.

SCROLLS APPEAR
Pause the game press Up Right Down Left A A A B B B B.

HAGGLE MAN 2

STAGE SELECT
At the title screen, hold A and press Up, Right, Right, Down, Down, Left, Left.

FULL POWER
Pause the game and press Up, Down, Up, Down, B, A, A.

SCROLLS APPEAR
Pause the game and press Down, Up, Up, A, A, B.

CONTINUE
At the Game Over scree

HAGGLE MAN 3

9999 GEARS
Pause the game and press B, A, B, A, Right. Left, Right, Left.

99 LIVES
Pause the game and press A, B, B, Left, Right, Left, Right.

WARP TO BOSS
Pause the game and press B, B, A, Left, Left, Right, Right.

RALLY KING

INVINCIBILITY

At the title screen, press Select + Left.

CARS DISAPPEAR

At the title screen, hold Select and press Down/Right.

START AT COURSE 2

At the title screen, press A, B, A, B, Up + Select.

START AT COURSE 3

At the title screen, press A, B, A, B, Left + Select.

START AT COURSE 4

At the title screen, press A, B, A, B, Down + Select.

STAR PRINCE

INVINCIBILITY

At the title screen, hold Up and press A, A, A. Then, hold Down and press B, B, B.

CONTINUE

At the Game Over screen, hold Left and press Start.

RHYTHM HEAVEN

RHYTHM TOYS - TELEPHONE NUMBERS

Enter the following numbers into the telephone in Rhythm Toys to unlock sounds from Rhythm Tengoku:

5553282338
5557325937
5557268724
5557625688

RUBIK'S PUZZLE WORLD

ALL LEVELS AND CUBIES

At the main menu, press X, Y, Y, X, X.

SCOOBY-DOO! FIRST FRIGHTS

DAPHNE'S SECRET COSTUME

Select Codes from the Extras menu and enter 2839.

FRED'S SECRET COSTUME

Select Codes from the Extras menu and enter 4826.

SCOOBY DOO'S SECRET COSTUME

Select Codes from the Extras menu and enter 1585.

SHAGGY'S SECRET COSTUME

Select Codes from the Extras menu and enter 3726.

VELMA'S SECRET COSTUME

Select Codes from the Extras menu and enter 6588.

SIMCITY CREATOR

99999999 MONEY

Enter MONEYBAGS as a password.

AMERICAN PROSPERITY AGE MAP

Enter NEWWORLD as a password.

ASIA AGE MAP

Enter SAMURAI as a password.

ASIA AGE BONUS MAP

Enter FEUDAL as a password.

DAWN OF CIVILIZATION MAP

Enter ANCIENT as a password.

GLOBAL WARMING MAP

Enter MODERN as a password.

GLOBAL WARMING BONUS MAP

Enter BEYOND as a password.

RENAISSANCE BONUS MAP

Enter HEREANDNOW as a password.

SIMCITY DS

LANDMARK BUILDINGS

Select Landmark Collection from the Museum menu. Choose Password and enter the following:

BUILDING	PASSWORD	BUILDING	PASSWORD
Anglican Cathedral (UK)	kipling	Melbourne Cricket Ground (Australia)	damemelba
Arc de Triomphe (France)	gaugin	Metropolitan Cath. (UK)	austen
Atomic Dome (Japan)	kawabata	Moai (Chile)	allende
Big Ben (UK)	orwell	Mt. Fuji (Japan)	hiroshige
Bowser Castle (Nintendo)	hanafuda	National Museum (Taiwan)	yuantlee
Brandenburg Gate (Germany)	gropius	Neuschwanstein Castle (Germany)	beethoven
Coit Tower	kerouac	Notre Dame (France)	hugo
Conciergerie (France)	rodin	Palace of Fine Arts (USA)	bunche
Daibutsu (Japan)	mishima	Palacio Real (Spain)	cervantes
Edo Castle (Japan)	shonagon	Paris Opera (France)	daumier
Eiffel Tower (France)	camus	Parthenon (Greece)	callas
Gateway Arch (USA)	twain	Pharos of Alexandria (Egypt)	zewail
Grand Central Station (USA)	f.scott	Rama IX Royal Park (Thailand)	phu
Great Pyramids (Egypt)	mahfouz	Reichstag (Germany)	goethe
Hagia Sofia (Turkey)	ataturk	Sagrada Familia (Spain)	dali
Helsinki Cathedral (Finland)	kivi	Shuri Castle (Japan)	basho
Himeji Castle (Japan)	hokusai	Smithsonian Castle (USA)	pauling
Holstentor (Germany)	durer	Sphinx (Egypt)	haykal
Independence Hall (USA)	mlkingjr	St Paul's Cathedral (UK)	defoe
Jefferson Memorial (USA)	thompson	St. Basil's Cathedral (Russia)	tolstoy
Kokkai (Japan)	soseki	St. Stephen's Cathedral (Austria)	mozart
LA Landmark (USA)	hemingway	Statue of Liberty (USA)	pollack
Lincoln Memorial (USA)	melville	Stockholm Palace (Sweden)	bergman
Liver Building (UK)	dickens	Taj Mahal (India)	tagore

BUILDING	PASSWORD	BUILDING	PASSWORD
Tower of London (UK)	maugham	Washington Monument	capote
Trafalgar Square (UK)	joyce	Westminster Abbey (UK)	greene
United Nations (UN)	amnesty	White House (USA)	Steinbeck
United States Capitol (USA)	poe		

THE SIMS 2

MONGOO MONKEY FOR THE CASINO

Start the game with Sims 2 in the GBA slot of your Nintendo DS.

THE SIMS 2 APARTMENT PETS

$10,000

From the PDA screen, select the disk icon. Then choose Unlockable from the Options and enter Cash.

SKATE IT

EMO CRYS

At the Credits screen, press Up, Up, Left, Left, Down, Down, Right, Right.

JACK KNIFE

At the Credits screen, press X, A, X, Y, Up, Left, Down, Right.

JAY JAY

At the Credits screen, press L, R, A, Left, Right, Y, R, L.

LIL' ROB

At the Credits screen, press L, Left, Y, R, Right, A, Up, X.

SPITBALL

At the Credits screen, press Up, Up, Down, Down, L, R, L, R.

SOUL BUBBLES

REVEAL ALL CALABASH LOCATIONS

Pause the game and press A, L, L, R, A, Down, A, R.

ALL LEVELS

At the World Select, press L, Up, X, Up, R, Y.

ALL GALLERY ITEMS

At the Gallery, press B, Up, B, B, L, Y.

SPECTROBES

CARD INPUT SYSTEM

When the Upsilon Cube is unearthed and shown to Aldous, the Card Input System feature becomes available. This will allow you to input data from Spectrobe Cards. These give you new Spectrobes and Custom Parts. If you get your hands on a Spectrobe Card and the system is unlocked, investigate the card input system in the spaceship's lower deck.

Follow the instructions on the upper screen to match the four corner points of the card to the corners of the touch screen. Touch the screen through the seven holes in the card in the order indicated on the card. If the code you input is correct, you receive Spectrobes, custom Parts, minerals or Cubes.

You can input the same card a maximum of four times. This means that you can only obtain four of the same Spectrobes from a single card. You can only input cards once. And some cards cannot be input until you have reached a certain point in the game.

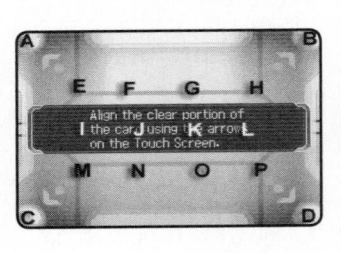

The following table gives you a seven character code which refers to the spots you touch in order. The first four characters have you touching the four corners and the final three are spots among the 12 in the middle. To get Cyclone Geo, Hammer Geo, Ice Geo, Plasma Geo, or Thunder Geo, you must first beat the game.

EFFECT	CODE	EFFECT	CODE
Aobasat Apex	BACD HEP	Sapphire Mineral	ABDC FJO
Cyclone Geo	CDAB LGM	Sequlos Propos	CDAB KIH
Danaphant Tuska	ABDC ELI	Sequslice	CDAB GKP
Danilob	DABC GLO	Shakor Bristle	DABC MLK
Emerald Mineral	BACD FKN	Sigma Cube	CDAB PML
Grilden Biblad	ABDC FIH	Tau Cube	DABC LIF
Grildragos Drafly	CDAB MHK	Thunder Geo	DABC MEL
Gristar	BACD EJN	Vilagrisp (Custom Part)	DABC EIN
Hammer Geo	ABDC ELH	Vilakroma	BACD NLM
Harumitey Lazos	DABC ILM	Vilakroma (Custom Color 1)	CDAB LJI
Ice Geo	CDAB HEK	Vilakroma (Custom Color 2)	DABC EGP
Inataflare Auger	ABDC IGH	Windora	ABDC MGP
Inkalade	ABDC GLP	Windora (Custom Color 1)	DABC EHG
Iota Cube	ABDC OHE	Windora (Custom Color 2)	CDAB JPM
Komainu	CDAB HMJ	Windora Ortex	BACD IPG
Kugaster Sonara	DABC LOE	Windora Ortex (Custom Color 1)	ABDC MPH
Mossax Jetspa (Custom Color 1)	BACD JML	Windora Ortex (Custom Color 2)	DABC MGH
Naglub	ABDC EJM	Windora Sordina	CDAB PEO
Plasma Geo	BACD KLE	Windora Sordina (Custom Color 1)	BACD MOH
Rho Cube	BACD PNI	Windora Sordina (Custom Color 2)	ABDC LEN
Ruby Mineral	CDAB FKO	Wing Geo (must beat game)	DABC MNP
Samukabu	ABDC OIL		
Samurite Voltar	BACD LHM		

SPIDER-MAN 2

ALL SPECIAL MOVES

Load the game with Spider-Man: Mysterio's Menace for Game Boy Advance in the Nintendo DS.

SPONGEBOB SQUAREPANTS
FEATURING NICKTOONS: GLOBS OF DOOM

INFINITE HEALTH

Select Unlock Codes from the Options and enter Tak, Tlaloc, Jimmy Neutron, Beautiful Gorgeous.

INSTANT KO

Select Unlock Codes from the Options and enter Dib, Tak, Beautiful Gorgeous, Plankton.

EXTRA ATTACK

Select Unlock Codes from the Options and enter Dib, Plankton, Technus, Jimmy Neutron.

EXTRA DEFENSE

Select Unlock Codes from the Options and enter Zim, Danny Phantom, Plankton, Beautiful Gorgeous.

MAX DEFENSE

Select Unlock Codes from the Options and enter Plankton, Dib, Beautiful Gorgeous, Plankton.

ITEMS +

Select Unlock Codes from the Options and enter Danny Phantom, Beautiful Gorgeous, Jimmy Neutron, Technus.

ITEMS ++

Select Unlock Codes from the Options and enter SpongeBob, Tlaloc, SpongeBob, Danny Phantom.

NO HEALTH ITEMS

Select Unlock Codes from the Options and enter Tak, SpongeBob, Technus, Danny Phantom.

LOWER PRICES

Select Unlock Codes from the Options and enter Tlaloc, Zim, Beautiful Gorgeous, SpongeBob.

SUPER BEAUTIFUL GORGEOUS

Select Unlock Codes from the Options and enter Beautiful Gorgeous, Technus, Jimmy Neutron, Beautiful Gorgeous.

SUPER DANNY PHANTOM

Select Unlock Codes from the Options and enter Danny Phantom, Zim, Danny Phantom, Beautiful Gorgeous.

SUPER DIB

Select Unlock Codes from the Options and enter Zim, Plankton, Dib, Plankton.

SUPER JIMMY

Select Unlock Codes from the Options and enter Technus, Danny Phantom, Jimmy Neutron, Technus.

SUPER PLANKTON

Select Unlock Codes from the Options and enter Tak, Plankton, Dib, Technus.

SUPER SPONGEBOB

Select Unlock Codes from the Options and enter Technus, SpongeBob, Technus, Tlaloc.

SUPER TAK

Select Unlock Codes from the Options and enter Danny Phantom, Jimmy Neutron, Tak, Tlaloc.

SUPER TECHNUS

Select Unlock Codes from the Options and enter Danny Phantom, Technus, Tak, Technus.

SUPER TLALOC

Select Unlock Codes from the Options and enter Tlaloc, Beautiful Gorgeous, Dib, SpongeBob.

SUPER ZIM

Select Unlock Codes from the Options and enter Plankton, Zim, Technus, SpongeBob.

SUPER JETPACK

Select Unlock Codes from the Options and enter Beautiful Gorgeous, Tlaloc, Jimmy Neutron, Jimmy Neutron.

COLORLESS ENEMIES

Select Unlock Codes from the Options and enter Technus, Jimmy Neutron, Tlaloc, Plankton.

BLUE ENEMIES

Select Unlock Codes from the Options and enter Beautiful Gorgeous, Zim, Plankton, Technus.

RED ENEMIES

Select Unlock Codes from the Options and enter SpongeBob, Tak, Jimmy Neutron, Danny Phantom.

DIFFICULT ENEMIES

Select Unlock Codes from the Options and enter SpongeBob, Dib, Dib, Technus.

DIFFICULT BOSSES

Select Unlock Codes from the Options and enter Plankton, Beautiful Gorgeous, Technus, Tlaloc.

INVINCIBLE PARTNER

Select Unlock Codes from the Options and enter Plankton, Tak, Beautiful Gorgeous, SpongeBob.

STAR TREK: TACTICAL ASSAULT

KLINGON CAMPAIGN

At the Main menu, press Up, Down, Left, Right, Select, Start, X.

UNLOCK MISSIONS

At the Main menu, press Up, Down, Left, Right, Select, Start, Start.

EXTRA CREW UPGRADES

At the Main menu, press Up, Down, Left, Right, Select, Start, Select.

ALL SHIPS IN SKIRMISH AND MULTIPLAYER

At the Main menu, press Up, Down, Left, Right, Select, Start, Y.

ANY SHIP IN MISSIONS

At the Main menu, press Up, Down, Left, Right, Select, Start, B.

STAR WARS: THE FORCE UNLEASHED

INCREASED HEALTH

Select Unleashed Codes from the Extras menu and enter QSSPVENXO.

UNLIMITED FORCE ENERGY

Select Unleashed Codes from the Extras menu and enter TVENCVMJZ.

MAX OUT FORCE POWERS

Select Unleashed Codes from the Extras menu and enter CPLOOLKBF.

MORE POWERFUL LIGHTSABER

Select Unleashed Codes from the Extras menu and enter lightsaber.

UBER LIGHTSABER
Select Unleashed Codes from the Extras menu and enter MOMIROXIW.

ROM KOTA
Select Unleashed Codes from the Extras menu and enter mandalore.

CEREMONIAL JEDI ROBES
Select Unleashed Codes from the Extras menu and enter CURSEZRUX.

DAD'S ROBES
Select Unleashed Codes from the Extras menu and enter wookiee.

DARTH VADER'S COSTUME
Select Unleashed Codes from the Extras menu and enter HRMXRKVEN.

KENTO'S ROBE
Select Unleashed Codes from the Extras menu and enter KBVMSEVNM.

KOTA'S OUTFIT
Select Unleashed Codes from the Extras menu and enter EEDOPVENG.

SITH ROBE
Select Unleashed Codes from the Extras menu and enter ZWSFVENXA.

SITH ROBES
Select Unleashed Codes from the Extras menu and enter holocron.

SITH STALKER ARMOR
Select Unleashed Codes from the Extras menu and enter CPLZKMZTD.

STAR WARS EPISODE III: REVENGE OF THE SITH

MASTER DIFFICULTY
Defeat the game.

ANAKIN'S STARFIGHTER
Beat the Anakin bot in multiplayer.

DARTH VADER'S TIE FIGHTER
Defeat the Darth Vader bot in multiplayer.

GENERAL GREVIOUS'S STARFIGHTER
Defeat the General Grevious bot in multiplayer.

MILLENIUM FALCON
Defeat the Solo bot in multiplayer.

SLAVE I
Defeat the Fett bot in multiplayer.

X-WING
Defeat the Luke bot in multiplayer.

SUPER ROBOT TAISEN OG SAGA: ENDLESS FRONTIER

NEW GAME +
After you have finished the game and saved, load your save and start again with your items and money.

OG1 CHOKER
Start a new game or load a saved file with the GBA game Super Robot Taisen: Original Generation in the GBA slot. This item boosts your SP by 100.

OG2 PENDANT
Start a new game or load a saved file with the GBA game Super Robot Taisen 2: Original Generation in the GBA slot. This item boosts your HP by 250.

TAMAGOTCHI CONNECTION: CORNER SHOP 3

DOUBLE LAYERED CAKE
Select Enter Code from the Special menu and enter R6194BJD6F.

TIGER WOODS PGA TOUR 2005

EMERALD DRAGON
Earn $1,000,000.

GREEK ISLES
Earn $1,500,000.

PARADISE COVER
Earn $2,000,000.

EA SPORTS FAVORITES
Earn $5,000,000

MEAN8TEEN
Earn $10,000,000.

FANTASY SPECIALS
Earn $15,000,000.

LEGEND COMPILATION 1
Defeat Hogan in Legend Tour.

LEGEND COMPILATION 2
Defeat Gary Player in Legend Tour.

LEGEND COMPILATION 3
Defeat Ballesteros in Legend Tour.

LEGEND COMPILATION 4
Defeat Palmer in Legend Tour.

LEGEND COMPILATION 5
Defeat Nicklaus in Legend Tour.

THE HUSTLER'S DREAM 18
Defeat The Hustler in Legend Tour.

TIGER'S DREAM 18
Defeat Tiger Woods in Legend Tour.

TOM CLANCY'S SPLINTER CELL CHAOS THEORY

UNLIMITED AMMO/GADGETS
Defeat the game.

CHARACTER SKINS
Defeat the game.

TONY HAWK'S DOWNHILL JAM

ALWAYS SNOWSKATE
Select Buy Stuff from the Skateshop. Choose Enter Code and enter SNOWSK8T.

MIRRORED MAPS
Select Buy Stuff from the Skateshop. Choose Enter Code and enter MIRRORBALL.

ABOMINABLE SNOWMAN OUTFIT
Select Buy Stuff from the Skateshop. Choose Enter Code and enter BIGSNOWMAN.

ZOMBIE SKATER OUTFIT
Select Buy Stuff from the Skateshop. Choose Enter Code and enter ZOMBIEALIVE.

THE URBZ: SIMS IN THE CITY

CLUB XIZZLE
Once you gain access to Club Xizzle, enter with the password "bucket."

WORLD CHAMPIONSHIP POKER

UNLOCK CASINOS
At the Title screen, press Y, X, Y, B, L, R. Then press the following direction:

DIRECTION	CASINO
Left	Amazon
Right	Nebula
Down	Renaissance

YU-GI-OH! NIGHTMARE TROUBADOUR

CREDITS

Unlock the Password Machine by defeating the Expert Cup. Enter the Duel Shop and select the Slot maching. Enter 00000375.

SOUND TEST

Unlock the Password Machine by defeating the Expert Cup. Enter the Duel Shop and select the Slot maching. Enter 57300000.

YU-GI-OH! WORLD CHAMPIONSHIP 2007

CARD PASSWORDS

Select Password from the Shop and enter one of the Card Passwords. You must already have that card or have it in a pack list for the password to work. Refer to the Card List for YU-GI-OH! GX TAG FORCE for PSP. All cards may not be available in World Championship 2007.

YU-GI-OH! WORLD CHAMPIONSHIP 2008

CARD PASSWORDS

Enter the following in the password machine to receive the corresponding card. You must already have the card to use the password.

PASSWORD EFFECT

CARD	PASSWORD	CARD	PASSWORD
7	67048711	Aqua Madoor	85639257
7 Colored Fish	23771716	Aqua Spirit	40916023
7 Completed	86198326	Archfiend of Gilfer	50287060
A Feint Plan	68170903	Armed Changer	90374791
A Hero Emerges	21597117	Armed Ninja	09076207
Abyss Soldier	18318842	Armored Glass	21070956
Acid Rain	21323861	Armored Zombie	20277860
Acid Trap Hole	41356845	Array of Revealing Light	69296555
Adhesive Explosive	53828196	Arsenal Bug	42364374
Agido	16135253	Arsenal Robber	55348096
Airknight Parshath	18036057	Assault on GHQ	62633180
Aitsu	48202661	Asura Priest	02134346
Alkana Knight Joker	06150044	Attack and Receive	63689843
Alligator's Sword	64428736	Autonomous Action Unit	71453557
Alligator's Sword Dragon	03366982	Axe of Despair	40619825
Alpha the Magnet Warrior	99785935	Axe Raider	48305365
Altar for Tribute	21070956	B. Skull Dragon	11901678
Amazon Archer	91869203	Baby Dragon	88819587
Amazoness Archers	67987611	Back to Square One	47453433
Amazoness Blowpiper	73574678	Backfire	82705573
Amazoness Chain Master	29654737	Bad Reaction to Simochi	40633297
Amazoness Fighter	55821894	Bait Doll	07165085
Amazoness Paladin	47480070	Ballista of Rampart Smashing	00242146
Amazoness Spellcaster	81325903	Banisher of the Light	61528025
Amazoness Swords Woman	94004268	Banner of Courage	10012614
Amazoness Tiger	10979723	Bark of The Dark Ruler	41925941
Amphibian Beast	67371383	Baron of the Fiend Sword	86325596
Amplifier	00303660	Barrel Behind the Door	78783370
Anti-Spell	53112492	Barrel Dragon	81480460

CARD	PASSWORD	CARD	PASSWORD
Battery Charger	61181383	Castle Walls	44209392
Batteryman AA	63142001	Catapult Turtle	95727991
Batteryman C	19733961	Ceasefire	36468556
Batteryman D	55401221	Celtic Guardian	91152256
Battle Ox	05053103	Cemetery Bomb	51394546
Battle Warrior	55550921	Centrifugal Field	01801154
Beast Fangs	46009906	Cestus of Dagla	28106077
Beast Soul Swap	35149085	Chain Destruction	01248895
Beastking of the Swamps	99426834	Chain Disappearance	57139487
Beautiful Headhuntress	16899564	Chain Energy	79323590
Beckoning Light	16255442	Chaos Command Magician	72630549
Berfomet	77207191	Chaos End	61044390
Berserk Gorilla	39168895	Chaos Greed	97439308
Beta the Magnet Warrior	39256679	Chimera the Flying Mythical Beast	04796100
Bickuribox	25655502	Chiron the Mage	16956455
Big Bang Shot	61127349	Chorus of Sanctuary	81380218
Big Eye	16768387	Chthonian Alliance	46910446
Big Shield Gardna	65240384	Chthonian Blast	18271561
Birdface	45547649	Chthonian Polymer	72287557
Black Illusion Ritual	41426869	Clay Charge	22479888
Black Luster Ritual	55761792	Cocoon of Evolution	40240595
Black Luster Soldier	72989439	Coffin Seller	65830223
Black Magic Ritual	76792184	Cold Wave	60682203
Black Pendant	65169794	Command Knight	10375182
Bladefly	28470714	Conscription	31000575
Blast Held by a Tribute	89041555	Continuous Destruction Punch	68057622
Blast Magician	21051146	Contract with Exodia	33244944
Blast Sphere	26302522	Contract with the Dark Master	96420087
Blast with Chain	98239899	Convulsion of Nature	62966332
Blasting the Ruins	21466326	Copycat	26376390
Blessings of the Nile	30653173	Cosmo Queen	38999506
Blowback Dragon	25551951	Covering Fire	74458486
Blue Medicine	20871001	Crass Clown	93889755
Blue-Eyes Toon Dragon	53183600	Crawling Dragon #2	38289717
Blue-Eyes Ultimate Dragon	23995346	Crimson Sunbird	46696593
Blue-Eyes White Dragon	80906030	Crush Card Virus	57728570
Blue-Eyes White Dragon	80906030	Curse of Anubis	66742250
Book of Taiyou	38699854	Curse of Darkness	84970821
Bottomless Trap Hole	29401950	Curse of Dragon	28279543
Bowganian	52090844	Curse of the Masked Beast	94377247
Bracchio-Raidus	16507828	Cursed Seal of the Forbidden Spell	58851034
Brain Control	87910978	Cyber Raider	39978267
Breaker the Magical Warrior	71413901	Cyber Shield	63224564
Breath of Light	20101223	Cyber-Tech Alligator	48766543
Bright Castle	82878489	D.D. Borderline	60912752
Burning Land	24294108	D.D. Designator	33423043
Burning Spear	18937875	D.D. Assailant	70074904
Burst Return	27191436	D.D. Dynamite	08628798
Burst Stream of Destruction	17655904	D.D. Trap Hole	05606466
Buster Rancher	84740193	D.D. Warrior	37043180
Cannon Soldier	11384280	D.D. Warrior Lady	07572887
Cannonball Spear Shellfish	95614612	D. Tribe	02833249
Card Destruction	72892473	Dark Artist	72520073
Card of Sanctity	04266498	Dark Deal	65824822
Card Shuffle	12183332	Dark Dust Spirit	89111398
Castle of Dark Illusions	00062121	Dark Elf	21417692

CARD	PASSWORD
Dark Energy	04614116
Dark Factory of Mass Production	90928333
Dark Jeroid	90980792
Dark Magic Attack	02314238
Dark Magic Curtain	99789342
Dark Magician	46986414
Dark Magician Girl	38033121
Dark Magician of Chaos	40737112
Dark Master - Zorc	97642679
Dark Mimic LV1	74713516
Dark Mimic LV3	01102515
Dark Mirror Force	20522190
Dark Necrofear	31829185
Dark Paladin	98502113
Dark Rabbit	99261403
Dark Room of Nightmare	85562745
Dark Sage	92377303
Dark Snake Syndrome	47233801
Dark Spirit of the Silent	93599951
Dark World Lightning	93554166
Darkness Approaches	80168720
Dark-Piercing Light	45895206
Deck Devastation Virus	35027493
Decoy Dragon	02732323
Dedication through Light and Darkness	69542930
De-Fusion	95286165
Delta Attacker	39719977
Despair from the Dark	71200730
De-Spell	19159413
Destiny Board	94212438
Destruction Ring	21219755
Dian Keto the Cure Master	84257639
Dice Re-Roll	83241722
Different Dimension Capsule	11961034
Different Dimension Dragon	50939127
Different Dimension Gate	56460688
Diffusion Wave-Motion	87880531
Dimension Fusion	23557835
Dimension Wall	67095270
Dimensional Prison	70342110
Dimensionhole	22959079
Disappear	24623598
Disarmament	20727787
Divine Sword - Phoenix Blade	31423101
Divine Wrath	49010598
DNA Surgery	74701381
Doomcaliber Knight	78700060
Double Coston	44436472
Double Snare	03682106
Double Spell	24096228
Dragged Down into the Grave	16435235
Dragon Capture Jar	50045299
Dragon Seeker	28563545
Dragon Treasure	01435851
Dragonic Attack	32437102

CARD	PASSWORD
Dragon's Mirror	71490127
Draining Shield	43250041
Dramatic Rescue	80193355
Dream Clown	13215230
Drill Bug	88733579
Driving Snow	00473469
Drop Off	55773067
Dunames Dark Witch	12493482
Dust Barrier	31476755
Dust Tornado	60082867
Earth Chant	59820352
Earthbound Spirit's Invitation	65743242
Earthquake	82828051
Eatgaboon	42578427
Ectoplasmer	97342942
Ekibyo Drakmord	69954399
Electro-Whip	37820550
Elegant Egotist	90219263
Elemental Hero Avian	21844576
Elemental Hero Burstinatrix	58932615
Elemental Hero Clayman	84327329
Elemental Hero Flame Wingman	35809262
Elemental Hero Rampart Blaster	47737087
Elemental Hero Sparkman	20721928
Elemental Hero Thunder Giant	61204971
Embodiment of Apophis	28649820
Emergency Provisions	53046408
Enchanted Arrow	93260132
Enchanting Fitting Room	30531525
Enemy Controller	98045062
Energy Drain	56916805
Enervating Mist	26022485
Enraged Battle Ox	76909279
Eradicating Aerosol	94716515
Eternal Drought	56606928
Eternal Rest	95051344
Exarion Universe	63749102
Exchange	05556668
Exhausting Spell	95451366
Exodia Necross	12600382
Exodia the Forbidden One	33396948
Fairy Box	21598948
Fairy King Truesdale	45425051
Fairy Meteor Crush	97687912
Fairy's Hand Mirror	17653779
Fake Trap	03027001
Feather Shot	19394153
Feather Wind	71060915
Fengsheng Mirror	37406863
Feral Imp	41392891
Fiend Comedian	81172176
Fiend Skull Dragon	66235877
Fiend's Hand Mirror	58607704
Fiend's Sanctuary	24874630
Final Countdown	95308449
Final Destiny	18591904

32

CARD	PASSWORD	CARD	PASSWORD
Firewing Pegasus	27054370	Granadora	13944422
Fissure	66788016	Grand Tiki Elder	13676474
Flame Cerebrus	60862676	Gravedigger Ghoul	82542267
Flame Manipulator	34460851	Gravekeeper's Assailant	25262697
Flame Swordsman	40502030	Gravekeeper's Cannonholder	99877698
Flying Kamakiri #1	84834865	Gravekeeper's Chief	62473983
Foolish Burial	81439173	Gravekeeper's Commandant	17393207
Forced Ceasefire	97806240	Gravekeeper's Curse	50712728
Forest	87430998	Gravekeeper's Guard	37101832
Fortress Whale	62337487	Gravekeeper's Servant	16762927
Fortress Whale's Oath	77454922	Gravekeeper's Spear Soldier	63695531
Frozen Soul	57069605	Gravekeeper's Spy	24317029
Fulfillment of the Contract	48206762	Gravekeeper's Vassal	99690140
Full Salvo	70865988	Gravekeeper's Watcher	26084285
Fusilier Dragon, the Duel-Mode Beast	51632798	Gravity Axe - Grarl	32022366
Fusion Gate	24094653	Gravity Bind	85742772
Fusion Sage	26902560	Great Moth	14141448
Fusion Sword Murasame Blade	37684215	Greed	89405199
Gaia Power	56594520	Green Baboon, Defender of the Forest	46668237
Gaia the Dragon Champion	66889139	Greenkappa	61831093
Gaia the Fierce Knight	06368038	Ground Collapse	90502999
Gamma the Magnet Warrior	11549357	Gust	73079365
Garoozis	14977074	Gust Fan	55321970
Garuda the Wind Spirit	12800777	Gyaku-Gire Panda	09817927
Gazelle the King of Mythical Beasts	05818798	Hammer Shot	26412047
Gear Golem the Moving Fortress	30190809	Hand Collapse	74519184
Gearfried the Iron Knight	00423705	Hannibal Necromancer	05640330
Gearfried the Swordmaster	57046845	Harpie Lady	76812113
Gemini Elf	69140098	Harpie Lady 1	91932350
Generation Shift	34460239	Harpie Lady 2	27927359
Germ Infection	24668830	Harpie Lady 3	54415063
Getsu Fuhma	21887179	Harpie Lady Sisters	12206212
Giant Flea	41762634	Harpies' Hunting Ground	75782277
Giant Germ	95178994	Harpie's Pet Dragon	52040216
Giant Rat	97017120	Headless Knight	5434080
Giant Red Seasnake	58831685	Heart of Clear Water	64801562
Giant Soldier of Stone	13039848	Heart of the Underdog	35762283
Giant Trunade	42703248	Heavy Mech Support Platform	23265594
Gigantes	47606319	Heavy Slump	52417194
Gilasaurus	45894482	Heavy Storm	19613556
Gilford the Legend	69933858	Helpoemer	76052811
Gilford the Lightning	36354007	Hercules Beetle	52584282
Gil Garth	38445524	Hero Kid	32679370
Goblin Attack Force	78658564	Hero Signal	22020907
Goblin Fan	04149689	Hidden Book of Spell	21840375
Goblin King	18590133	Hieroglyph Lithograph	10248192
Goblin Thief	45311864	Hinotama	46130346
Goblin's Secret Remedy	11868825	Hiro's Shadow Scout	81863068
Goddess of Whim	67959180	Hitotsu-Me Giant	76184692
Goddess with the Third Eye	53493204	Horn Imp	69669405
Gokibore	15367030	Horn of Light	38552107
Gorgon's Eye	52648457	Horn of the Unicorn	64047146
Graceful Dice	74137509	Hoshiningen	67629977
Gradius' Option	14291024	House of Adhesive Tape	15083728
		Human-Wave Tactics	30353551

CARD	PASSWORD
Illusionist Faceless Mage	28546905
Impenetrable Formation	96631852
Inferno	74823665
Inferno Fire Blast	52684508
Infinite Cards	94163677
Infinite Dismissal	54109233
Injection Fairy Lily	79575620
Insect Armor with Laser Cannon	03492538
Insect Barrier	23615409
Insect Imitation	96965364
Insect Queen	91512835
Inspection	16227556
Interdimensional Matter Transporter	36261276
Invigoration	98374133
Jack's Knight	90876561
Jade Insect Whistle	95214051
Jam Breeding Machine	21770260
Jam Defender	21558682
Jar of Greed	83968380
Jigen Bakudan	90020065
Jinzo	77585513
Jinzo #7	77585513
Jowgen the Spiritualist	41855169
Jowls of Dark Demise	05257687
Judge Man	30113682
Judgment of the Pharaoh	55948544
Just Desserts	24068492
Kabazauls	51934376
Kabazauls	51934376
Kanan the Swordsmistress	12829151
Killer Needle	88979991
Kinetic Soldier	79853073
King of the Skull Servants	36021814
King of the Swamp	79109599
King Tiger Wanghu	83986578
King's Knight	64788463
Koitsu	69456283
Krokodilus	76512652
Kryuel	82642348
Kunai with Chain	37390589
Kuriboh	40640057
Kycoo the Ghost Destroyer	88240808
Labyrinth of Nightmare	66526672
Labyrinth Tank	99551425
Larvae Moth	87756343
Laser Cannon Armor	77007920
Last Day of the Witch	90330453
Launcher Spider	87322377
Lava Battleguard	20394040
Lava Golem	00102380
Left Arm of the Forbidden One	07902349
Left Leg of the Forbidden One	44519536
Legacy of Yata-Garasu	30461781
Legendary Sword	61854111
Level Conversion Lab	84397023

CARD	PASSWORD
Level Limit - Area A	54976796
Level Limit - Area B	03136426
Level Modulation	61850482
Level Up!	25290459
Light of Judgment	44595286
Lighten the Load	37231841
Lightforce Sword	49587034
Lightning Vortex	69162969
Little Chimera	68658728
Luminous Soldier	57482479
Luminous Spark	81777047
Luster Dragon	11091375
Machine Duplication	63995093
Machine King	46700124
Mad Sword Beast	79870141
Mage Power	83746708
Magic Cylinder	62279055
Magic Drain	59344077
Magic Formula	67227834
Magic Jammer	77414722
Magical Arm Shield	96008713
Magical Dimension	28553439
Magical Explosion	32723153
Magical Hats	81210420
Magical Stone Excavation	98494543
Magical Thorn	53119267
Magician of Black Chaos	30208479
Magician of Faith	31560081
Magician's Circle	00050755
Magician's Unite	36045450
Magician's Valkyria	80304126
Maha Vailo	93013676
Maharaghi	40695128
Maiden of the Aqua	17214465
Major Riot	09074847
Malevolent Catastrophe	01224927
Malevolent Nuzzler	99597615
Malfunction	06137091
Malice Dispersion	13626450
Man-Eater Bug	54652250
Man-Eating Treasure Chest	13723605
Manga Ryu-Ran	38369349
Marauding Captain	02460565
Marie the Fallen One	57579381
Marshmallon	31305911
Marshmallon Glasses	66865880
Mask of Brutality	82432018
Mask of Darkness	28933734
Mask of Dispel	20765952
Mask of Restrict	29549364
Mask of the Accursed	56948373
Mask of Weakness	57882509
Masked Sorcerer	10189126
Mass Driver	34906152
Master Kyonshee	24530661
Mataza the Zapper	22609617

CARD	PASSWORD	CARD	PASSWORD
Mausoleum of the Emperor	80921533	Mystical Space Typhoon	05318639
Mechanicalchaser	07359741	Narrow Pass	40172183
Mega Ton Magical Cannon	32062913	Necrovalley	47355498
Megamorph	22046459	Needle Wall	38299233
Melchid the Four-Faced Beast	86569121	Needle Worm	81843628
Meltiel, Sage of the Sky	49905576	Negate Attack	14315573
Mesmeric Control	48642904	Neo the Magic Swordsman	50930991
Messenger of Peace	44656491	Newdoria	04335645
Metal Detector	75646520	Next to be Lost	07076131
Metal Reflect Slime	26905245	Nightmare Wheel	54704216
Metalmorph	68540058	Nimble Momonga	22567609
Metalzoa	50705071	Nitro Unit	23842445
Meteor Black Dragon	90660762	Non Aggression Area	76848240
Meteor Dragon	64271667	Non-Fusion Area	27581098
Michizure	37580756	Non-Spellcasting Area	20065549
Micro Ray	18190572	Numinous Healer	02130625
Millennium Shield	32012841	Nuvia the Wicked	12953226
Milus Radiant	07489323	Obnoxious Celtic Guard	52077741
Mind Control	37520316	Ojama Black	79335209
Mind Crush	15800838	Ojama Delta Hurricane!!	08251996
Miracle Dig	63434080	Ojama Green	12482652
Miracle Kids	55985014	Ojama King	90140980
Miracle Restoring	68334074	Ojama Trio	29843091
Mirror Force	44095762	Ojama Yellow	42941100
Mispolymerization	58392024	Ojamagic	24643836
Mist body	47529357	Ojamuscle	98259197
Moisture Creature	75285069	Ominous Fortunetelling	56995655
Mokey Mokey	27288416	Ookazi	19523799
Mokey Mokey King	13803864	Opti-Camouflage Armor	44762290
Mokey Mokey Smackdown	01965724	Order to Charge	78986941
Molten Destruction	19384334	Order to Smash	39019325
Monster Gate	43040603	Otohime	39751093
Monster Recovery	93108433	Overpowering Eye	60577362
Monster Reincarnation	74848038	Panther Warrior	42035044
Mooyan Curry	58074572	Paralyzing Potion	50152549
Morphing Jar	33508719	Parasite Paracide	27911549
Morphing Jar #2	79106360	Parrot Dragon	62762898
Mother Grizzly	57839750	Patrician of Darkness	19153634
Mountain	50913601	Pendulum Machine	24433920
Muka Muka	46657337	Penguin Knight	36039163
Multiplication of Ants	22493811	Penguin Soldier	93920745
Multiply	40703222	Perfectly Ultimate Great Moth	48579379
Mushroom Man	14181608	Petit Moth	58192742
My Body as a Shield	69279219	Pharaoh's Treasure	63571750
Mysterious Puppeteer	54098121	Pigeonholing Books of Spell	96677818
Mystic Box	25774450	Pikeru's Second Sight	58015506
Mystic Horseman	68516705	Pinch Hopper	26185991
Mystic Probe	49251811	Pitch-Black Power Stone	34029630
Mystic Swordsman LV2	47507260	Poison Fangs	76539047
Mystic Swordsman LV4	74591968	Poison of the Old Man	08842266
Mystic Swordsman LV6	60482781	Polymerization	35550694
Mystic Tomato	83011277	Pot of Avarice	67169062
Mystical Elf	15025844	Premature Burial	70828912
Mystical Moon	36607978	Prepare to Strike Back	04483989
Mystical Refpanel	35563539	Prevent Rat	00549481
Mystical Sheep #1	30451366	Princess of Tsurugi	51371017

CARD	PASSWORD	CARD	PASSWORD
Prohibition	43711255	Ryu Kokki	57281778
Protector of the Sanctuary	24221739	Ryu-Kishin	15303296
Pumpking the King of Ghosts	29155212	Ryu-Ran	02964201
Queen's Knight	25652259	Sage's Stone	13604200
Rabid Horseman	94905343	Saggi the Dark Clown	66602787
Radiant Jeral	84177693	Sakuretsu Armor	56120475
Radiant Mirror Force	21481146	Salamandra	32268901
Raigeki Break	04178474	Salvage	96947648
Rapid-Fire Magician	06337436	Sangan	26202165
Ray of Hope	82529174	Sasuke Samurai #3	77379481
Ready for Intercepting	31785398	Sasuke Samurai #4	64538655
Really Eternal Rest	28121403	Satellite Cannon	50400231
Reaper of the Cards	33066139	Second Coin Toss	36562627
Reckless Greed	37576645	Sengenjin	76232340
Recycle	96316857	Serial Spell	49398568
Red Archery Girl	65570596	Serpentine Princess	71829750
Red Medicine	38199696	Seven Tools of the Bandit	03819470
Red-Eyes B. Chick	36262024	Shadow Ghoul	30778711
Red-Eyes Black Dragon	74677422	Shadow of Eyes	58621589
Red-Eyes Black Metal Dragon	64335804	Share the Pain	56830749
Reflect Bounder	02851070	Shield & Sword	52097679
Reinforcement of the Army	32807846	Shield Crush	30683373
Reinforcements	17814387	Shift	59560625
Release Restraint	75417459	Shifting Shadows	59237154
Relieve Monster	37507488	Shinato, King of a Higher Plane	86327225
Relinquished	64631466	Shinato's Ark	60365591
Remove Trap	51482758	Shining Abyss	87303357
Respect Play	08951260	Shining Angel	95956346
Restructer Revolution	99518961	Shooting Star Bow - Ceal	95638658
Reversal Quiz	05990062	Shrink	55713623
Reverse Trap	77622396	Silver Bow and Arrow	01557499
Revival Jam	31709826	Simultaneous Loss	92219931
Right Arm of the Forbidden One	70903634	Skilled Dark Magician	73752131
Right Leg of the Forbidden One	08124921	Skilled White Magician	46363422
Rigorous Reaver	39180960	Skull Dice	00126218
Ring of Magnetism	20436034	Skull Servant	32274490
Riryoku Field	70344351	Skull-Mark Ladybug	64306248
Rising Energy	78211862	Skyscraper	63035430
Rite of Spirit	30450531	Slate Warrior	78636495
Ritual Weapon	54351224	Slot Machine	03797883
Robbin' Goblin	88279736	Smashing Ground	97169186
Robbin' Zombie	83258273	Smoke Grenade of the Thief	63789924
Robotic Knight	44203504	Snake Fang	00596051
Rock Bombardment	20781762	Sogen	86318356
Rocket Warrior	30860696	Solar Ray	44472639
Rod of Silence - Kay'est	95515060	Solemn Judgment	41420027
Rogue Doll	91939608	Solemn Wishes	35346968
Roll Out!	91597389	Sorcerer of the Doomed	49218300
Royal Command	33950246	Soul Absorption	68073522
Royal Decree	51452091	Soul Demolition	76297408
Royal Magical Library	70791313	Soul Exchange	68005187
Royal Oppression	93016201	Soul of Purity and Light	77527210
Royal Surrender	56058888	Soul of the Pure	47852924
Royal Tribute	72405967	Soul Release	05758500
Rude Kaiser	26378150	Soul Resurrection	92924317
Rush Recklessly	70046172	Soul Reversal	78864369

CARD	PASSWORD	CARD	PASSWORD
Soul Taker	81510157	The Gross Ghost of Fled Dreams	68049471
Spark Blaster	97362768	The Illusory Gentleman	83764996
Spatial Collapse	20644748	The Inexperienced Spy	81820689
Special Hurricane	42598242	The Last Warrior from Another Planet	86099788
Spell Absorption	51481927		
Spell Reproduction	29228529	The Law of the Normal	66926224
Spell Vanishing	29735721	The League of Uniform Nomenclature	55008284
Spellbinding Circle	18807108		
Spell-stopping Statute	10069180	The Little Swordsman of Aile	25109950
Spiral Spear Strike	49328340	The Masked Beast	49064413
Spirit Message "A"	94772232	The Portrait's Secret	32541773
Spirit Message "I"	31893528	The Regulation of Tribe	00296499
Spirit Message "L"	30170981	The Reliable Guardian	16430187
Spirit Message "N"	67287533	The Rock Spirit	76305638
Spirit of Flames	13522325	The Sanctuary in the Sky	56433456
Spirit of the Pharaoh	25343280	The Second Sarcophagus	04081094
Spirit's Invitation	92394653	The Secret of the Bandit	99351431
Spiritual Earth Art - Kurogane	70156997	The Shallow Grave	43434803
Spiritual Energy Settle Machine	99173029	The Snake Hair	29491031
Spiritual Fire Art - Kurenai	42945701	The Spell Absorbing Life	99517131
Spiritual Water Art - Aoi	06540606	The Statue of Easter Island	10261698
Spiritual Wind Art - Miyabi	79333300	The Third Sarcophagus	78697395
Spiritualism	15866454	The Unhappy Girl	27618634
St. Joan	21175632	The Unhappy Maiden	51275027
Staunch Defender	92854392	The Warrior Returning Alive	95281259
Steel Ogre Grotto #2	90908427	The Wicked Worm Beast	06285791
Steel Scorpion	13599884	Thestalos the Firestorm Monarch	26205777
Stim-Pack	83225447	Thousand Dragon	41462083
Stone Statue of the Aztecs	31812496	Thousand Energy	05703682
Stop Defense	63102017	Thousand Knives	63391643
Stray Lambs	60764581	Thousand-Eyes Idol	27125110
Stumbling	34646691	Threatening Roar	36361633
Swamp Battleguard	40453765	Three-Headed Geedo	78423643
Swift Gaia the Fierce Knight	16589042	Thunder Crash	69196160
Sword of Deep-Seated	98495314	Thunder Dragon	31786629
Sword of the Soul-Eater	05371656	Thunder Nyan Nyan	70797118
Swords of Concealing Light	12923641	Time Machine	80987696
Swords of Revealing Light	72302403	Time Wizard	06285791
Swordsman of Landstar	03573512	Token Feastevil	83675475
System Down	07672244	Toon Alligator	59383041
Tailor of the Fickle	43641473	Toon Cannon Soldier	79875176
Terraforming	73628505	Toon Dark Magician Girl	90960358
The A. Forces	00403847	Toon Defense	43509019
The Agent of Force - Mars	91123920	Toon Gemini Elf	42386471
The Agent of Judgement - Saturn	91345518	Toon Goblin Attack Force	15270885
The Big March of Animals	01689516	Toon Masked Sorcerer	16392422
The Bistro Butcher	71107816	Toon Mermaid	65458948
The Cheerful Coffin	41142615	Toon Summoned Skull	91842653
The Creator	61505339	Toon Table of Contents	89997728
The Creator Incarnate	97093037	Toon World	15259703
The Dark Door	30606547	Tornado	61068510
The Earl of Demise	66989694	Tornado Wall	18605135
The Fiend Megacyber	66362965	Torpedo Fish	90337190
The First Sarcophagus	31076103	Tower of Babel	94256039
The Flute of Summoning Kuriboh	20065322	Tragedy	35686187
The Forgiving Maiden	84080938	Transcendent Wings	25573054

CARD	PASSWORD
Trap Hole	04206964
Trap Jammer	19252988
Trap Master	46461247
Tremendous Fire	46918794
Triage	30888983
Triangle Ecstasy Spark	12181376
Triangle Power	32298781
Tribute Doll	02903036
Tribute to the Doomed	79759861
Tri-Horned Dragon	39111158
Twin Swords of Flashing Light - Tryce	21900719
Twin-Headed Behemoth	43586926
Twin-Headed Thunder Dragon	54752875
Two-Headed King Rex	94119974
Two-Pronged Attack	83887306
Tyhone	72842870
Type Zero Magic Crusher	35346968
UFO Turtle	60806437
Ultimate Offering	80604091
Ultra Evolution Pill	22431243
Umiiruka	82999629
Union Attack	60399954
United We Stand	56747793
Unity	14731897
Upstart Goblin	70368879
Uraby	01784619
Valkyrion the Magna Warrior	75347539
Versago the Destroyer	50259460
Vile Germs	39774685
Vorse Raider	14898066
Waboku	12607053
Wall of Illusion	13945283

CARD	PASSWORD
Wall of Revealing Light	17078030
Wall Shadow	63162310
Warrior Elimination	90873992
Warrior Lady of the Wasteland	05438492
Wasteland	98239899
Weapon Change	10035717
Weather Report	72053645
Weed Out	28604635
White Magical Hat	15150365
White-Horned Dragon	73891874
Wicked-Breaking Flamberge - Baou	68427465
Widespread Ruin	77754944
Wild Nature's Release	61166988
Winged Dragon, Guardian of the Fortress #1	87796900
Winged Kuriboh	57116033
Winged Kuriboh LV10	98585345
Witch's Apprentice	80741828
Wolf	49417509
Wolf Axwielder	56369281
Woodland Sprite	06979239
World Suppression	12253117
Xing Zhen Hu	76515293
Yamata Dragon	76862289
Yami	59197169
Yellow Luster Shield	04542651
Yu-Jo Friendship	81332143
Zaborg the Thunder Monarch	51945556
Zero Gravity	83133491
Zoa	24311372
Zolga	16268841
Zombie Warrior	31339260

ZOO KEEPER

GEKIMUZU DIFFICULTY

Earn a high score in all 4 modes.
Here are the high scores needed for each mode:

MODE	SCORE
Zoo keeper	200000
Tokoton 100	800000
Quest mode	10000
Time attack	600000

ZOO TYCOON DS

UNLOCK EVERYTHING

At the Main menu, press Up, Up, Down, Down, Left, Right, Left, Right, Up, Up, Down , Down, Left, Right, Left, Right.

PLAYSTATION® PORTABLE

CONTENTS

ASTRO BOY: THE VIDEO GAME

INVULNERABLE
Pause the game and press Up, Down, Down, Up, L1, R.

MAX STATS
Pause the game and press Left, Left, R, Down, Down, L1.

INFINITE SUPERS
Pause the game and press Left, L1, Right, L1, Up, Down.

INFINITE DASHES
Pause the game and press R, R, L1, R, Left, Up.

DISABLE SUPERS
Pause the game and press L1, L1, R, R, L1, Left.

COSTUME SWAP (ARENA AND CLASSIC COSTUMES)
Pause the game and press R, Up, L1, Up, Down, R.

UNLOCK LEVELS
Pause the game and press Up, L1, Right, L1, Down, L1. This allows you to travel to any level from the Story menu.

BEN 10: ALIEN FORCE THE GAME

LEVEL LORD
Enter Gwen, Kevin, Big Chill, Gwen as a code.

INVINCIBILITY
Enter Kevin, Big Chill, Swampfire, Kevin as a code.

ALL COMBOS
Enter Swampfire, Gwen, Kevin, Ben as a code.

INFINITE ALIENS
Enter Ben, Swampfire, Gwen, Big Chill as a code.

BEN 10: PROTECTOR OF EARTH

INVINCIBILITY
Select a game from the Continue option. Go to the Map Selection screen, press Start and choose Extras. Select Enter Secret Code and enter XLR8, Heatblast, Wildvine, Fourarms.

ALL COMBOS
Select a game from the Continue option. Go to the Map Selection screen, press Start and choose Extras. Select Enter Secret Code and enter Cannonblot, Heatblast, Fourarms, Heatblast.

ALL LOCATIONS
Select a game from the Continue option. Go to the Map Selection screen, press Start and choose Extras. Select Enter Secret Code and enter Heatblast, XLR8, XLR8, Cannonblot.

DNA FORCE SKINS
Select a game from the Continue option. Go to the Map Selection screen, press Start and choose Extras. Select Enter Secret Code and enter Wildvine, Fourarms, Heatblast, Cannonbolt.

DARK HEROES SKINS
Select a game from the Continue option. Go to the Map Selection screen, press Start and choose Extras. Select Enter Secret Code and enter Cannonbolt, Cannonbolt, Fourarms, Heatblast.

ALL ALIEN FORMS

Select a game from the Continue option. Go to the Map Selection screen, press Start and choose Extras. Select Enter Secret Code and enter Wildvine, Fourarms, Heatblast, Wildvine.

MASTER CONTROL

Select a game from the Continue option. Go to the Map Selection screen, press Start and choose Extras. Select Enter Secret Code and enter Cannonbolt, Heatblast, Wildvine, Fourarms.

CAPCOM CLASSICS COLLECTION REMIXED

UNLOCK EVERYTHING

At the title screen, press Left on D-pad, Right on D-pad, Left on Analog stick, Right on Analog stick, ●, ●, Up on D-pad, Down on D-pad.

CAPCOM PUZZLE WORLD

SUPER BUSTER BROS.

LEVEL SELECT IN TOUR MODE

At the Main menu, highlight Tour Mode, hold Down and press ❽.

SUPER PUZZLE FIGHTER

PLAY AS AKUMA

At the character select, highlight Hsien-Ko and press Down.

PLAY AS DAN

At the character select, highlight Donovan and press Down.

PLAY AS DEVILOT

At the character select, highlight Morrigan and press Down.

PLAY AS ANITA

At the character select, hold L + R and choose Donovan.

PLAY AS HSIEN-KO'S TALISMAN

At the character select, hold L + R and choose Hsien-Ko.

PLAY AS MORRIGAN AS A BAT

At the character select, hold L + R and choose Morrigan.

CARS

BONUS SPEEDWAY (REVERSED) IN CUSTOM RACE

At the Main menu hold L and press ✖, ●, ▲, ✖, ▲, ●.

ALL CARS, PAINTJOBS, TRACKS, MOVIE CLIPS AND MODES

At the main menu, hold L and press ▲, ●, ✖, ●, ▲, ✖, ●, ▲, ●, ✖.

UNLIMITED NITROUS

At the main menu, hold L and ✖, ●, ●, ●, ●, ▲, ●, ✖.

CASTLEVANIA: THE DRACULA X CHRONICLES

ORIGINAL RONDO OF BLOOD

LEVEL SELECT

Enter X-X!V''Q as your player name

SYMPHONY OF THE NIGHT

PLAY AS ALUCARD WITH 99 LUCK AND LAPIS LAZULI

Start a new game with the name X-X!V''Q.

PLAY AS ALUCARD WITH AXE LORD ARMOR

After clearing the game once, start a new game with the name AXEARMOR.

PLAY AS MARIA RENARD

After clearing the game once, start a new game with the name MARIA.

PLAY AS RICHTER BELMONT

After clearing the game once, start a new game with the name RICHTER.

CRASH: MIND OVER MUTANT

A cheat can be deactivated by re-entering the code.

FREEZE ENEMIES WITH TOUCH

Pause the game, hold R and press Down, Down, Down, Up.

ENEMIES DROP X4 DAMAGE

Pause the game, hold R and press Up, Up, Up, Left.

ENEMIES DROP PURPLE FRUIT

Pause the game, hold R and press Up, Down, Down, Up.

ENEMIES DROP SUPER KICK

Pause the game, hold R and press Up, Right, Down, Left.

ENIMIES DROP WUMPA FRUIT

Pause the game, hold R and press Right, Right, Right, Up.

SHADOW CRASH

Pause the game, hold R and press Left, Right, Left, Right.

DEFORMED CRASH

Pause the game, hold R and press Left, Left, Left, Down.

CRISIS CORE—FINAL FANTASY VII

NEW GAME+

After completing the game, you'll be prompted to make a new save. Loading a game from this new save will begin a New Game+, starting the game over while allowing Zack to retain almost everything he's earned.

The following items transfer to a New Game+:

Level, Experience, SP, Gil, Playtime, Non-Key Items, Materia, and DMW Completion Rate

The following items do not transfer:

Key Items, Materia/Accessory Slot Expansion, Ability to SP Convert, DMW Images, Mission Progress, Mail, and Unlocked Shops

DISGAEA 2: DARK HERO DAYS

AXEL MODE

Highlight New Game and press ⬠, ⬛, ⬤, ⬠, ⬛, ⬤, ✖.

FINAL FANTASY TACTICS: THE WAR OF THE LIONS

MUSIC TEST MODE

Enter the main character's name as PolkaPolka at the name entry screen.

FLATOUT: HEAD ON

1 MILLION CREDITS

Select Enter Code from the Extras menu and enter GIVECASH.

ALL CARS AND 1 MILLION CREDITS

Select Enter Code from the Extras menu and enter GIEVEPIX.

BIG RIG

Select Enter Code from the Extras menu and enter ELPUEBLO.

BIG RIG TRUCK

Select Enter Code from the Extras menu and enter RAIDERS.

FLATMOBILE CAR

Select Enter Code from the Extras menu and enter WOTKINS.

MOB CAR

Select Enter Code from the Extras menu and enter BIGTRUCK.

PIMPSTER CAR

Select Enter Code from the Extras menu and enter RUTTO.

ROCKET CAR

Select Enter Code from the Extras menu and enter KALJAKOPPA.

SCHOOL BUS

Select Enter Code from the Extras menu and enter GIEVCARPLZ.

G.I. JOE: THE RISE OF COBRA

CLASSIC DUKE

At the main menu, press Left, Up, Square, Up, Right, ▲.

CLASSIC SCARLET

At the main menu, press Right, Up, Down, Down, ▲.

HOT BRAIN

119.99 TEMPERATURE IN ALL 5 CATEGORIES

Select New Game and enter Cheat.

HOT SHOTS GOLF 2

UNLOCK EVERYTHING

Enter 2gsh as your name.

IRON MAN

Iron Man's different armor suits are unlocked by completing certain missions.

COMPLETE MISSION	SUIT UNLOCKED
1, Escape	Mark I
2, First Flight	Mark II
3, Fight Back	Mark III
5, Maggia Compound	Gold Tin Can
8, Frozen Ship	Classic
11, Island Meltdown	Stealth
13, Showdown	Titanium Man

PSP MINIGAMES

Minigames can be unlocked by completing the following missions. Access the minigames through the Bonus menu.

COMPLETE MISSION	PSP MINIGAME UNLOCKED	COMPLETE MISSION	PSP MINIGAME UNLOCKED
1, Escape	Tin Can Challenge 1 + 2	8, Frozen Ship	SPEED KILL: FROZEN SHIP / SURVIVAL: FROZEN SHIP
2, First Flight	DEATH RACE: STARK INDUSTRY	9, Home Front	BOSS FIGHT: TITANIUM MAN
3, Fight Back	BOSS FIGHT: DREADNOUGHT	10, Save Pepper	DEATH RACE: DAM BASSIN
4, Weapons Transport	DEATH RACE: AFGHAN DESERT / BOSS FIGHT: WHIPLASH	11, Island Meltdown	SPEED KILL: GREEK ISLANDS / SURVIVAL: GREEK ISLANDS
5, Maggia Compound	DEATH RACE: MAGGIA MANSION	12, Battlesuit Factory	SPEED KILL: TINMEN FACTORY / SURVIVAL: TINMEN FACTORY
6, Flying Fortress	SPEED KILL: FLYING FORTRESS / SURVIVAL: FLYING FORTRESS	13, Showdown	BOSS FIGHT: IRON MONGER
7, Nuclear Winter	DEATH RACE: ARTIC CIRCLE		

CONCEPT ART

As you progress through the game and destroy the Weapon Crates, bonuses are unlocked. You can find all of these in the Bonus menu once unlocked.

CONCEPT ART UNLOCKED	NUMBER OF WEAPON CRATES FOUND
Environments Set 1	6
Environments Set 2	12
Iron Man	18
Environments Set 3	24
Enemies	30
Environments Set 4	36
Villains	42
Vehicles	48
Covers	50

JUICED 2: HOT IMPORT NIGHTS

LAST MAN STANDING CHALLENGE AND AN ASCARI KZ1

Select Cheats and Challenges from the DNA Lab menu and enter KNOX. Defeat the challenge to earn the Ascari KZ1.

SPECIAL CHALLENGE AND AN AUDI TT 1.8 QUATTRO

Select Cheats and Challenges from the DNA Lab menu and enter YTHZ. Defeat the challenge to earn the Audi TT 1.8 Quattro.

SPECIAL CHALLENGE AND A BMW Z4

Select Cheats and Challenges from the DNA Lab menu and enter GVDL. Defeat the challenge to earn the BMW Z4.

SPECIAL CHALLENGE AND A HOLDEN MONARO

Select Cheats and Challenges from the DNA Lab menu and enter RBSG. Defeat the challenge to earn the Holden Monaro.

SPECIAL CHALLENGE AND A HYUNDAI COUPE 2.7 V6

Select Cheats and Challenges from the DNA Lab menu and enter BSLU. Defeat the challenge to earn the Hyundai Coupe 2.7 V6.

SPECIAL CHALLENGE AND AN INFINITY G35

Select Cheats and Challenges from the DNA Lab menu and enter MRHC. Defeat the challenge to earn the Infinity G35.

SPECIAL CHALLENGE AND AN INFINITY RED G35

Select Cheats and Challenges from the DNA Lab menu and enter MNCH. Defeat the challenge to earn the Infinity G35.

SPECIAL CHALLENGE AND A KOENIGSEGG CCX

Select Cheats and Challenges from the DNA Lab menu and enter KDTR. Defeat the challenge to earn the Koenigsegg CCX.

SPECIAL CHALLENGE AND A MITSUBISHI PROTOTYPE X

Select Cheats and Challenges from the DNA Lab menu and enter DOPX. Defeat the challenge to earn the Mitsubishi Prototype X.

SPECIAL CHALLENGE AND A NISSAN 350Z

Select Cheats and Challenges from the DNA Lab menu and enter PRGN. Defeat the challenge to earn the Nissan 350Z.

SPECIAL CHALLENGE AND A NISSAN SKYLINE R34 GT-R

Select Cheats and Challenges from the DNA Lab menu and enter JWRS. Defeat the challenge to earn the Nissan Skyline R34 GT-R.

SPECIAL CHALLENGE AND A SALEEN S7

Select Cheats and Challenges from the DNA Lab menu and enter WIKF. Defeat the challenge to earn the Saleen S7.

SPECIAL CHALLENGE AND A SEAT LEON CUPRA R

Select Cheats and Challenges from the DNA Lab menu and enter FAMQ. Defeat the challenge to earn the Seat Leon Cupra R.

LEGO BATMAN

BATCAVE CODES

Using the computer in the Batcave, select Enter Code and enter the following codes.

CHARACTERS

CHARACTER	CODE	CHARACTER	CODE
Alfred	ZAQ637	Penguin Henchman	BJH782
Batgirl	JKR331	Penguin Minion	KJP748
Bruce Wayne	BDJ327	Poison Ivy Goon	GTB899
Catwoman (Classic)	M1AAWW	Police Marksman	HKG984
Clown Goon	HJK327	Police Officer	JRY983
Commissioner Gordon	DDP967	Riddler Goon	CRY928
Fishmonger	HGY748	Riddler Henchman	XEU824
Freeze Girl	XVK541	S.W.A.T.	HTF114
Joker Goon	UTF782	Sailor	NAV592
Joker Henchman	YUN924	Scientist	JFL786
Mad Hatter	JCA283	Security Guard	PLB946
Man-Bat	NYU942	The Joker (Tropical)	CCB199
Military Policeman	MKL382	Yeti	NJL412
Nightwing	MVY759	Zoo Sweeper	DWR243
Penguin Goon	NKA238		

VEHICLES

VEHICLE	CODE	VEHICLE	CODE
Bat-Tank	KNTT4B	Mr. Freeze's Kart	BCT229
Bruce Wayne's Private Jet	LEA664	Penguin Goon Submarine	BTN248
Catwoman's Motorcycle	HPL826	Police Bike	LJP234
Garbage Truck	DUS483	Police Boat	PLC999
Goon Helicopter	GCH328	Police Car	KJL832
Harbor Helicopter	CHP735	Police Helicopter	CWR732
Harley Quinn's Hammer Truck	RDT637	Police Van	MAC788
Mad Hatter's Glider	HS000W	Police Watercraft	VJD328
Mad Hatter's Steamboat	M4DM4N	Riddler's Jet	HAHAHA
Mr. Freeze's Iceberg	ICYICE	Robin's Submarine	TTF453
The Joker's Van	JUK657	Two-Face's Armored Truck	EFE933

CHEATS

CHEAT	CODE
More Batarang Targets	XWP645
Piece Detector	KHJ554
Power Brick Detector	MMN786
Regenerate Hearts	HJHZHJ
Score x2	N4NR3E
Score x4	CX9MAT
Score x6	MLVNFZ
Score x8	WCC089
Score x10	18HW07

CHEAT	CODE
Always Score Multiply	9LR6NB
Fast Batarangs	JRBDCB
Fast Walk	ZOLM6N
Flame Batarang	DB8VWH
Freeze Batarang	XPN4NG
Extra Hearts	ML3KHP
Fast Build	EVG26J
Immune to Freeze	JXUDY4
Invincibility	WYD5CP
Minikit Detector	ZXGH9J

LEGO INDIANA JONES: THE ORIGINAL ADVENTURES

CHARACTERS

Approach the blackboard in the classroom and enter the following codes.

CHARACTER	CODE
Bandit	12N68W
Bandit Swordsman	1MK4RT
Barranca	04EM94
Bazooka Trooper (Crusade)	MK83R7
Bazooka Trooper (Raiders)	S93Y5R
Bellog	CHN3VU
Bellog (Jungle)	TDR197
Bellog (Robes)	VEO29L
British Commander	B73EUA
British Officer	VJ5T19
British Soldier	DJ5I2W
Captain Katanga	VJ3T13
Chatter Lal	ENW936
Chatter Lal (Thuggee)	CNH4RY
Chen	3NK481
Colonel Dietrich	2K9RK5
Colonel Vogel	8EAL4H
Dancing Girl	C7EJ21
Donovan	3NFTU8
Elsa (Desert)	JSNR19
Elsa (Officer)	VMJ5US
Enemy Boxer	8246RB
Enemy Butler	VJ48W3
Enemy Guard	VJ7R51
Enemy Guard (Mountains)	YR47WM
Enemy Officer	572E61
Enemy Officer (Desert)	2MK450
Enemy Pilot	B84ELP
Enemy Radio Operator	1MF94R
Enemy Soldier (Desert)	4NSU70

CHARACTER	CODE
Fedora	V75YSP
First Mate	0GIN24
Grail Knight	NE6THI
Hovitos Tribesman	H0V1SS
Indiana Jones (Desert Disguise)	4J8S4M
Indiana Jones (Officer)	VJ8SOS
Jungle Guide	24PF34
Kao Kan	WMO46I
Kazim	NRHZ3I
Kazim (Desert)	3M29TI
Lao Che	2NK479
Maharajah	NFKSN2
Major Toht	13NS01
Masked Bandit	N48SFO
Mola Ram	FJUR31
Monkey Man	3RF6YJ
Pankot Assassin	2NKTT2
Pankot Guard	VN28RH
Sherpa Brawler	VJ37WJ
Sherpa Gunner	ND762W
Slave Child	0E3ENW
Thuggee	VM683E
Thuggee Acolyte	T2R3F9
Thuggee Slave Driver	VBS76W
Village Dignitary	KD481N
Village Elder	4682E1
Willie (Dinner Suit)	VK9387
Willie (Pajamas)	MEN4IP
Wu Han	3NSL1B

EXTRAS

Approach the blackboard in the Classsroom and enter the following codes. Some cheats need to be enabled by selecting Extras from the pause menu.

CHEAT	CODE	CHEAT	CODE
Artifact Detector	VIKED7	Regenerate Hearts	MDLP69
Beep Beep	VNF59Q	Secret Characters	3X44AA
Character Treasure	VIES2R	Silhouettes	3HE85H
Disarm Enemies	VKRNS9	Super Scream	VN3R7S
Disguises	4ID1N6	Super Slap	OP1TA5
Fast Build	V83SLO	Treasure Magnet	H86LA2
Fast Dig	378RS6	Treasure x10	VI3PS8
Fast Fix	FJ59WS	Treasure x2	VM4TS9
Fertilizer	B1GW1F	Treasure x4	VLWEN3
Ice Rink	33GM7J	Treasure x6	V84RYS
Parcel Detector	VUT673	Treasure x8	A72E1M
Poo Treasure	WWQ1SA		

LEGO STAR WARS II: THE ORIGINAL TRILOGY

BEACH TROOPER

At Mos Eisley Canteena, select Enter Code and enter UCK868. You still need to select Characters and purchase this character for 20,000 studs.

BEN KENOBI (GHOST)

At Mos Eisley Canteena, select Enter Code and enter BEN917. You still need to select Characters and purchase this character for 1,100,000 studs.

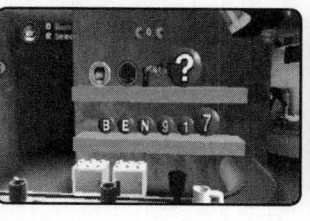 

BESPIN GUARD

At Mos Eisley Canteena, select Enter Code and enter VHY832. You still need to select Characters and purchase this character for 15,000 studs.

BIB FORTUNA

At Mos Eisley Canteena, select Enter Code and enter WTY721. You still need to select Characters and purchase this character for 16,000 studs.

BOBA FETT

At Mos Eisley Canteena, select Enter Code and enter HLP221. You still need to select Characters and purchase this character for 175,000 studs.

DEATH STAR TROOPER

At Mos Eisley Canteena, select Enter Code and enter BNC332. You still need to select Characters and purchase this character for 19,000 studs.

EWOK

At Mos Eisley Canteena, select Enter Code and enter TTT289. You still need to select Characters and purchase this character for 34,000 studs.

GAMORREAN GUARD

At Mos Eisley Canteena, select Enter Code and enter YZF999. You still need to select Characters and purchase this character for 40,000 studs.

GONK DROID

At Mos Eisley Canteena, select Enter Code and enter NFX582. You still need to select Characters and purchase this character for 1,550 studs.

GRAND MOFF TARKIN

At Mos Eisley Canteena, select Enter Code and enter SMG219. You still need to select Characters and purchase this character for 38,000 studs.

GREEDO

At Mos Eisley Canteena, select Enter Code and enter NAH118. You still need to select Characters and purchase this character for 60,000 studs.

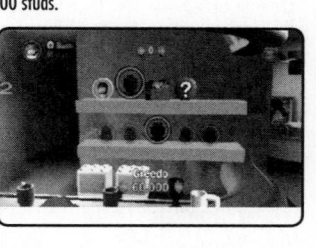

HAN SOLO (HOOD)

At Mos Eisley Canteena, select Enter Code and enter YWM840. You still need to select Characters and purchase this character for 20,000 studs.

IG-88

At Mos Eisley Canteena, select Enter Code and enter NXL973. You still need to select Characters and purchase this character for 30,000 studs.

IMPERIAL GUARD

At Mos Eisley Canteena, select Enter Code and enter MMM111. You still need to select Characters and purchase this character for 45,000 studs.

IMPERIAL OFFICER

At Mos Eisley Canteena, select Enter Code and enter BBV889. You still need to select Characters and purchase this character for 28,000 studs.

IMPERIAL SHUTTLE PILOT

At Mos Eisley Canteena, select Enter Code and enter VAP664. You still need to select Characters and purchase this character for 29,000 studs.

IMPERIAL SPY

At Mos Eisley Canteena, select Enter Code and enter CVT125. You still need to select Characters and purchase this character for 13,500 studs.

JAWA

At Mos Eisley Canteena, select Enter Code and enter JAW499. You still need to select Characters and purchase this character for 24,000 studs.

LOBOT

At Mos Eisley Canteena, select Enter Code and enter UUB319. You still need to select Characters and purchase this character for 11,000 studs.

PALACE GUARD

At Mos Eisley Canteena, select Enter Code and enter SGE549. You still need to select Characters and purchase this character for 14,000 studs.

REBEL PILOT

At Mos Eisley Canteena, select Enter Code and enter CYG336. You still need to select Characters and purchase this character for 15,000 studs.

REBEL TROOPER (HOTH)

At Mos Eisley Canteena, select Enter Code and enter EKU849. You still need to select Characters and purchase this character for 16,000 studs.

SANDTROOPER

At Mos Eisley Canteena, select Enter Code and enter YDV451. You still need to select Characters and purchase this character for 14,000 studs.

SKIFF GUARD

At Mos Eisley Canteena, select Enter Code and enter GBU888. You still need to select Characters and purchase this character for 12,000 studs.

SNOWTROOPER

At Mos Eisley Canteena, select Enter Code and enter NYU989. You still need to select Characters and purchase this character for 16,000 studs.

STROMTROOPER

At Mos Eisley Canteena, select Enter Code and enter PTR345. You still need to select Characters and purchase this character for 10,000 studs.

THE EMPEROR

At Mos Eisley Canteena, select Enter Code and enter HHY382. You still need to select Characters and purchase this character for 275,000 studs.

TIE FIGHTER

At Mos Eisley Canteena, select Enter Code and enter HDY739. You still need to select Characters and purchase this character for 60,000 studs.

TIE FIGHTER PILOT

At Mos Eisley Canteena, select Enter Code and enter NNZ316. You still need to select Characters and purchase this character for 21,000 studs.

TIE INTERCEPTOR

At Mos Eisley Canteena, select Enter Code and enter QYA828. You still need to select Characters and purchase this character for 40,000 studs.

TUSKEN RAIDER

At Mos Eisley Canteena, select Enter Code and enter PEJ821. You still need to select Characters and purchase this character for 23,000 studs.

UGNAUGHT

At Mos Eisley Canteena, select Enter Code and enter UGN694. You still need to select Characters and purchase this character for 36,000 studs.

MARVEL SUPER HERO SQUAD

IRON MAN BONUS COSTUMES
Select Enter Code from the Options and enter 111111.

HULK BONUS COSTUMES
Select Enter Code from the Options and enter 222222.

WOLVERINE BONUS COSTUMES
Select Enter Code from the Options and enter 333333.

THOR BONUS COSTUMES
Select Enter Code from the Options and enter 444444.

SILVER SURFER BONUS COSTUMES
Select Enter Code from the Options and enter 555555.

FALCON BONUS COSTUMES
Select Enter Code from the Options and enter 666666.

CHEAT SUPER KNOCKBACK
Select Enter Code from the Options and enter 777777.

CHEAT NO BLOCK MODE
Select Enter Code from the Options and enter 888888.

DR. DOOM BONUS COSTUMES
Select Enter Code from the Options and enter 999999.

MARVEL ULTIMATE ALLIANCE

UNLOCK ALL SKINS
At the Team menu, press Up, Down, Left, Right, Left, Right, Start.

UNLOCKS ALL HERO POWERS
At the Team menu, press Left, Right, Up, Down, Up, Down, Start.

ALL HEROES TO LEVEL 99
At the Team menu, press Up, Left, Up, Left, Down, Right, Down, Right, Start.

UNLOCK ALL HEROES
At the Team menu, press Up, Up, Down, Down, Left, Left, Left, Start.

UNLOCK DAREDEVIL
At the Team menu, press Left, Left, Right, Right, Up, Down, Up, Down, Start.

UNLOCK SILVER SURFER
At the Team menu, press Down, Left, Left, Up, Right, Up, Down, Left, Start.

GOD MODE
During gameplay, press Up, Down, Up, Down, Up, Left, Down, Right, Start.

TOUCH OF DEATH
During gameplay, press Left, Right, Down, Down, Right, Left, Start.

SUPER SPEED
During gameplay, press Up, Left, Up, Right, Down, Right, Start.

FILL MOMENTUM
During gameplay, press Left, Right, Right, Left, Up, Down, Down, Up, Start.

UNLOCK ALL COMICS

At the Review menu, press Left, Right, Right, Left, Up, Up, Right, Start.

UNLOCK ALL CONCEPT ART

At the Review menu, press Down, Down, Down, Right, Right, Left, Down, Start.

UNLOCK ALL CINEMATICS

At the Review menu, press Up, Left, Left, Up, Right, Right, Up, Start.

UNLOCK ALL LOAD SCREENS

At the Review menu, press Up, Down, Right, Left, Up, Up Down, Start.

UNLOCK ALL COURSES

At the Comic Missions menu, press Up, Right, Left, Down, Up, Right, Left, Down, Start.

MARVEL: ULTIMATE ALLIANCE 2

GOD MODE

At any point during a game, press Up, Up, Down, Down, Left, Right, Down.

GIVE MONEY

At the Team Select or Hero Details screen press Up, Up, Down, Down, Up, Up, Up, Down.

UNLOCK ALL POWERS

At the Team Select or Hero Details screen press Up, Up, Down, Down, Left, Right, Right, Left.

ADVANCE ALL CHARACTERS TO L99

At the Hero Details screen press Down, Up, Left, Up, Right, Up, Left, Down.

UNLOCK ALL BONUS MISSIONS

While using the Bonus Mission Simulator, press Up, Right, Down, Left, Left, Right, Up, Up.

ADD 1 CHARACTER LEVEL

During a game, press Down, Up, Right, Up, Right, Up, Right, Down.

ADD 10 CHARACTER LEVELS

During a game, press Down, Up, Left, Up, Left, Up, Left, Down.

MLB 07: THE SHOW

SILVER ERA AND GOLD ERA TEAMS

At the Main menu, press Left, Up, Right, Down, Down, Left, Up, Down.

MAX BREAK PITCHES

Pause the game and press Right, Up, Right, Down, Up, Left, Left, Down.

MAX SPEED PITCHES

Pause the game and press Up, Left, Down, Up, Left, Right, Left, Down.

MLB 08: THE SHOW

CLASSIC FREE AGENTS AT THE PLAYER MOVEMENT MENU

At the main menu, press Left, Right, Up, Left, Right, Up, Right, Down.

SILVER ERA AND GOLDEN ERA TEAMS

At the main menu, press Right, Up, Right, Down, Down, Left, Up, Down.

BIG BALL

Pause the game and press Right, Down, Up, Left, Right, Left, Down, Up.

BIG HEAD MODE
Pause the game and press Right, Left, Down, Up, Left, Up, Down, Left.

SMALL HEAD MODE
Pause the game and press Left, Right, Down, Up, Right, Left, Down, Left.

N+

25 EXTRA LEVELS
At the main menu, hold L + R and press ✖, ⦿, ✖, ⦿, ✖, ✖, ⦿.

NBA 2K10

ABA BALL
Select Codes from Options and enter payrespect.

2K CHINA TEAM
Select Codes from Options and enter 2kchina.

NBA 2K TEAM
Select Codes from Options and enter nba2k.

2K SPORTS TEAM
Select Codes from Options and enter 2ksports.

VISUAL CONCEPTS TEAM
Select Codes from Options and enter vcteam.

NEED FOR SPEED CARBON: OWN THE CITY

UNLOCK EVERYTHING
At the start menu, press X, X, Right, Left, Square, Up, Down.

JET CAR
At the start menu, press Up, Down, Left, R1, L1, Circle, Triangle.

LAMBORGINI MERCIALAGO
At the start menu, press X, X, Up, Down, Left, Right, Circle, Circle.

TRANSFORMERS CAR
At the start menu, press X, X, X, Square, Triangle, Triangle, Up, Down.

NEOPETS PETPET ADVENTURE: THE WAND OF WISHING

START GAME WITH 5 CHOCOLATE TREATS
Enter treat4u as your Petpet's name. You can then rename name your character. The chocolate treats are shaped according to the character you chose.

POCKET POOL

ALL PICTURES AND VIDEOS
At the title screen, press L, R, L, L, R, R, L (x3), R (x3), L (x4), R (x4).

PRINNY: CAN I REALLY BE THE HERO?

START A NEW GAME WITH THE ALTERNATE STORYLINE

At the main menu, highlight New Game and press ▲, ■, ●, ▲, ■, ●, ✖.

SECRET AGENT CLANK

ACTIVATE CHALICE OF POWER

Press Up, Up, Down, Down, Left, Right, Left, Right to regain health once per level.

SEGA GENESIS COLLECTION

Before using the following cheats, select the ABC Control option. This sets the controller to the following: ■ is A, ✖ is B, ● is C.

ALTERED BEAST

OPTIONS MENU

At the title screen, hold ✖ and press Start.

LEVEL SELECT

After enabling the Options menu, select a level from the menu. At the title screen, hold ■ and press Start.

BEAST SELECT

At the title screen, hold ■ + ✖ + ● + Down/Left and then press Start

SOUND TEST

At the title screen, hold ■ + ● + Up/Right and press Start.

COMIX ZONE

INVINCIBILITY

At the jukebox screen, press C on the following sounds:

3, 12, 17, 2, 2, 10, 2, 7, 7, 11

LEVEL SELECT

At the jukebox screen, press C on the following sounds:

14, 15, 18, 5, 13, 1, 3, 18, 15, 6

Press C on the desired level.

ECCO THE DOLPHIN

INVINCIBILITY

When the level name appears, hold ■ + Start until the level begins.

DEBUG MENU

Pause the game with Ecco facing the screen and press Right, ✖, ●, ✖, ●, Down, ●, Up.

INFINITE AIR

Enter LIFEFISH as a password

PASSWORDS

LEVEL	PASSWORD	LEVEL	PASSWORD
The Undercaves	WEFIDNMP	Open Ocean	YWGTTJNI
The Vents	BQDPXJDS	Ice Zone	HZIFZBMF
The Lagoon	JNSBRIKY	Hard Water	LRFJRQLI
Ridge Water	NTSBZTKB	Cold Water	UYNFRQLC

LEVEL	PASSWORD	LEVEL	PASSWORD
Island Zone	LYTIOQLZ	Origin Beach	EGRIUNLB
Deep Water	MNOPOQLR	Trilobite Circle	IELMUNLB
The Marble	RJNTQQLZ	Dark Water	RKEQUNLN
The Library	RTGXQQLE	City of Forever 2	HPQIGPLA
Deep City	DDXPQQLJ	The Tube	JUMFKMLB
City of Forever	MSDBRQLA	The Machine	GXUBKMLF
Jurassic Beach	IYCBUNLB	The Last Fight	TSONLMLU
Pteranodon Pond	DMXEUNLI		

FLICKY

ROUND SELECT

Begin a new game. Before the first round appears, hold ⬤ + ⬤ + Up + Start. Press Up or Down to select a Round.

GAIN GROUND

LEVEL SELECT

At the Options screen, press ⬤, ⬤, ⬤, ⬤.

GOLDEN AXE

LEVEL SELECT

Select Arcade Mode. At the character select, hold Down/Left +⬤ and press Start. Press Up or Down to select a level.

RISTAR

Select Passwords from the Options menu and enter the following:

LEVEL SELECT
ILOVEU

BOSS RUSH MODE
MUSEUM

TIME ATTACK MODE
DOFEEL

TOUGHER DIFFICULTY
SUPER

ONCHI MUSIC
MAGURO. Activate this from the Sound Test.

CLEARS PASSWORD
XXXXXX

GAME COPYRIGHT INFO
AGES

SONIC THE HEDGEHOG

LEVEL SELECT

At the title screen, press Up, Down, Left, Right. Hold ⬤ and press Start.

SONIC THE HEDGEHOG 2

LEVEL SELECT

Select Sound Test from the options. Press C on the following sounds in order: 19, 65, 09, 17. At the title screen, hold ⬤ and press Start.

VECTORMAN

DEBUG MODE

At the options screen, press ⬤, ⬤, ⬤, ⬤, Down, ⬤, ⬤, ⬤, ⬤.

REFILL LIFE

Pause the game and press ⬤, ⬤, Right, ⬤, ⬤, ⬤, Down, ⬤, ⬤, Right, ⬤.

55

VECTORMAN 2

LEVEL SELECT
Pause the game and press Up, Right, ●, ✖, ●, Down, Left, ●, Down.

EXTRA LIFE
Pause the game and press Right, Up, ✖, ●, Down, Up, ✖, Down, Up, ✖. Repeat for more lives.

FULL ENERGY
Pause the game and press ✖, ●, ✖, ●, Left, Up, Up.

NEW WEAPON
Pause the game and press ●, ●, Left, Left, Down, ●, Down. Repeat for more weapons.

SHREK THE THIRD

10,000 BONUS COINS
Press Up, Up, Down, Up, Right, Left at the Gift Shop.

THE SIMPSONS GAME

UNLIMITED POWER FOR ALL CHARACTERS
At the Extras menu, press ▲, Left, Right, ▲, ●, L.

ALL MOVIES
At the Extras menu, press ●, Left, ●, Right, ▲, R.

ALL CLICHÉS
At the Extras menu, press Left, ●, Right, ▲, Right, L.

THE SIMS 2: CASTAWAY

CHEAT GNOME
During a game, press L, R, Up, ✖, R. You can now use this Gnome to get the following during Live mode:

ALL PLANS
During a game, press ✖, R, ✖, R, ✖.

ALL CRAFT AND RESOURCES
During a game, press ●, ▲, R, Down, Down, Up.

MAX FOOD AND RESOURCES
During a game, press ● (x4), L.

E SIMS 2: PETS

CHEAT GNOME
During a game, press L, L, R, ✖, ✖, Up. Now you can enter the following cheats:

VANCE TIME 6 HOURS
ing a game, press Up, Left, Down, Right, R.

E SIM PET POINTS
ing a game, press ▲, ●, ✖, ●, L, R.

0,000
During a game, press ▲, Up, Left, Down, Right.

SPIDER-MAN: FRIEND OR FOE

NEW GOBLIN

At the stage complete screen, hold L + R and press ●, Down, ✖, Right, ●, Up, ▲, Left.

STAR WARS: THE FORCE UNLEASHED

CHEATS

Once you have accessed the Rogue Shadow, select Enter Code from the Extras menu. Now you can enter the following codes:

CHEAT	CODE
Invincibility	CORTOSIS
Unlimited Force	VERGENCE
1,000,000 Force Points	SPEEDER
All Force Powers	TYRANUS
Max Force Power Level	KATARN
Max Combo Level	COUNTDOOKU
Amplified Lightsaber Damage	LIGHTSABER

COSTUMES

Once you have accessed the Rogue Shadow, select Enter Code from the Extras menu. Now you can enter the following codes:

COSTUME	CODE	COSTUME	CODE
All Costumes	GRANDMOFF	Juno Eclipse	ECLIPSE
501st Legion	LEGION	Kento's Robe	WOOKIEE
Aayla Secura	AAYLA	Kleef	KLEEF
Admiral Ackbar	ITSATWAP	Lando Calrissian	SCOUNDREL
Anakin Skywalker	CHOSENONE	Luke Skywalker	T16WOMPRAT
Asajj Ventress	ACOLYTE	Luke Skywalker (Yavin)	YELLOWJCKT
Ceremonial Jedi Robes	DANTOOINE	Mace Windu	JEDIMASTER
Chop'aa Notimo	NOTIMO	Mara Jade	MARAJADE
Classic stormtrooper	TK421	Maris Brook	MARISBROOD
Count Dooku	SERENNO	Navy commando	STORMTROOP
Darth Desolous	PAUAN	Obi Wan Kenobi	BENKENOBI
Darth Maul	ZABRAK	Proxy	HOLOGRAM
Darth Phobos	HIDDENFEAR	Qui Gon Jinn	MAVERICK
Darth Vader	SITHLORD	Shaak Ti	TOGRUTA
Drexl Roosh	DREXLROOSH	Shadow trooper	INTHEDARK
Emperor Palpatine	PALPATINE	Sith Robes	HOLOCRON
General Rahm Kota	MANDALORE	Sith Stalker Armor	KORRIBAN
Han Solo	NERFHERDER	Twi'lek	SECURA
Heavy trooper	SHOCKTROOP		

STAR WARS: LETHAL ALLIANCE

ALL LEVELS

Select Create Profile from the Profiles menu and enter HANSOLO.

ALL LEVELS AND REFILL HEALTH WHEN DEPLETED

Select Create Profile from the Profiles menu and enter JD1MSTR.

REFILL HEALTH WHEN DEPLETED

Select Create Profile from the Profiles menu and enter BOBAF3T.

STRIKERS 1945 PLUS PORTABLE

XP-55 ASCENDER
At the random select, press Down, Up, Down, Up, Down, Down, Down, Down, Up.

SUPER MONKEY BALL ADVENTURE

ALL CARDS
At the mode select, press ■, ▲, ●, ■, ▲, ●, ■, ▲, ●, ■, ▲, ●.

THRILLVILLE: OFF THE RAILS

$50,000
During a game, press ■, ●, ▲, ■, ●, ▲, ✕. Repeat this code as much as desired.

ALL PARKS
During a game, press ■, ●, ▲, ■, ●, ▲, ■.

ALL RIDES
During a game, press ■, ●, ▲, ■ ●, ▲, ▲. Some rides still need to be researched.

COMPLETE MISSIONS
During a game, press ■, ●, ▲, ■, ●, ▲, ●. Then, at the Missions menu, highlight a mission and press ■ to complete that mission. Some missions have Bronze, Silver, and Gold objectives. For these missions the first press of ■ earns the Bronze, the second earns the Silver, and the third earns the Gold.

TIGER WOODS PGA TOUR 09

UNLOCK PGA TOUR EVENTS
Enter BEATIT as a password.

$1,000,000
Enter JACKPOT as a password.

UNLOCK ALL CLOTHING AND EQUIPMENT
Enter SHOP2DROP as a password.

MAX SKILL POINTS AND ALL CLOTHING AND EQUIPMENT
Enter IAMRUBBISH as a password.

UNLOCK ALL COVER STORIES
Enter HEADLINER as a password.

TOMB RAIDER: LEGEND

You need to unlock the following cheats before they can be used.

BULLETPROOF
During a game, hold L and press ✕, R, ▲, R, ●, R.

DRAW ENEMY HEALTH
During a game, hold L and press ■, ●, ✕, R, R, ▲.

INFINITE ASSUALT RIFLE AMMO
During a game, hold L and press ✕, O, ✕, R, ■, ▲.

INFINITE GRENADE LAUNCHER

During a game, hold L and press R, ▲, R, ◉, R, ■.

INFINITE SHOTGUN AMMO

During a game, hold L and press R, ◉, ■, R, ■, ✖.

INFINITE SMG AMMO

During a game, hold L and press ◉, ▲, R, R, ✖, ◉.

ONE SHOT KILL

During a game, hold L and press ▲, ✖, ▲, ■, R, ◉.

TEXTURELESS MODE

hold L and press R, ✖, ◉, ✖, ▲, R.

WIELD EXCALIBUR

During a game, hold L and press ▲, ✖, ◉, R, ▲, R.

VIRTUA TENNIS 3

ALL COURTS

At the Game Mode screen, press Up, Up, Down, Down, Left, Right, Left, Right.

ALL GEAR

At the Game Mode screen, press Left, Right, ◉, Left, Right, ◉, Up, Down.

KING & DUKE

At the Game Mode screen, press Up, Up, Down, Down, Left, Right, L, R.

WALL-E

KILL ALL

Select Cheats and then Secret Codes. Enter BOTOFWAR.

UNDETECTED BY ENEMIES

Select Cheats and then Secret Codes. Enter STEALTHARMOR.

LASERS CHANGE COLORS

Select Cheats and then Secret Codes. Enter RAINBOWLAZER.

CUBES ARE EXPLOSIVE

Select Cheats and then Secret Codes. Enter EXPLOSIVEWORLD.

LIGHTEN DARK AREAS

Select Cheats and then Secret Codes. Enter GLOWINTHEDARK.

GOGGLES

Select Cheats and then Secret Codes. Enter BOTOFMYSTERY.

GOLD TRACKS

Select Cheats and then Secret Codes. Enter GOLDENTRACKS.

WORLD CHAMPIONSHIP POKER 2: FEATURING HOWARD LEDERER

SKIP WEEK AND MONEY CHEATS

At the career world map, hold **R1**. Hold **L1** and release **R1**. Hold Up and release **L1**. Hold **L1** and release Up. Hold **R1** and release **L1**. While still holding **R1**, press Up/Down to skip weeks and Right/Left for money.

WRC: FIA WORLD RALLY CHAMPIONSHIP

UNLOCK EVERYTHING

Create a new profile with the name PADLOCK.

EXTRA AVATARS

Create a new profile with the name UGLYMUGS.

GHOST CAR

Create a new profile with the name SPOOKY.

SUPERCHARGER

Create a new profile with the name MAXPOWER.

TIME TRIAL GHOST CARS

Create a new profile with the name AITRIAL.

BIRD CAMERA

Create a new profile with the name dovecam.

REVERSES CONTROLS

Create a new profile with the name REVERSE.

WWE SMACKDOWN VS. RAW 2010

THE ROCK

Select Cheat Codes from the Options and enter The Great One.

VINCE'S OFFICE AND DIRT SHEET FOR BACKSTAGE BRAWL

Select Cheat Codes from the Options menu and enter BonusBrawl.

SHAWN MICHAELS' NEW COSTUME

Select Cheat Codes from the Options menu and enter Bow Down.

RANDY ORTON'S NEW COSTUME

Select Cheat Codes from the Options menu and enter ViperRKO.

TRIPLE H'S NEW COSTUME

Select Cheat Codes from the Options menu and enter Suck IT!.

X-MEN LEGENDS II: RISE OF APOCALYPSE

ALL CHARACTERS

At the Team Management screen, press Right, Left, Left, Right, Up, Up, Up, Start.

LEVEL 99 CHARACTERS

At the Team Management screen, press Up, Down, Up, Down, Left, Up, Left, Right, Start.

ALL SKILLS

At the Team Management screen, press Left, Right, Left, Right, Down, Up, Start.

SUPER SPEED

Pause the game and press Up, Up, Up, Down, Up, Down, Start.

UNLIMITED XTREME POWER

Pause the game and press Left, Down, Right, Down, Up, Up, Down, Up Start.

100,000 TECHBITS

At Forge or Beast's equipment screen, press Up, Up, Up, Down, Right, Right, Start.

ALL CINEMATICS

A the Review menu, press Left, Right, Right, Left, Down, Down, Left, Start.

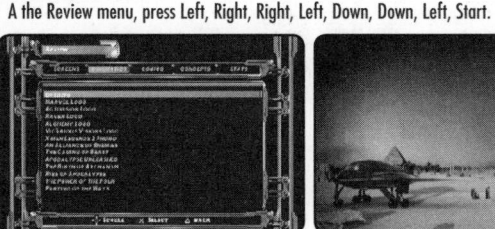 

ALL COMIC BOOKS

At the Review menu, press Right, Left, Left, Right, Up, Up, Right, Start.

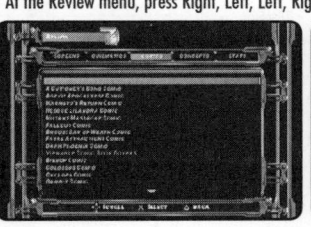 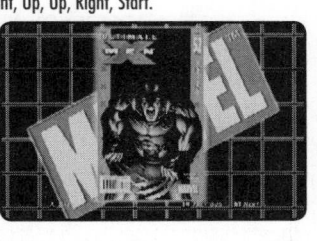

YU-GI-OH! GX TAG FORCE

BOOSTER PACK

At the card shop, press Up, Up, Down, Down, Left, Right, Left, Right, ✖, ⬤.

YU-GI-OH! GX TAG FORCE 2

MIDDDAY CONSTELLATION BOOSTER PACK

When buying booster packs, press Up, Up, Down, Down, Left, Right, Left, Right, ✖, ⬤.

YU-GI-OH! CARD PASSWORDS

Enter the following in the Password Machine to obtain for rental:

PASSWORD	EFFECT	PASSWORD	EFFECT
4-Starred Ladybug of Doom	83994646	Abyss Soldier	18318842
7 Colored Fish	23771716	Abyssal Designator	89801755
A Cat of Ill Omen	24140059	Acid Trap Hole	41356845
A Deal With Dark Ruler	06850209	Acrobat Monkey	47372349
A Feather of the Phoenix	49140998	Adhesion Trap Hole	62325062
A Feint Plan	68170903	Adhesive Explosive	53828396
A Hero Emerges	21597117	After the Struggle	25345186
A Legendary Ocean	00295517	Agido	16135253
A Man With Wdjat	51351302	Airknight Parshath	18036057
A Rival Appears!	05728014	Aitsu	48202661
A Wingbeat of Giant Dragon	28596933	Alkana Knight Joker	06150044
A-Team: Trap Disposal Unit	13026402	Alpha the Magnet Warrior	99785935
Abare Ushioni	89718302	Altar for Tribute	21070956
Absolute End	27744077	Amazon Archer	91869203
Absorbing Kid From the Sky	49771608	Amazoness Archers	67987611

CHEAT CODE EXPLOSION FOR HANDHELDS

PLAYSTATION® PORTABLE

PASSWORD	EFFECT
73515478	Amazoness Blowpiper
95452737	Amazoness Chain Master
47480070	Amazoness Paladin
94002668	Amazoness Swords Woman
10979723	Amazoness Tiger
98677691	Ambulance Rescueroid
81728213	Ambulanceroid
95714353	Amebo
67371383	Amphibian Beast
64342551	Amphibious Bugroth MK-3
23265594	An Owl of Luck
31552106	Ancient Elf
31557782	Ancient Gear
10509340	Ancient Gear Beast
80045583	Ancient Gear Cannon
92001300	Ancient Gear Castle
67829249	Ancient Gear Drill
83104731	Ancient Gear Golem
60549745	Ancient Gear Soldier
54912797	Ancient Lamp
43206477	Ancient Lizard Warrior
13468468	Andro Sphinx
13250922	Anteatereatingant
90564143	Anti-Aircraft Flower
51211264	Anti-Spell
60195135	Apprentice Magician
48539234	Appropriate
58963752	Aqua Madoor
40916093	Aqua Spirit
55007420	Arcane Archer of the Forest
07082760	Archfiend of Gilfer
98811766	Archfiend Soldier
18258287	Archlord Zerato
53152481	Armaill
90374761	Armed Changer
00608602	Armed Dragon LV 3
46384674	Armed Dragon LV 5
73879377	Armed Dragon LV 7
59646453	Armed Dragon LV10
84430650	Armed Samurai - Ben Kei
07080418	Armor Axe
79616965	Armor Break
15808851	Armored Lizard
17535588	Armored Starfish
20277860	Armored Zombie
29966555	Array of Revealing Light
42364374	Arsenal Bug
55348065	Arsenal Robber
96068958	Arsenal Summoner
62633180	Assault on GHQ
37053871	Astral Barrier
02134346	Asura Priest
88260974	Aswan Apparition
87340660	Atomic Firefly
63689843	Attack and Receive
18769616	Attack Reflector Unit
37976040	Aussa the Earth Charmer
71453557	Autonomous Action Unit
99782860	Avatar of the Pot
84916494	Axe Dragonute
40619085	Axe of Despair
80161068	B. Skull Dragon
15317640	B.E.S. Covered Core
22790227	B.E.S. Crystal Core
44659628	B.E.S. Tetran
18861857	Baby Dragon
47453433	Back to Square One
82755072	Backfire
36280194	Backup Soldier
40963297	Bad Reaction to Simochi
07165085	Bait Doll
77042146	Ballista of Rampart Smashing
51280725	Banisher of the Light
41629169	Bark of Dark Ruler
81840860	Barrel Dragon
61811838	Basic Insect
63142001	Batteryman AA
19733961	Batteryman C
55401221	Batteryman D
48094997	Battle Footballer
05050103	Battle Ox
94463200	Battle-Scarred
40135311	Bazoo the Soul-Eater
35149085	Beast Soul Swap
52457812	Beaver Warrior
12255442	Beckoning Light
45228489	Beelze Frog
20374520	Begone, Knave
22996376	Behemoth the King of All Animals
31310120	Beige, Vanguard of Dark World
98568950	Berserk Dragon
91688685	Berserk Gorilla
39256629	Beta the Magnet Warrior
25565502	Bickuribox
62117349	Big Bang Shot
54723621	Big Burn
14140969	Big Core
42129512	Big Koala
52620384	Big Shield Gardna
51575916	Big Wave Small Wave
59300081	Big-Tusked Mammoth
59896829	Bio-Mage
45546549	Birdface
41412689	Black Illusion Ritual
72989439	Black Luster Soldier - Envoy of the beginning
65169794	Black Pendant
38670435	Black Tyranno
62763752	Blackland Fire Dragon
39507162	Blade Knight
52868433	Blade Rabbit
97023549	Blade Skater

PASSWORD	EFFECT	PASSWORD	EFFECT
Bladefly	28470714	Castle of Dark Illusions	00062121
Blast Held By a Tribute	89041555	Cat's Ear Tribe	95841282
Blast Magician	21051146	Catapult Turtle	95727991
Blast with Chain	98239899	Cathedral of Nobles	29762407
Blasting the Ruins	21466326	Catnipped Kitty	96501677
Blazing Inpachi	05464695	Cave Dragon	93220472
Blind Destruction	32015116	Ceasefire	36468556
Blindly Loyal Goblin	35215622	Celtic Guardian	91152256
Block Attack	25880422	Cemetery Bomb	51394546
Blockman	48115277	Centrifugal	01801154
Blowback Dragon	25551951	Ceremonial Bell	20228463
Blue-Eyes Shining Dragon	53347303	Cetus of Dagala	28106077
Blue-Eyes Toon Dragon	53183600	Chain Burst	48276469
Blue-Eyes Ultimate Dragon	23995346	Chain Destruction	01248895
Blue-Eyes White Dragon	89631139	Chain Disappearance	57139487
Blue-Winged Crown	41396436	Chain Energy	79323590
Bokoichi the Freightening Car	08715625	Chain Thrasher	88190453
Bombardment Beetle	57409948	Chainsaw Insect	77252217
Bonding - H2O	45898858	Change of Heart	04031928
Boneheimer	98456117	Chaos Command Magician	72630549
Book of Life	02204140	Chaos Emperor Dragon - Envoy of the End	82301904
Book of Moon	14087893		
Book of Taiyou	38699854	Chaos End	61044390
Boss Rush	66947414	Chaos Greed	97439308
Bottom Dweller	81386177	Chaos Necromancer	01434352
Bottomless Shifting Sand	76532077	Chaos Sorcerer	09596126
Bottomless Trap Hole	29401950	Chaosrider Gutaph	47829960
Bountiful Artemis	32296881	Charcoal Inpachi	13179332
Bowganian	52090844	Charm of Shabti	50412166
Bracchio-Raidus	16507828	Charubin the Fire Knight	37421579
Brain Control	87910978	Chiron the Mage	16956455
Brain Jacker	40267580	Chopman the Desperate Outlaw	40884383
Branch!	30548775	Chorus of Sanctuary	81380218
Breaker the Magical Warrior	71413901	Chthonian Alliance	46910446
Broww, Huntsman of Dark World	79126789	Chthonian Blast	18271561
Brron, Mad King of Dark World	06214884	Chthonian Polymer	72287557
Bubble Blaster	53586134	Chu-Ske the Mouse Fighter	08508055
Bubble Illusion	80075749	Clay Charge	22479888
Bubble Shuffle	61968753	Cliff the Trap Remover	06967870
Bubonic Vermin	06104968	Cobra Jar	86801871
Burning Algae	41859700	Cobraman Sakuzy	75109441
Burning Beast	59364406	Cold Wave	60682203
Burning Land	24294108	Collected Power	07565547
Burst Breath	80163754	Combination Attack	08964854
Burst Return	27191436	Command Knight	10375182
Burst Stream of Destruction	17655904	Commander Covington	22666164
Buster Blader	78193831	Commencement Dance	43417563
Buster Rancher	84740193	Compulsory Evacuation Device	94192409
Butterfly Dagger - Elma	69243953	Confiscation	17375316
Byser Shock	17597059	Conscription	31000575
Call of The Haunted	97077563	Continuous Destruction Punch	68057622
Call of the Mummy	04861205	Contract With Exodia	33244944
Cannon Soldier	11384280	Contract With the Abyss	69035382
Cannonball Spear Shellfish	95614612	Contract with the Dark Master	96420087
Card of Safe Return	57953380	Convulsion of Nature	62966332
Card Shuffle	12183332	Cost Down	23265313

PASSWORD	EFFECT
Covering Fire	74458486
Crab Turtle	91782219
Crass Clown	93889755
Creature Swap	31036355
Creeping Doom Manta	52571838
Crimson Ninja	14618326
Criosphinx	18654201
Cross Counter	37083210
Crush D. Gandra	64681432
Cure Mermaid	85802526
Curse of Aging	41398771
Curse of Anubis	66742250
Curse of Darkness	84970821
Curse of Dragon	28279543
Curse of the Masked Beast	94377247
Curse of Vampire	34294855
Cyber Dragon	70095154
Cyber End Dragon	01546123
Cyber Twin Dragon	74157028
Cyber-Dark Edge	77625948
Cyber-Stein	69015963
Cyberdark Dragon	40418351
Cyberdark Horn	41230939
Cyberdark Keel	03019642
D - Shield	62868900
D - Time	99075257
D. D. Assailant	70074904
D. D. Borderline	60912752
D. D. Crazy Beast	48148828
D. D. Dynamite	08628798
D. D. M. - Different Dimension Master	82112775
D. D. Trainer	86498013
D. D. Trap Hole	05606466
D. D. Warrior Lady	07572887
Dancing Fairy	90925163
Dangerous Machine TYPE-6	76895648
Dark Artist	72520073
Dark Bat	67049542
Dark Blade	11321183
Dark Blade the Dragon Knight	86805855
Dark Driceratops	65287621
Dark Dust Spirit	89111398
Dark Elf	21417692
Dark Energy	04614116
Dark Factory of Mass Production	90928333
Dark Flare Knight	13722870
Dark Hole	53129443
Dark Magic Attack	02314238
Dark Magic Ritual	76792184
Dark Magician	46986414
Dark Magician Girl	38033121
Dark Magician of Chaos	40737112
Dark Magician's Tome of Black Magic	67227834
Dark Master - Zorc	97642679

PASSWORD	EFFECT
Dark Mirror Force	20522190
Dark Paladin	98502113
Dark Room of Nightmare	85562745
Dark Sage	92377303
Dark Snake Syndrome	47233801
Dark-Piercing Light	45895206
Darkfire Dragon	17881964
Darkfire Soldier #1	05388481
Darkfire Soldier #2	78861134
Darkworld Thorns	43500484
De-Spell	19159413
Deal of Phantom	69122763
Decayed Commander	10209545
Dedication Through Light And Darkness	69542930
Deepsea Shark	28593363
Dekoichi the Battlechanted Locomotive	87621407
Delinquent Duo	44763025
Demotion	72575145
Des Counterblow	39131963
Des Croaking	44883830
Des Dendle	12965761
Des Feral Imp	81985784
Des Frog	84451804
Des Kangaroo	78613627
Des Koala	69579761
Des Lacooda	02326738
Des Wombat	09637706
Desert Sunlight	93747864
Destertapir	13409151
Destiny Board	94212438
Destiny Hero - Captain Tenacious	77608643
Destiny Hero - Diamond Dude	13093792
Destiny Hero - Doom Lord	41613948
Destiny Hero - Dreadmaster	40591390
Destiny Signal	35464895
Destroyer Golem	73481154
Destruction Ring	21219755
Dian Keto the Cure Master	84257639
Dice Jar	03549275
Dimension Distortion	95194279
Dimensional Warrior	37043180
Disappear	24623598
Disarmament	20727787
Disc Fighter	19612721
Dissolverock	40826495
Divine Dragon Ragnarok	62113340
Divine Wrath	49010598
DNA Surgery	74701381
DNA Transplant	56769674
Doitsu	57062206
Dokurorider	99721536
Dokuroyaiba	30325729
Don Turtle	03493978
Don Zaloog	76922029

PASSWORD	EFFECT	PASSWORD	EFFECT
Doriado	84916669	Eternal Draught	56606928
Doriado's Blessing	23965037	Eternal Rest	95051344
Dragon Seeker	28563545	Exhausting Spell	95451366
Dragon Treasure	01435851	Exile of the Wicked	26725158
Dragon Zombie	66672569	Exiled Force	74131780
Dragon's Mirror	71490127	Exodia Necross	12600382
Dragon's Rage	54178050	Exodia the Forbidden One	33396948
Dragoness the Wicked Knight	70681994	Fairy Box	21598948
Draining Shield	43250041	Fairy Dragon	20315854
Dream Clown	13215230	Fairy King Truesdale	45425051
Drillago	99050989	Fairy Meteor Crush	97687912
Drillroid	71218746	Faith Bird	75582395
Dunames Dark Witch	12493482	Fatal Abacus	77910045
Dust Tornado	60082867	Fenrir	00218704
Earth Chant	59820352	Feral Imp	41392891
Earthbound Spirit	67105242	Fiber Jar	78706415
Earthquake	82828051	Fiend Comedian	81172176
Eatgaboon	42578427	Fiend Scorpion	26566878
Ebon Magician Curran	46128076	Fiend's Hand	52800428
Electro-Whip	37820550	Fiend's Mirror	31890399
Elegant Egotist	90219263	Final Countdown	95308449
Element Dragon	30314994	Final Destiny	18591904
Elemental Burst	61411502	Final Flame	73134081
Elemental Hero Avian	21844576	Final Ritual of the Ancients	60369732
Elemental Hero Bladedge	59793705	Fire Darts	43061293
Elemental Hero Bubbleman	79979666	Fire Eye	88435542
Elemental Hero Burstinatrix	58932615	Fire Kraken	46534755
Elemental Hero Clayman	84327329	Fire Princess	64752646
Elemental Hero Electrum/ Erekshieler	29343734	Fire Reaper	53581214
		Fire Sorcerer	27132350
Elemental Hero Flame Wingman	35809262	Firegrass	53293545
Elemental Hero Mariner	14225239	Firewing Pegasus	27054370
Elemental Hero Necroid Shaman	81003500	Fireyarou	71407486
Elemental Hero Neos	89943723	Fissure	66788016
Elemental Hero Phoenix Enforcer	41436536	Five God Dragon (Five Headed Dragon)	99267150
Elemental Hero Shining Flare Wingman	25366484		
		Flame Cerebrus	60862676
Elemental Hero Shining Phoenix Enforcer	88820235	Flame Champion	42599677
		Flame Dancer	12883044
Elemental Hero Sparkman	20721928	Flame Ghost	58528964
Elemental Hero Thunder Giant	61204971	Flame Manipulator	34460851
Elemental Mistress Doriado	99414158	Flame Swordsman	45231177
Elemental Recharge	36586443	Flame Viper	02830619
Elf's Light	39897277	Flash Assailant	96890582
Emblem of Dragon Destroyer	06390406	Flower Wolf	95952802
Embodiment of Apophis	28649820	Flying Fish	31987274
Emergency Provisions	53046408	Flying Kamakiri #1	84834865
Emes the Infinity	43580269	Flying Kamakiri #2	03134241
Empress Judge	15237615	Follow Wind	98252586
Empress Mantis	58818411	Foolish Burial	81439173
Enchanted Javelin	96355986	Forest	87430998
Enchanting Mermaid	75376965	Fortress Whale	62337487
Enemy Controller	98045062	Fortress Whale's Oath	77454922
Enraged Battle Ox	76909279	Frenzied Panda	98818516
Enraged Muka Muka	91862578	Frozen Soul	57069605
Eradicating Aerosol	94716515	Fruits of Kozaky's Studies	49998907

PASSWORD	EFFECT
Fuh-Rin-Ka-Zan	01781310
Fuhma Shuriken	09373534
Fulfillment of the Contract	48206762
Fushi No Tori	38538445
Fusion Gate	33550694
Fusion Recovery	18511384
Fusion Sage	26902560
Fusion Weapon	27967615
Fusionist	01641883
Gadget Soldier	86281779
Gagagigo	49003308
Gaia Power	56594520
Gaia the Dragon Champion	66889139
Gaia the Fierce Knight	06368038
Gale Dogra	16229315
Gale Lizard	77491079
Gamble	37313786
Gamma the Magnet Warrior	11549357
Garma Sword	90844184
Garma Sword Oath	78577570
Garoozis	14977074
Garuda the Wind Spirit	12800777
Gatling Dragon	87751584
Gazelle the King of Mythical Beasts	05818798
Gear Golem the Moving Fortress	30190809
Gearfried the Iron Knight	00423705
Gearfried the Swordmaster	57046845
Gemini Elf	69140098
Getsu Fuhma	21887179
Giant Axe Mummy	78266168
Giant Germ	95178994
Giant Kozaky	58185394
Giant Orc	73698349
Giant Rat	97017120
Giant Red Seasnake	58831685
Giant Soldier of Stone	13039848
Giant Trunade	42703248
Gift of the Mystical Elf	98299011
Giga Gagagigo	43793530
Giga-Tech Wolf	08471389
Gigantes	47606319
Gigobyte	53776525
Gil Garth	38445524
Gilasaurus	45894482
Giltia the D. Knight	51828629
Girochin Kuwagata	84620194
Goblin Attack Force	78658564
Goblin Calligrapher	12057781
Goblin Elite Attack Force	85306040
Goblin Thief	45311864
Goblin's Secret Remedy	11868825
Gogiga Gagagigo	39674352
Golem Sentry	82323207
Good Goblin Housekeeping	09744376
Gora Turtle	80233946
Graceful Charity	79571449

PASSWORD	EFFECT
Graceful Dice	74137509
Gradius	10992251
Gradius' Option	14291024
Granadora	13944422
Grand Tiki Elder	13676474
Granmarg the Rock Monarch	60229110
Gravedigger Ghoul	82542267
Gravekeeper's Cannonholder	99877698
Gravekeeper's Curse	50712728
Gravekeeper's Guard	37101832
Gravekeeper's Servant	16762927
Gravekeeper's Spear Soldier	63695531
Gravekeeper's Spy	24317029
Gravekeeper's Vassal	99690140
Graverobber's Retribution	33737664
Gravity Bind	85742772
Gray Wing	29618570
Great Angus	11813953
Great Long Nose	02356994
Great Mammoth of Goldfine	54622031
Green Gadget	41172955
Gren Maju Da Eiza	36584821
Ground Attacker Bugroth	58314394
Ground Collapse	90502999
Gruesome Goo	65623423
Gryphon Wing	55608151
Gryphon's Feather Duster	34370473
Guardian Angel Joan	68007326
Guardian of the Labyrinth	89272878
Guardian of the Sea	85448931
Guardian Sphinx	40659562
Guardian Statue	75209824
Gust Fan	55321970
Gyaku-Gire Panda	09817927
Gyroid	18325492
Hade-Hane	28357177
Hamburger Recipe	80811661
Hammer Shot	26412047
Hamon	32491822
Hand of Nephthys	98446407
Hane-Hane	07089711
Hannibal Necromancer	05640330
Hard Armor	20060230
Harpie Girl	34100324
Harpie Lady 1	91932350
Harpie Lady 2	27927359
Harpie Lady 3	54415063
Harpie Lady Sisters	12206212
Harpie's Brother	30532390
Harpies' Hunting Ground	75782277
Hayabusa Knight	21015833
Headless Knight	05434080
Heart of Clear Water	64801562
Heart of the Underdog	35762283
Heavy Mech Support Platform	23265594
Heavy Storm	19613556

PASSWORD	EFFECT	PASSWORD	EFFECT
Helios - The Primordial Sun	54493213	Infinite Dismissal	54109233
Helios Duo Megistus	80887952	Injection Fairy Lily	79575620
Helios Tris Megiste	17286057	Inpachi	97923414
Helping Robo for Combat	47025270	Insect Armor with Laser Cannon	03492538
Hero Barrier	44676200	Insect Barrier	23615409
HERO Flash!!	00191749	Insect Imitation	96965364
Hero Heart	67951831	Insect Knight	35052053
Hero Kid	32679370	Insect Princess	37957847
Hero Ring	26647858	Insect Queen	91512835
Hero Signal	22020907	Insect Soldiers of the Sky	07019529
Hidden Book of Spell	21840375	Inspection	16227556
Hidden Soldier	02047519	Interdimensional Matter Transporter	36261276
Hieracosphinx	82260502	Invader From Another Dimension	28450915
Hieroglyph Lithograph	10248192	Invader of Darkness	56647086
High Tide Gyojin	54579801	Invader of the Throne	03056267
Hiita the Fire Charmer	00759393	Invasion of Flames	26082229
Hino-Kagu-Tsuchi	75745607	Invigoration	98374133
Hinotama Soul	96851799	Iron Blacksmith Kotetsu	73431236
Hiro's Shadow Scout	81863068	Island Turtle	04042268
Hitotsu-Me Giant	76184692	Jack's Knight	90876561
Holy Knight Ishzark	57902462	Jade Insect Whistle	95214051
Homunculus the Alchemic Being	40410110	Jam Breeding Machine	21770260
Horn of Heaven	98069388	Jam Defender	21558682
Horn of Light	38552107	Jar of Greed	83968380
Horn of the Unicorn	64047146	Jar Robber	33784505
Horus The Black Flame Dragon LV4	75830094	Javelin Beetle	26932788
Horus The Black Flame Dragon LV6	11224103	Javelin Beetle Pact	41182875
Horus The Black Flame Dragon LV8	48229808	Jellyfish	14851496
Hoshiningen	67629977	Jerry Beans Man	23635815
House of Adhesive Tape	15083728	Jetroid	43697559
Howling Insect	93107608	Jinzo	77585513
Huge Revolution	65396880	Jinzo #7	32809211
Human-Wave Tactics	30353551	Jirai Gumo	94773007
Humanoid Slime	46821314	Jowgen the Spiritualist	41855169
Humanoid Worm Drake	05600127	Jowls of Dark Demise	05257687
Hungry Burger	30243636	Judge Man	30113682
Hydrogeddon	22587018	Judgment of Anubis	55256016
Hyena	22873798	Just Desserts	24068492
Hyozanryu	62397231	KA-2 Des Scissors	52768103
Hyper Hammerhead	02671330	Kabazauls	51934376
Hysteric Fairy	21297224	Kagemusha of the Blue Flame	15401633
Icarus Attack	53367095	Kaibaman	34627841
Illusionist Faceless Mage	28546905	Kaiser Dragon	94566432
Impenetrable Formation	96631852	Kaiser Glider	52824910
Imperial Order	61740673	Kaiser Sea Horse	17444133
Inaba White Rabbit	77084837	Kaminari Attack	09653271
Incandescent Ordeal	33031674	Kaminote Blow	97570038
Indomitable Fighter Lei Lei	84173492	Kamionwizard	41544074
Infernal Flame Emperor	19847532	Kangaroo Champ	95789089
Infernal Queen Archfiend	08581705	Karate Man	23289281
Inferno	74823665	Karbonala Warrior	54541900
Inferno Fire Blast	52684508	Karma Cut	71587526
Inferno Hammer	17185260	Kelbek	54878498
Inferno Reckless Summon	12247206	Keldo	80441106
Inferno Tempest	14391920	Killer Needle	88979991
Infinite Cards	94163677	Kinetic Soldier	79853073

PASSWORD	EFFECT
King Dragun	13756293
King Fog	84686841
King of the Skull Servants	36021814
King of the Swamp	79109599
King of Yamimakai	69455834
King Tiger Wanghu	83986578
King's Knight	64788463
Kiryu	84814897
Kiseitai	04266839
Kishido Spirit	60519422
Knight's Title	87210505
Koitsu	69456283
Kojikocy	01184620
Kotodama	19406822
Kozaky	99171160
Kozaky's Self-Destruct Button	21908319
Kryuel	82642348
Kumootoko	56283725
Kurama	85705804
Kuriboh	40640057
Kuwagata Alpha	60802233
Kwagar Hercules	95144193
Kycoo The Ghost Destroyer	88240808
La Jinn The Mystical Genie of The Lamp	97590747
Labyrinth of Nightmare	66526672
Labyrinth Tank	99551425
Lady Assailant of Flames	90147755
Lady Ninja Yae	82005435
Lady of Faith	17358176
Larvas	94675535
Laser Cannon Armor	77007920
Last Day of Witch	90330453
Last Turn	28566710
Launcher Spider	87322377
Lava Battleguard	20394040
Lava Golem	00102380
Layard the Liberator	67468948
Left Arm of the Forbidden One	07902349
Left Leg of the Forbidden One	44519536
Legendary Black Belt	96438440
Legendary Flame Lord	60258960
Legendary Jujitsu Master	25773409
Legendary Sword	61854111
Leghul	12472242
Lekunga	62543393
Lesser Dragon	55444629
Lesser Fiend	16475472
Level Conversion Lab	84397023
Level Limit - Area A	54976796
Level Limit - Area B	03136426
Level Modulation	61850482
Level Up!	25290459
Levia-Dragon	37721209
Light of Intervention	62867251
Light of Judgment	44595286

PASSWORD	EFFECT
Lighten the Load	37231841
Lightforce Sword	49587034
Lightning Blade	55226821
Lightning Conger	27671321
Lightning Vortex	69162969
Limiter Removal	23171610
Liquid Beast	93108297
Little Chimera	68658728
Little-Winguard	90790253
Lizard Soldier	20831168
Lord of D.	17985575
Lord of the Lamp	99510761
Lost Guardian	45871897
Luminous Soldier	57282479
Luminous Spark	81777047
Luster Dragon	11091375
Luster Dragon #2	17658803
M-Warrior #1	56342351
M-Warrior #2	92731455
Machine Conversion Factory	25769732
Machine Duplication	63995093
Machine King	46700124
Machine King Prototype	89222931
Machiners Defender	96384007
Machiners Force	58054262
Machiners Sniper	23782705
Machiners Soldier	60999392
Mad Dog of Darkness	79182538
Mad Lobster	97240270
Mad Sword Beast	79870141
Mage Power	83746708
Magic Drain	59344077
Magic Jammer	77414722
Magical Cylinder	62279055
Magical Dimension	28553439
Magical Explosion	32723153
Magical Hats	81210420
Magical Labyrinth	64389297
Magical Marionette	08034697
Magical Merchant	32362575
Magical Plant Mandragola	07802006
Magical Scientist	34206604
Magical Thorn	53119267
Magician of Black Chaos	30208479
Magician of Faith	31560081
Magician's Circle	00050755
Magician's Unite	36045450
Magician's Valkyrie	80304126
Magnet Circle	94940436
Maha Vailo	93013676
Maharaghi	40695128
Maiden of the Aqua	17214465
Maji-Gire Panda	60102563
Maju Garzett	08794435
Makiu	27827272
Makyura the Destructor	21593977

PASSWORD	EFFECT	PASSWORD	EFFECT
Malevolent Nuzzler	99597615	Metalmorph	68540058
Malfunction	06137095	Metalzoa	50705071
Malice Ascendant	14255590	Metamorphosis	46411259
Malice Dispersion	13626450	Meteor B. Dragon	90660762
Mammoth Graveyard	40374923	Meteor Dragon	64271667
Man Eater	93553943	Meteor of Destruction	33767325
Man-Eater Bug	54652250	Meteorain	64274292
Man-Eating Black Shark	80727036	Michizure	37580756
Man-Eating Treasure Chest	13723605	Micro-Ray	18190572
Man-Thro' Tro'	43714890	Mid Shield Gardna	75487237
Manga Ryu-Ran	38369349	Mighty Guard	62327910
Manju of the Ten Thousand Hands	95492061	Mikazukinoyaiba	38277918
Manticore of Darkness	77121851	Millennium Golem	47986555
Marauding Captain	02460565	Millennium Scorpion	82482194
Marie the Fallen One	57579381	Millennium Shield	32012841
Marine Beast	29929832	Milus Radiant	07489323
Marshmallon	31305911	Minar	32539892
Marshmallon Glasses	66865880	Mind Control	37520316
Maryokutai	71466592	Mind Haxorz	75392615
Masaki the Legendary Swordsman	44287299	Mind on Air	66690411
Mask of Brutality	82432018	Mind Wipe	52718046
Mask of Darkness	28933734	Mine Golem	76321376
Mask of Restrict	29549364	Minefield Eruption	85519211
Mask of Weakness	57882509	Minor Goblin Official	01918087
Masked Dragon	39191307	Miracle Dig	06343408
Masked of the Accursed	56948373	Miracle Fusion	45906428
Masked Sorcerer	10189126	Miracle Kid	55985014
Mass Driver	34906152	Miracle Restoring	68334074
Master Kyonshee	24530661	Mirage Dragon	15960641
Master Monk	49814180	Mirage Knight	49217579
Master of Dragon Knight	62873545	Mirage of Nightmare	41482598
Master of Oz	27134689	Mirror Force	44095762
Mataza the Zapper	22609617	Mirror Wall	22359980
Mavelus	59036972	Misfortune	01036974
Maximum Six	30707994	Mispolymerization	58392024
Mazera DeVille	06133894	Mistobody	47529357
Mech Mole Zombie	63545455	Moai Interceptor Cannons	45159319
Mecha-Dog Marron	94667532	Mobius the Frost Monarch	04929256
Mechanical Hound	22512237	Moisture Creature	75285069
Mechanical Snail	34442949	Mokey Mokey	27288416
Mechanical Spider	45688586	Mokey Mokey King	13803864
Mechanicalchaser	07359741	Mokey Mokey Smackdown	01965724
Meda Bat	76211194	Molten Behemoth	17192817
Medusa Worm	02694423	Molten Destruction	19384334
Mefist the Infernal General	46820049	Molten Zombie	04732017
Mega Thunderball	21817254	Monk Fighter	03810071
Mega Ton Magical Cannon	32062913	Monster Egg	36121917
Megamorph	22046459	Monster Eye	84133008
Megarock Dragon	71544954	Monster Gate	43040603
Melchid the Four-Face Beast	86569121	Monster Reborn	83764718
Memory Crusher	48700891	Monster Recovery	93108433
Mermaid Knight	24435369	Monster Reincarnation	74848038
Messenger of Peace	44656491	Mooyan Curry	58074572
Metal Armored Bug	65957473	Morale Boost	93671934
Metal Dragon	09293977	Morphing Jar	33508719
Metallizing Parasite	07369217	Morphing Jar #2	79106360

PASSWORD	EFFECT	PASSWORD	EFFECT
Mother Grizzly	57839750	Niwatori	07805359
Mountain	50913601	Nobleman of Crossout	71044499
Mr. Volcano	31477025	Nobleman of Extermination	17449108
Mudora	82108372	Nobleman-Eater Bug	65878864
Muka Muka	46657337	Non Aggression Area	76848240
Multiplication of Ants	22493811	Non-Fusion Area	27581098
Multiply	40703222	Non-Spellcasting Area	20065549
Musician King	56907389	Novox's Prayer	43694075
Mustering of the Dark Scorpions	68191243	Nubian Guard	51616747
Mysterious Puppeteer	54098121	Numinous Healer	02130625
Mystic Horseman	68516705	Nutrient Z	29389368
Mystic Lamp	98049915	Nuvia the Wicked	12953226
Mystic Plasma Zone	18161786	O - Oversoul	63703130
Mystic Swordsman LV 2	47507260	Obnoxious Celtic Guardian	52077741
Mystic Swordsman LV 4	74591968	Ocubeam	86088138
Mystic Swordsman LV 6	60482781	Offerings to the Doomed	19230407
Mystic Tomato	83011277	Ojama Black	79335209
Mystic Wok	80161395	Ojama Delta Hurricane	08251996
Mystical Beast Serket	89194033	Ojama Green	12482652
Mystical Elf	15025844	Ojama King	90140980
Mystical Knight of Jackal	98745000	Ojama Trio	29843091
Mystical Moon	36607978	Ojama Yellow	42941100
Mystical Sand	32751480	Ojamagic	24643836
Mystical Sheep #2	30451366	Ojamuscle	98259197
Mystical Shine Ball	39552864	Old Vindictive Magician	45141844
Mystical Space Typhoon	05318639	Ominous Fortunetelling	56995655
Mystik Wok	80161395	Oni Tank T-34	66927994
Mythical Beast Cerberus	55424270	Opti-Camaflouge Armor	44762290
Nanobreaker	70948327	Opticlops	14531242
Necklace of Command	48576951	Option Hunter	33248692
Necrovalley	47355498	Orca Mega-Fortress of Darkness	63120904
Needle Ball	94230224	Ordeal of a Traveler	39537362
Needle Burrower	98162242	Order to Charge	78986941
Needle Ceiling	38411870	Order to Smash	39019325
Needle Wall	38299233	Otohime	39751093
Needle Worm	81843628	Outstanding Dog Marron	11548522
Negate Attack	14315573	Overdrive	02311603
Nemuriko	90963488	Oxygeddon	58071123
Neo Aqua Madoor	49563947	Painful Choice	74191942
Neo Bug	16587243	Paladin of White Dragon	73398797
Neo the Magic Swordsman	50930991	Pale Beast	21263083
Neo-Space	40215635	Pandemonium	94585852
Neo-Spacian Aqua Dolphin	17955766	Pandemonium Watchbear	75375465
Newdoria	04335645	Parasite Paracide	27911549
Next to be Lost	07076131	Parasitic Ticky	87978805
Night Assailant	16226786	Patrician of Darkness	19153634
Nightmare Horse	59290628	Patroid	71930383
Nightmare Penguin	81306586	Penguin Knight	36039163
Nightmare Wheel	54704216	Penumbral Soldier Lady	64751286
Nightmare's Steelcage	58775978	People Running About	12143771
Nimble Momonga	22567609	Perfect Machine King	18891691
Nin-Ken Dog	11987744	Performance of Sword	04849037
Ninja Grandmaster Sasuke	04041838	Petit Angel	38142739
Ninjitsu Art of Decoy	89628781	Petit Dragon	75356564
Ninjitsu Art of Transformation	70861343	Petit Moth	58192742
Nitro Unit	23842445	Phantasmal Martyrs	93224848

PASSWORD	EFFECT
07526514	Rareguild Armor
12503902	Rare Metalmorph
06337436	Rapid-Fire Magician
11125118	Rancer Dragonute
41382147	Rallis the Star Bird
21347810	Rainbow Flower
66719324	Rain Of Mercy
04178474	Raigeki Break
12580477	Raigeki
90261085	Raging Flame Sprite
31440542	Rafflesia Seduction
94905343	Rabid Horseman
25652259	Queen's Knight
77044671	Pyramid Turtle
53569894	Pyramid of Light
74703140	Punished Eagle
29155212	Pumpking the King of Ghosts
26439782	Proto-Cyber Dragon
10071456	Protector of the Throne
24721739	Protector of the Sanctuary
11678191	Protective Soul Ailin
75917880	Princess Pikeru
51370117	Princess of Tsurugi
02316198	Princess Curran
23701465	Primal Seed
91559748	Prickle Fairy
00549451	Prevent Rat
04483989	Prepare to Strike Back
70828912	Premature Burial
68304813	Precious Card from Beyond
54289683	Power Capsule
37630732	Power Bond
55144522	Pot of Greed
70278545	Pot of Generosity
67169062	Pot of Avarice
52860176	Possessed Dark Soul
24094653	Polymerization
08842266	Poison of the Old Man
43716289	Poison Mummy
76539047	Poison Fangs
56856508	Poison Draw Frog
47415292	Pitch-Dark Dragon
88975532	Pitch-Black Warwolf
34029630	Pitch-Black Power Stone
50823978	Piranha Army
90669916	Pineapple Blast
26185991	Pinch Hopper
58107506	Pikeru's Second Sight
74270067	Pikeru's Circle of Enchantment
66607691	Photon Generator Unit
63356631	Phoenix Wing Wind Blast
89959538	Pharonic Protector
52550093	Pharaoh's Servant
07576264	Phantom Beast Wild-Horn
34961968	Phantom Beast Thunder-Pegasus
71181155	Phantom Beast Cross-Wing

PASSWORD	EFFECT
69906967	Raviel, Lord of Phantasms
85309439	Ray & Temperature
82527174	Ray of Hope
74694807	Re-fusion
31785398	Ready For Intercepting
28121403	Ready Eternal Rest
33066182	Reaper of the Cards
85684223	Reaper of the Nightmare
58725038	Reasoning
23412244	Reborn Zombie
37564645	Reckless Greed
96389191	Recycle
65570955	Red Archery Girl
86445498	Red Gadget
38199696	Red Medicine
56387350	Red Moon Baby
36262024	Red-Eyes B. Chick
74677422	Red-Eyes B. Dragon
64335804	Red-Eyes Black Metal Dragon
96561011	Red-Eyes Darkness Dragon
02057010	Reflect Bounder
70821187	Regenerating Mummy
32807846	Reinforcement of the Army
75417459	Release Restraint
64631466	Relinquished
22589918	Reload
51482758	Remove Trap
14878871	Rescue Cat
31551595	Rescued
62420419	Reshef the Dark Being
08915260	Respect Play
27174286	Return from the Different Dimension
19827717	Return of the Doomed
17484499	Reversal of Graves
05500629	Reversal Quiz
31709826	Revival Jam
70903634	Right Arm of the Forbidden One
08124921	Right Leg of the Forbidden One
58519905	Ring of Defense
83555666	Ring of Destruction
20436034	Ring of Magnetism
70344351	Kiryoku Field
45378982	Rising Air Current
78271861	Rising Energy
30450531	Rite of Spirit
54351225	Ritual Weapon
88279736	Robbin' Goblin
83258273	Robbin' Zombie
92721852	Robolady
44203304	Robotic Knight
38916461	Roboyarou
20781762	Rock Bombardment
68846917	Rock Ogre Grotto
53890795	Rocket Jumper
30860096	Rocket Warrior

PASSWORD	EFFECT
37620434	Shadow Tamer
58621589	Shadow Of Eyes
30778111	Shadow Ghoul
03819470	Seven tools of the Bandit
07792265	Servant of Catobolism
71829750	Serpentine Princess
66516792	Serpent Night Dragon
49398568	Serial Spell
60391679	Senri Eye
57585212	Self-Destruct Button
27053506	Secret Barrel
11068549	Second Goblin
36562627	Second Coin Toss
02618169	Seamaster Meiser
42071342	Sea Serpent Warrior of Darkness
63035430	Scyscraper
56035209	Scroll of Bewitchment
67532912	Science soldier
05498296	Scorr, Scout of Dark World
73915051	Scapegoat
17832827	Satellite canon
64558595	Sasuke Samurai #4
77379481	Sasuke Samurai #3
11760174	Sasuke Samurai #2
16272245	Sasuke Samurai
53539634	Sanwitch
26202915	Sangan
73648243	Sand Moth
50593156	Sand Gambler
44782772	Samsara
96974648	Salvage
32210691	Salamandra
56120475	Sakuretsu Armor
96607287	Sogai the Dark Clown
61441708	Sacred Phoenix of Nephthys
05644564	Sacred Crane
49645990	Saber Beetle
24611934	Ryu-Kishin Powered
42647539	Ryu-Kishin Clown
49988263	Ryu Senshi
81122977	Ryu kokki
70042172	Rush Recklessly
46427957	Ruin, Queen of Oblivion
72405967	Royal Tribute
56058888	Royal Surrender
70791313	Royal Magical Library
68208350	Royal Knight
16060093	Royal Keeper
51420091	Royal Decree
33950246	Royal Command
88303689	Roulette Barrel
37383718	Rope of Spirit
93382620	Rope of Life
39004808	Root Water
91591389	Roll Out!
94793422	Rod of the Mind's Eye

EFFECT	PASSWORD
Soul Exchange	0098050187
Soul Absorption	68073522
Sorcerer of Dark Magic	88619463
Sonic Jammer	84552005
Sonic Duck	84696266
Solomon's Lawbook	23471572
Solemn Wishes	35346968
Solemn Judgment	41420027
Solar Ray	44472639
Solar Flare Dragon	45985838
Sotsu	60294171
Sogen	86318356
Snatch Steal	45986093
Smoke Grenade of the Thief	63789924
Smashing Ground	97169176
Slate Warrior	78636495
Skyscraper	63035240
Skull-Mark LadyBug	64306948
Skull Zoma	79852326
Skull Servant	32274490
Skull Red Bird	10202894
Skull Mariner	05265750
Skull Lair	06733059
Skull Invitation	18139712
Skull Dog Marron	86652646
Skull Descovery Knight	78000000
Skull Archfiend of Lightning	61370518
Skilled White Magician	46363422
Skilled Dark Magician	73752131
Skill Drain	82732705
Sixth Sense	03280747
Sinister Serpent	08131171
Simultaneous Loss	92266931
Simorgh, Bird of Divinity	14989021
Silver Fang	90357090
Sillpheed	2300101
Silva, Warlord of Dark World	32619582
Silent Swordsman LV7	37267042
Silent Swordsman LV5	74388397
Silent Swordsman LV3	01199658
Silent Magician LV8	72543549
Silent Magician Lv4	73615916
Silent Insect	40867519
Shooting Star Bow - (eal)	95838658
Shining Angel	95346956
Shining Abyss	75353037
Shinato, King of a Higher Plane	52272829
Shinato's Ark	60955691
Shifting Shadows	59237154
Shift	59590525
Shien's Spy	07072244
Shield Crash	30890373
Shield & Sword	52097679
Share the Pain	56830749
Shadowslayer	20939559
Shadowknight Archfiend	09630356

PASSWORD	EFFECT	PASSWORD	EFFECT
Soul of Purity and Light	77527210	Stray Lambs	60764581
Soul Release	05758500	Strike Ninja	41006930
Soul Resurrection	92924317	Stronghold	13955608
Soul Reversal	78864369	Stumbling	34646691
Soul Tiger	15734813	Success Probability 0%	06859683
Soul-Absorbing Bone Tower	63012333	Summon Priest	00423585
Souleater	31242786	Summoned Skull	70781052
Souls Of The Forgotten	04920010	Summoner of Illusions	14644902
Space Mambo	36119641	Super Conductor Tyranno	85520851
Spark Blaster	97362768	Super Rejuvenation	27770341
Sparks	76103675	Super Robolady	75923050
Spatial Collapse	20644748	Super Roboyarou	01412158
Spear Cretin	58551308	Supply	44072894
Spear Dragon	31553716	Susa Soldier	40473581
Spell Canceller	84636823	Swarm of Locusts	41872150
Spell Economics	04259068	Swarm of Scarabs	15383415
Spell Purification	01669772	Swift Gaia the Fierce Knight	16589042
Spell Reproduction	29228529	Sword Hunter	51345461
Spell Shield Type-8	38275183	Sword of Deep-Seated	98495314
Spell Vanishing	29735721	Sword of Dragon's Soul	61405855
Spell-Stopping Statute	10069180	Sword of the Soul Eater	05371656
Spellbinding Circle	18807108	Swords of Concealing Light	12923641
Spherous Lady	52121290	Swords of Revealing Light	72302403
Sphinx Teleia	51402177	Swordsman of Landstar	03573512
Spiral Spear Strike	49328340	Symbol of Heritage	45305419
Spirit Barrier	53239672	System Down	18895832
Spirit Caller	48659020	T.A.D.P.O.L.E.	10456559
Spirit Message A	94772232	Tactical Espionage Expert	89698120
Spirit Message I	31893528	Tailor of the Fickle	43641473
Spirit Message L	30170981	Taunt	90740329
Spirit Message N	67287533	Tenkabito Shien	41589166
Spirit of Flames	13522325	Terra the Terrible	63308047
Spirit of the Breeze	53530069	Terraforming	73628505
Spirit of the Harp	80770678	Terrorking Archfiend	35975813
Spirit of the Pharaoh	25343280	Terrorking Salmon	78060096
Spirit Reaper	23205979	Teva	16469012
Spirit Ryu	67957315	The Agent of Creation - Venus	64734921
Spiritual Earth Art - Kurogane	70156997	The Agent of Force - Mars	91123920
Spiritual Energy Settle Machine	99173029	The Agent of Judgment - Saturn	91345518
Spiritual Fire Art - Kurenai	42945701	The Agent of Wisdom - Mercury	38730226
Spiritual Water Art - Aoi	06540606	The All-Seeing White Tiger	32269855
Spiritual Wind Art - Miyabi	79333300	The Big March of Animals	01689516
Spiritualism	15866454	The Bistro Butcher	71107816
St. Joan	21175632	The Cheerful Coffin	41142615
Stamping Destruction	81385346	The Creator	61505339
Star Boy	08201910	The Creator Incarnate	97093037
Statue of the Wicked	65810489	The Dark - Hex Sealed Fusion	52101615
Staunch Defender	92854392	The Dark Door	30606547
Stealth Bird	03510565	The Dragon Dwelling in the Cave	93346024
Steam Gyroid	05368615	The Dragon's Bead	92408984
Steamroid	44729197	The Earl of Demise	66989694
Steel Ogre Grotto #1	29172562	The Earth - Hex Sealed Fusion	88696724
Steel Ogre Grotto #2	90908427	The Emperor's Holiday	68400115
Stim-Pack	83225447	The End of Anubis	65403020
Stop Defense	63102017	The Eye Of Truth	34694160
Storming Wynn	29013526	The Fiend Megacyber	66362965

PASSWORD	EFFECT
The Flute of Summoning Dragon	43973174
The Flute of Summoning Kuriboh	20065322
The Forceful Sentry	42829885
The Forces of Darkness	29826127
The Forgiving Maiden	84080938
The Furious Sea King	18710707
The Graveyard in the Fourth Dimension	88089103
The Gross Ghost of Fled Dreams	68049471
The Hunter With 7 Weapons	01525329
The Illusionary Gentleman	83764996
The Immortal of Thunder	84926738
The Kick Man	90407382
The Last Warrior From Another Planet	86099788
The Law of the Normal	66926224
The League of Uniform Nomenclature	55008284
The Legendary Fisherman	03643300
The Light - Hex Sealed Fusion	15717011
The Little Swordsman of Aile	25109950
The Masked Beast	49064413
The Portrait's Secret	32541773
The Regulation of Tribe	00296499
The Reliable Guardian	16430187
The Rock Spirit	76305638
The Sanctuary in the Sky	56433456
The Second Sarcophagus	04081094
The Secret of the Bandit	99351431
The Shallow Grave	43434803
The Spell Absorbing Life	99517131
The Thing in the Crater	78243409
The Third Sarcophagus	78697395
The Trojan Horse	38479725
The Unhappy Girl	27618634
The Unhappy Maiden	51275027
The Warrior Returning Alive	95281259
Theban Nightmare	51838385
Theinen the Great Sphinx	87997872
Thestalos the Firestorm Monarch	26205777
Thousand Dragon	41462083
Thousand Energy	05703682
Thousand Needles	33977496
Thousand-Eyes Idol	27125110
Thousand-Eyes Restrict	63519819
Threatening Roar	36361633
Three-Headed Geedo	78423643
Throwstone Unit	76075810
Thunder Crash	69196160
Thunder Dragon	31786629
Thunder Nyan Nyan	70797118
Thunder of Ruler	91781589
Time Seal	35316708
Time Wizard	71625222
Timeater	44913552
Timidity	40350910

PASSWORD	EFFECT
Token Festevil	83675475
Token Thanksgiving	57182235
Tongyo	69572024
Toon Cannon Soldier	79875176
Toon Dark Magician Girl	90960358
Toon Defense	43509019
Toon Gemini Elf	42386471
Toon Goblin Attack Force	15270885
Toon Masked Sorcerer	16392422
Toon Mermaid	65458948
Toon Summoned Skull	91842653
Toon Table of Contents	89997728
Toon World	15259703
Tornado Bird	71283180
Tornado Wall	18605135
Torpedo Fish	90337190
Torrential Tribute	53582587
Total Defense Shogun	75372290
Tower of Babel	94256039
Tragedy	35686187
Transcendent Wings	25573054
Trap Dustshoot	64697231
Trap Hole	04206964
Trap Jammer	19252988
Treeborn Frog	12538374
Tremendous Fire	46918794
Tri-Horned Dragon	39111158
Triage	30888983
Trial of Nightmare	77827521
Trial of the Princesses	72709014
Triangle Ecstasy Spark	12181376
Triangle Power	32298781
Tribe-Infecting Virus	33184167
Tribute Doll	02903036
Tribute to The Doomed	79759861
Tripwire Beast	45042329
Troop Dragon	55013285
Tsukuyomi	34853266
Turtle Oath	76806714
Turtle Tiger	37313348
Twin Swords of Flashing Light	21900719
Twin-Headed Beast	82035781
Twin-Headed Behemoth	43586926
Twin-Headed Fire Dragon	78984772
Twin-Headed Thunder Dragon	54752875
Twin-Headed Wolf	88132637
Two Thousand Needles	83228073
Two-Man Cell Battle	25578802
Two-Mouth Darkruler	57305373
Two-Pronged Attack	83887306
Tyhone	72842870
Type Zero Magic Crusher	21237481
Tyranno Infinity	83235263
Tyrant Dragon	94568601
UFOroid	07602840
UFOroid Fighter	32752319

PASSWORD	EFFECT	PASSWORD	EFFECT
Ultimate Insect LV1	49441499	White Magician Pikeru	81383947
Ultimate Insect LV3	34088136	White Ninja	01571945
Ultimate Insect LV5	34830502	Wicked-Breaking Flameberge-Baou	68427465
Ultimate Insect LV7	19877898	Wild Nature's Release	61166988
Ultimate Obedient Fiend	32240937	Winged Dragon, Guardian of the Fortress #1	87796900
Ultimate Tyranno	15894048	Winged Kuriboh	57116033
Ultra Evolution Pill	22431243	Winged Kuriboh LV10	98585345
Umi	22702055	Winged Minion	89258225
Umiiruka	82999629	Winged Sage Falcos	87523462
Union Attack	60399954	Wingweaver	31447217
United Resistance	85936485	Witch Doctor of Chaos	75946257
United We Stand	56747793	Witch of the Black Forest	78010363
Unity	14731897	Witch's Apprentice	80741828
Unshaven Angler	92084010	Witty Phantom	36304921
Upstart Goblin	70368879	Wolf Axwielder	56369281
Uraby	01784619	Woodborg Inpachi	35322812
Uria, Lord of Sealing Flames	06007213	Woodland Sprite	06979239
V-Tiger Jet	51638941	Worm Drake	73216412
Valkyrion the Magna Warrior	75347539	Wroughtweiler	06480253
Vampire Genesis	22056710	Wynn the Wind Charmer	37744402
Vampire Lord	53839837	X-Head Cannon	62651957
Vampire Orchis	46571052	Xing Zhen Hu	76515293
Vengeful Bog Spirit	95220856	XY-Dragon Cannon	02111707
Victory D	44910027	XYZ-Dragon Cannon	91998119
Vilepawn Archfiend	73219648	XZ-Tank Cannon	99724761
VW-Tiger Catapult	58859575	Y-Dragon Head	65622692
VWXYZ-Dragon Catapult Cannon	84243274	Yamata Dragon	76862289
W-Wing Catapult	96300057	Yami	59197169
Waboku	12607053	Yata-Garasu	03078576
Wall of Revealing Light	17078030	Yellow Gadget	13839120
Wandering Mummy	42994702	Yellow Luster Shield	04542651
Warrior Dai Grepher	75953262	Yomi Ship	51534754
Warrior of Zera	66073051	YZ-Tank Dragon	25119460
Wasteland	23424603	Z-Metal Tank	64500000
Water Dragon	85066822	Zaborg the Thunder Monarch	51945556
Water Omotics	02483611	Zero Gravity	83133491
Wave Motion Cannon	38992735	Zoa	24311372
Weed Out	28604635	Zolga	16268841
Whiptail Crow	91996584	Zombie Tiger	47693640
Whirlwind Prodigy	15090429	Zombyra the Dark	88472456
White Dragon Ritual	09786492	Zure, Knight of Dark World	07459013
White Horn Dragon	73891874		
White Magical Hat	15150365		

YU-GI-OH! DUEL MONSTERS GX: TAG FORCE 3

MIDDAY CONSTELLATION BOOSTER PACK

At the store, get to the booster pack menu and press Up, Up, Down, Down, Left, Right, Left, Right, ✖, ⬤. The pack will now be available at the store.

75

GAME BOY® ADVANCE

TABLE OF CONTENTS

BANJO PILOT

GRUNTY

Defeat Grunty in the Broomstick battle race. Then, you can purchase Grunty from Cheato.

HUMBA WUMBA

Defeat Humba Wumba in the Jiggu battle race. Then, you can purchase Humba Wumba from Cheato.

JOLLY

Defeat Jolly in the Pumpkin battle race. Then, you can purchase Jolly from Cheato.

KLUNGO

Defeat Klungo in the Skull battle race. Then, you can purchase Klungo from Cheato.

BARBIE AS THE PRINCESS AND THE PAUPER

PASSWORDS

LEVEL	PASSWORD
1-2	Preminger, Wolfie, Erika, Serafina
1-3	Wolfie, Preminger, Serafania, Preminger
1-4	Preminger, Wolfie, Serfania, Wolfie
Boss 1	Serafina, Woflia. Erika, Preminger
2-1	Princess Anneliese, Preminger, Wolfie, Erika
2-2	Preminger, Princess Anneliese, Wolfie, Erika
2-3	Preminger, Serafina, Preminger, Erika
2-4	Serafina, Erika, Preminger, Wolfie
Boss 2	Preminger, Erika, Serafina, Wolfie

LEVEL	PASSWORD
3-1	Wolfie, Preminger, Wolfie, Erika
3-2	Serafina, Preminger, Erika, Serafina
3-3	Erika, Wolfie, Serafina, Princess Anneliese
3-4	Erika, Serafina, Erika, Preminger
Boss 3	Preminger, Serafina, Princess Anneliese, Serafina
4-1	Wolfie, Serafina, Preminger, Serafina
4-2	Preminger, Serafina, Princess Anneliese, Preminger
4-3	Wolfie, Serafina, Erika, Serafina
Boss 4	Erika, Serafina, Princess Anneliese, Wolfie
Final Boss	Erika, Princess Anneliese, Princess Anneliese, Man
Arcade Level	Princess Anneliese, Serafina, Erika, Wolfie

CASTLEVANIA: ARIA OF SORROW

NO ITEMS

Start a new game with the name NOUSE to use no items in the game.

NO SOULS

Start a new game with the name NOSOUL to use no souls in the game.

DK: KING OF SWING

ATTACK BATTLE 3

At the Title screen, press Up + L + A + B to bring up a password screen. Enter 65942922.

CLIMBING RACE 5

At the Title screen, press Up + L + A + B to bring up a password screen. Enter 55860327.

OBSTACLE RACE 4

At the Title screen, press Up + L + A + B to bring up a password screen. Enter 35805225.

UNLOCK TIME ATTACK

Complete the game as DK.

UNLOCK DIDDY MODE

Collect 24 medals as DK.

UNLOCK BUBBLES

Complete Diddy Mode with 24 Medals.

UNLOCK KREMLING

Collect 6 gold medals in Jungle Jam.

UNLOCK KING K. ROOL

Collect 12 gold medals in Jungle Jam.

DONKEY KONG COUNTRY 2: DIDDY KONG'S QUEST

ALL LEVELS

Select Cheats from the Options and enter freedom.

START WITH 15 LIVES

Select Cheats from the Options and enter helpme.

START WITH 55 LIVES

Select Cheats from the Options and enter weakling.

START WITH 10 BANANA COINS

Select Cheats from the Options and enter richman.

START WITH 50 BANANA COINS

Select Cheats from the Options and enter wellrich.

NO DK OR HALF WAY BARRELS

Select Cheats from the Options and enter rockard.

MUSIC PLAYER

Select Cheats from the Options and enter onetime.

CREDITS

Select Cheats from the Options and enter kredits.

FINAL FANTASY I & II: DAWN OF SOULS

FF I TILE GAME

During a game of Final Fantasy I and after you get the ship, hold A and press B about 55 times.

FF II CONCENTRATION GAME

Once you obtain the Snowcraft, hold B and press A about 20 times.

MONSTER FORCE

RESTART LEVEL

Pause the game, hold L + R and press A.

FINISH LEVEL

During a game, hold L + R + A and press Up.

PLAY AS MINA OR DREW

At the Character Select screen, hold L + R + B and press Right.

RATATOUILLE

INVINCIBILITY

Enter X4V!3RJ as a password.

ALL CHAPTERS

Enter H3L!X3! as a password. Press L or R at the Chapter Select screen.

ALL MINI-GAMES

Enter JV4ND1Z as a password.

ALL BONUS PICTURES

Enter 3R1CQRR as a password.

RIVER CITY RANSOM EX

Select the status menu and change your name to the following:

MAX STATS
DAMAX

$999999.99
PLAYA

CUSTOM CHAR
XTRA0

CUSTOM SELF
XTRA1

CUSTOM MOVE
XTRA2

CLEAR SAVE
ERAZE

TECHNIQUES 1
FUZZY. This group includes Mach Punch, Dragon Kick, Acro Circus, Grand Slam, Javelin Man, Slick Trick, Nitro Port, Twin Kick, Deadly Shot, Top Spin, Helicopter, Torpedo.

TECHNIQUES 2
WUZZY. This group includes Slap Happy, Pulper, Headbutt, Kickstand, Big Bang, Wheel Throw, Glide Chop, Head Bomb, Chain Chump, Jet Kick, Shuriken, Flip Throw.

TECHNIQUES 3
WAZZA. This group includes Boomerang, Charge It, Bat Fang, Flying Kick, Speed Drop, Bomb Blow, Killer Kick, Bike Kick, Slam Punk, Dragon Knee, God Fist, Hyperguard.

TECHNIQUES 4
BEAR*. This group includes PhoenixWing, Inlines, Springlines, Rocketeers, Air Merc's Narcishoes, Magic Pants, Pandora Box, Skaterz, Custom Fit.

STREET FIGHTER ALPHA 3

ALL FIGHTERS
At the Title screen, press Left, Right, Down, Right, L, L, A, L, L, B, R, A, Up.

ALL MODES
At the Title screen, press A, Up, A, L, R, Right, L, Right, A, Down, Right. Now press L, Right, A, R, Up,L, Right, B, A, Up, Right, Down, Right.

PLAY AS SUPER BISON
At the Character Select screen, hold Start and select Bison.

PLAY AS SHIN AKUMA
At the Character Select screen, hold Start and select Akuma.

ALTERNATE COSTUMES
At the Character Select screen, press L or R.

FINAL BATTLE
At the Speed Select option, hold A + B.

THAT'S SO RAVEN 2: SUPERNATURAL STYLE ™

COSTUME MODE
At the Title screen, press Left, Right, Up, Down, B, B, B, Up, Down.

UNLIMITED ENERGY MODE
At the Title screen, press B, B, L, R, Up, Down, Up, Left, Right.

TRON 2.0: KILLER APP

ALL MINIGAMES

At the Title screen, press Left, Left, Left, Left, Up, Right, Down, Down, Select.

YOSHI TOPSY-TURVY

CHALLENGE MODE AND CHALLENGE 1

Defeat Bowser for the second time in Story Mode.

CHALLENGES 2, 3, 4

Complete the Egg Gallery in Story Mode.

FINAL CHALLENGE

Earn all Golds in Story Mode.

YU-GI-OH! 7 TRIALS TO GLORY: WORLD CHAMPIONSHIP TOURNAMENT 2005

PURPLE TITLE SCREEN

Completing the game changes the Title screen from blue to purple. To switch it back, press Up, Up, Down, Down, Left, Right, Left, Right, B, A at the Title screen.

CREDITS

Defeat the game, then press Up, Up, Down, Down, Left, Right, Left, Right, B, A.

CARD PASSWORDS

At the password machine, press R and enter a password.

Refer to the Card List for YU-GI-OH! GX TAG FORCE for PSP. All cards are not available in World Championship Tournament 2005.

YU-GI-OH! ULTIMATE MASTERS: WORLD CHAMPIONSHIP TOURNAMENT 2006

CARD PASSWORDS

Enter the 8-digit codes at the Password screen to unlock that card for purchase.

Refer to the Card List for YU-GI-OH! GX TAG FORCE for PSP. All cards may not be available in World Championship Tournament 2006.

ONLINE GAMING FOR KIDS: A PARENT'S GUIDE

There are plenty of great games for kids on the web, but which ones are best for your child, and how can you ensure they don't visit a site that's inappropriate? Well, we've compiled a list of the most impressive and trusted gaming spots for kids, then categorized them by age. Visit these sites and choose which ones your family likes most. Once you've determined your favorites, you can then make accessing them safe and easy for your child in just three easy steps:

SAFE ONLINE GAMING FOR KIDS IS AS EASY AS 1-2-3

Here's how you can create an **Internet Games Page**—a clickable document that allows your child to safely and easily visit your family's favorite online gaming sites for kids:

1. Open a new document in Microsoft Word.

2. Type in the URLs (web site addresses) listed in this section that best suit your child's age and interests. After each URL, press ENTER to automatically create a Hyperlink. The address will then appear in blue, underlined text. That means you can now immediately go directly to that web site. Just simultaneously press CTRL and click on the blue text. See our note below for an even slicker way of doing this.

3. When your list of Hyperlinks is complete, save the file as "[Your Child's Name]'s Games" on your computer's desktop.

USER FRIENDLY LINKS

If you think your child might find it difficult to visit his or her favorite gaming sites by selecting from a list of long and sometimes unwieldy internet addresses, then customize the lists on your Internet Games Page by renaming them with something more easily recognizable. It's easy. Simply type the name you wish to use (LEGO, for example) and highlight the word with your mouse. Next, right-click on the highlighted word and select Hyperlink from the window that pops up. Another window appears with your cursor blinking in the empty Address field. Type in the proper URL here (in the case of LEGO, you would type *http://play.lego.com/en-US/games/default.aspx* into this field), then click OK. The word you highlighted on your Internet Games Page is now a Hyperlink. Using our example, that means your child can simply click on (left-click + CTRL) the word "LEGO" to visit the LEGO games site!

You can even dress up this document with colorful backgrounds and clip art to make it even more personal and appealing. You now have a resource that provides a quick and easy path for your child to access safe and entertaining gaming sites that you have seen and trust.

BEST ONLINE GAMING SITES FOR KIDS

AGES 6-7

Children in this age group may not be as computer savvy and certainly won't have as strong reading skills as older kids. So, you may need to get your child started until he or she is comfortable navigating these sites and properly understands the rules to the games.

Slime Slinger Online Game

http://www.scholastic.com/goosebumps/slimeslinger/game.asp

A fun game based on the popular Goosebumps series of books.

Highlights Kids Hidden Pictures

http://www.highlightskids.com/GamesandGiggles/HiddenPics/HIddenPixFlashObjects/h8hpiArchive.asp

More than just games, these puzzle-oriented offerings really work kids' brains.

CBeebies at BBC

http://www.bbc.co.uk/cbeebies/fun/

Lots of cute games for younger kids.

Yahooligans Games

http://kids.yahoo.com/games

Loads of fun for all ages here with a wide variety of games—puzzles, arcade, sports, and more!

Pauly's Playhouse Online Games

http://www.paulysplayhouse.com/paulys_playhouse/game_page/game.html

Wow! This site has loads of games! All pretty simple and most will have your child smiling from ear to ear.

Nick.com Games Online

http://www.nick.com/games/

Lots of good stuff here, all associated with Nick programming your child likely already enjoys.

Lego Club Games

http://play.lego.com/en-US/games/default.aspx

Great interactive fun that provides exciting scenarios that simulate playing with LEGO toys.

Barbie.com Games Online

http://barbie.everythinggirl.com/activities/fun_games/

Let's face it, most girls like Barbie as much as just about anything. The games your daughter plays on this site will not disappoint her.

EDUCATIONAL FUN!

Chicken Stacker

http://pbskids.org/lions/games/stacker.html

You can never go wrong with PBS when it comes to kids, and Between the Lions is one of many great programs. This game based on the show helps kids build their word power.

Play Kids Games.com

http://www.playkidsgames.com/

Everything from simple math to word and memory games. Plenty here for the next age group, too.

Scholastic Games

http://www.scholastic.com/kids/games.htm

Solve mysteries, answer trivia, collect rare items, and more! The fun here is all based on popular books with this age group.

Monkeybar TV

http://www.hasbro.com/monkeybartv/default.cfm?page=Entertainment/OnlineGames/GameHome

This site is operated by Hasbro, so the characters and toys associated with the games are all classics known and loved by kids and adults—including Transformers, Littlest Pet Shop, Monopoly, GI Joe, Star Wars, and others!

Cartoon Network Games Online

http://www.cartoonnetwork.com/games/index.html

Kids can't read and be active all the time, and cartoons nicely fill that need to laugh and take it easy. This is the place for hilarious games from hilarious toons.

I Spy Games Online

http://www.scholastic.com/ispy/play/

Another Scholastic gem that allows kids to use their powers of observation online!

Disney Channel Games Online

http://tv.disney.go.com/disneychannel/games/index.html

Have you ever met a fourth grader who isn't into Disney? Hannah Montana, Kim Possible, Zack & Cody... what's not to like? This site has plenty of familiar faces and fun stuff.

Kidnetics Active Online Games

http://www.kidnetic.com/

Fitness focused games and projects for kids.

EDUCATIONAL FUN!

Multiplication.com

http://www.multiplication.com/interactive_games.htm

Cute and entertaining games that help make multiplication tables a breeze.

Big Brainz

http://www.bigbrainz.com/index.php

Download a free version of Timez Attack, a great looking action video game that boosts multiplication skills!

If you're 10 years old, there's no reason you still can't have fun playing the games we've listed in the previous two age groups, but these will definitely appeal to the big kids.

ESPN Arcade

http://arcade.espn.go.com/

ESPN offers a great online gaming site for kids who are into sports.

Zeeks Board & Card Games

http://games.zeeks.com/games.php

Tons of free games. Not just entertaining, but a little edgy, too!

Battleship

http://www.creativecalendar.com/kids/Games/games_battleship.html

Everyone loves this game. Just as much fun online!

OTHER ONLINE GAMES

We've put these games in a separate category because they're not free. They either require a subscription or the purchase of a toy to play. However, you may consider these investments worthwhile, as they do provide some intriguing gameplay and learning opportunities. Plus, if your kids are into gaming or have friends who are, they're bound to mention these sites to you sooner or later, so you may want to see what they're all about for yourself.

Webkinz

http://www.webkinz.com/

Requires you to buy a toy before "adopting" one online, but the game experience is pretty cool. Webkinz allows kids to care for their pet, including improving and furnishing its home. Earn Kinz cash by answering trivia and doing other fun activities.

Club Penguin

http://www.clubpenguin.com/

This subscription-based online game is operated by Disney. It provides a kid-friendly virtual world where children can play games, have fun, and interact with each other...but it's not free.

A NOTE TO PARENTS

This book is an exclusive Scholastic edition that has been edited to remove all Mature-rated codes, as well as games that include excessive violence, sexual content, and inappropriate codes for children.

This book includes only E, E+, and T-rated games.

In addition, this book provides a listing of the ESRB ratings for all games included inside.

EARLY CHILDHOOD
Titles rated EC (Early Childhood) have content that may be suitable for ages 3 and older. Contains no material that parents would find inappropriate.

TEEN
Titles rated T (Teen) have content that may be suitable for ages 13 and older. Titles in this category may contain violence, suggestive themes, crude humor, minimal blood and/or infrequent use of strong language.

EVERYONE
Titles rated E (Everyone) have content that may be suitable for ages 6 and older. Titles in this category may contain minimal cartoon, fantasy or mild violence and/or infrequent use of mild language.

MATURE
Titles rated M (Mature) have content that may be suitable for persons ages 17 and older. Titles in this category may contain intense violence, blood and gore, sexual content, and/or strong language.

EVERYONE 10+
Titles rated E10+ (Everyone 10 and older) have content that may be suitable for ages 10 and older. Titles in this category may contain more cartoon, fantasy or mild violence, mild language, and/or minimal suggestive themes.

ADULTS ONLY
Titles rated AO (Adults Only) have content that should only be played by persons 18 years and older. Titles in this category may include prolonged scenes of intense violence and/or graphic sexual content and nudity.